The Platonic Conception of Immortality and its Connexion with the Theory of Ideas

CAMBRIDGE
UNIVERSITY PRESS

University Printing House, Cambridge CB2 8BS, United Kingdom

Published in the United States of America by Cambridge University Press, New York

Cambridge University Press is part of the University of Cambridge.

It furthers the University's mission by disseminating knowledge in the pursuit of education, learning and research at the highest international levels of excellence.

www.cambridge.org
Information on this title: www.cambridge.org/9781107688315

© Cambridge University Press 1904

First published 1904
First paperback edition 2014

A catalogue record for this publication is available from the British Library

ISBN 978-1-107-68831-5 Paperback

The Platonic Conception of Immortality and its Connexion with the Theory of Ideas

AN ESSAY WHICH OBTAINED THE HARE PRIZE, 1903

BY

R. K. GAYE, M.A.,

FELLOW OF TRINITY COLLEGE, CAMBRIDGE.

LONDON

C. J. CLAY AND SONS

CAMBRIDGE UNIVERSITY PRESS WAREHOUSE

AVE MARIA LANE

1904

ΜΙΜΕῖϲΘΑΙ ΔΕῖΝ ἩΜᾶϹ ΟἴΕΤΑΙ ΠᾶϹῌ ΜΗΧΑΝῌ ΤὸΝ ἐΠὶ ΤΟῦ
ΚΡόΝΟΥ ΛΕΓόΜΕΝΟΝ ΒίΟΝ, ΚΑὶ ὅϹΟΝ ἐΝ ἩΜῖΝ ἀΘΑΝΑϹίΑϹ ἔΝΕϹΤΙ,
ΤΟύΤῳ ΠΕΙΘΟΜέΝΟΥϹ ΔΗΜΟϹίᾳ ΚΑὶ ἰΔίᾳ ΤάϹ Τ' ΟἰΚήϹΕΙϹ ΚΑὶ ΤὰϹ
ΠόΛΕΙϹ ΔΙΟΙΚΕῖΝ, ΤὴΝ ΤΟῦ ΝΟῦ ΔΙΑΝΟΜὴΝ ἐΠΟΝΟΜάΖΟΝΤΑϹ ΝόΜΟΝ.

                                                       PLATO *Laws* 713 E.

Quand l'immortalité de l'âme seroit une erreur, je serois fâché
de ne pas la croire: j'avoue que je ne suis pas si humble que les
athées.   Je ne sais comment ils pensent; mais pour moi je ne veux
pas troquer l'idée de mon immortalité contre celle de la béatitude
d'un jour.   Je suis charmé de me croire immortel comme Dieu
même.   Indépendamment des idées révélées, les idées méta-
physiques me donnent une très-forte espérance de mon bonheur
éternel, à laquelle je ne voudrois pas renoncer.

                                       MONTESQUIEU *Pensées Diverses.*

PREFACE.

" A SCIENTIFIC basis was first given to the belief in immortality by Plato," says Zeller (*Pre-Socratics* I. 74). Commenting on this statement, Mr E. S. Thompson in his edition of the *Meno* (p. 289) remarks: "This basis is found in the doctrine of Ideas." My object here is to follow up a little more closely the connexion existing between these two theories with which the name of Plato will always be associated—the Theory of Ideas and the Theory of the Immortality of the Soul. In this way I hope to make clear the nature of Plato's conception of immortality and to determine in what sense, if any, he believed in the continued existence of the individual soul. But this main subject has inevitably involved the consideration of a larger question, namely the Platonic conception of the nature of the soul and more especially of the mutual relations of soul and body.

In the following pages, then, I have attempted to trace the rise and gradual development of the doctrine of immortality as it was formulated in Plato's mind and to indicate certain changes which, as it seems to me, he introduces into this doctrine in consequence of a modification of his theory of soul—a modification due, as I endeavour to prove, to changes in his metaphysical theories. My contention is that *mutatis mutandis* very much the same differences are to be found in his later as compared with his earlier theory of soul as those which Dr Henry Jackson has discovered in the later as compared with the earlier Theory of Ideas; and these differences must necessarily affect his views on the subject of immortality. The most important Dialogues of which we have to take account in this connexion are of course the *Phaedo* and the *Timaeus*, which, both from the standpoint of the theory of soul and from that of ontology, may fairly be regarded as typical respectively of what Dr Jackson would call Plato's earlier and later philosophical periods. But several others, notably the *Phaedrus*, the *Republic*, and the tenth book of the *Laws*, contain much that cannot be neglected in any attempt to fulfil the task which I have undertaken.

Mr R. D. Archer-Hind in the Introduction to his edition of the *Phaedo*, where he is discussing Plato's attitude towards the question of immortality, maintains that Plato, when he composed that dialogue, upheld the immortality of the individual soul. He proceeds, how-ever, to remark (p. 31): " I have made this defence of the literal interpretation not because I consider that the continued existence of the individual is of any real im-portance in the Platonic system—I should not go so far as to affirm that it was retained to the last—but because, in order that we may follow historically the development of Plato's thought, it is important for us to determine precisely what he means to set forth in each dialogue." In what follows I on the other hand hope not only to go so far as to affirm that a belief in individual im-mortality was retained by Plato to the last, but to show further that, though his philosophical system as a whole does not depend for its truth on the continued existence of the individual, he does nevertheless attach a real importance to the doctrine, and as a matter of fact goes out of his way to affirm it in one of the most important metaphysical parts of the *Timaeus*.

It will be seen throughout this essay how greatly I am indebted to Dr Jackson's papers in *The Journal of Philology* (vols. X, XI, XIII, XIV, XV) on "Plato's Later Theory of Ideas": and my obligation to Mr Archer-Hind's editions of the *Phaedo* and the *Timaeus* is hardly less obvious. It is to these sources almost entirely that I owe the view I take of the metaphysical significance of the Dialogues of the later period, that is to say the period represented by the *Parmenides*, *Philebus*, *Theaetetus*, *Sophist*, *Politicus*, and *Timaeus*. In fact, had it not been for the labours of these scholars in showing that Plato's Dialogues reflect two distinct stages of metaphysical opinion, this essay could never have been written, based as it is throughout on the assumption that there really was some such modification of Plato's philosophical doctrines as they hold to have taken place. If I have ventured in some points of detail to express a divergence of opinion, this in no way detracts from the value which I attach, and which, I imagine, all who are interested in the subject must attach, to their attempt (in my opinion successful) to obtain a rational interpretation of Platonic philosophy in accordance with the statements of Plato himself and the testimony of Aristotle. The main conclusions at which they have arrived seem to me, if not certain, to contain at least a very high degree of probability, and I have been content to presume them throughout.

I am also in a slighter degree a debtor to two other Platonic scholars: the late Dr W. H. Thompson, whose edition of the *Phaedrus* I have used with pleasure and, I hope, with profit; and Mr E. S. Thompson, whose instructive commentary on the *Meno* is most useful to any student of Plato. Though I do not think anything in what follows is directly derived from these editions, I have found them both very helpful for the understanding of Plato's language and philosophy.

I cannot conclude without reference to what is really my greatest debt, though it can be ascribed to no written source. I am sure that all who have studied under Dr Jackson will agree with me in acknowledging the immense help they have received from his oral instruction, not only in the lecture-room, but still more in those informal conversations in which they have attempted to play the part of Theaetetus. I could not venture to estimate the extent to which in this essay I have been consciously or unconsciously inspired by hints and suggestions which have come to me in this manner: but my indebtedness and, I hope, my gratitude are not the less because I am unable to acknowledge in detail my obligations to one who carries out so faithfully Plato's injunction to teachers—δεῖ δὲ εἰς δύναμιν μηδὲν παραλείπειν αὐτῷ, πάντα δὲ λόγον ἀφερμηνεύειν, ἵνα οὗτος τοῖς ἄλλοις μηνυτής τε ἅμα καὶ τροφεὺς γίγνηται.

R. K. GAYE.

TRINITY COLLEGE, CAMBRIDGE.
11 *October*, 1904.

CONTENTS.

INTRODUCTION.

Οὐκ ᾔσθησαι, ἦν δ’ ἐγώ, ὅτι ἀθάνατος ἡμῶν ἡ ψυχὴ καὶ οὐδέποτε ἀπόλλυται; Καὶ ὃς ἐμβλέψας μοι καὶ θαυμάσας εἶπε· Μὰ Δί’ οὐκ ἔγωγε· σὺ δὲ τοῦτ’ ἔχεις λέγειν ; Εἰ μὴ ἀδικῶ γ’, ἔφην· οἶμαι δὲ καὶ σύ· οὐδὲν γὰρ χαλεπόν.   PLATO *Republic* 608 D.

To anyone reading the above passage the question naturally suggests itself : Why is Glaucon made to express surprise at the mention of a doctrine which must have been familiar by this time to all who sat at Plato's feet? The *Republic*, so far as I am aware, is by no one considered to be the earliest of those Dialogues in which a belief in the immortality of the soul is expressed or implied. Such a belief is hinted at in the *Apology*, perhaps the earliest of Plato's extant works; it appears with greater definiteness in the *Crito* ; it forms the subject of a direct demonstration in the *Phaedrus* : and all these Dialogues are generally admitted to have been written before the *Republic*. To this question it is perhaps impossible to give a decisive answer. We must remember, however, that the *Republic* differs from all the preceding Dialogues in this, namely that in a truer sense than any of them it is a complete whole, an exhaustive statement of ethical, sociological, and educational opinions : and as such it sums up and co-ordinates all that is important in earlier works for the formulation of these

G.   1

opinions. In the *Republic* Plato lays before us a comprehensive system of Ethics constructed upon a plan
peculiar to himself and differing from all previous or
contemporary systems in that it professes to be founded
upon a definite metaphysical basis.

In the elaboration of this ethical system the doctrine
of the immortality of the soul plays an important part.
From the beginning, however, it must be clearly understood that Plato does not in the slightest degree depend
upon this doctrine for the formulation and justification
of his system of Ethics. This is quite clear to anyone
who follows the course of the discussion from the second
to the ninth book of the *Republic*. It is in this part of
the Dialogue that Plato works out in detail his educational system of Ethics, and here he expressly leaves out
of account all considerations derived from the expectation
of any future state of rewards and punishments. He
consistently refuses to make self-interest of this sort the
basis of the morality which he inculcates, holding as he
does that 'justice' is not only more *profitable* but in its
own essential nature *better* than 'injustice'; its superiority
is natural and not dependent upon any ulterior considerations.

Nevertheless the doctrine of the immortality of the
soul is a favourite one with Plato, and it is clear that for
some reason it possesses in his eyes an importance of its
own. We find him continually referring to it more or
less distinctly throughout the Dialogues; in some of
them it is one of the weightiest themes discussed; in one
—the *Phaedo*—it is actually the weightiest. It would
seem that when once the theory had begun to take shape
in his mind it was never long absent from his thoughts,
and he could not bring himself to leave the subject until

he had made the doctrine thoroughly his own. From this point of view, then, it is not surprising that in the *Republic*, where he could not consistently with his own principles bring it to bear directly on the details of his ethical scheme, he should feel constrained to introduce it in the form of an appendix to the main body of the work.

In the *Republic*, as has been said above, all that Plato considers to be philosophically important in the preceding Dialogues is summed up and worked together so as to form a single harmonious system of Ethics. Whereas these Dialogues have dealt for the most part with one particular point, the *Republic* combines their results and forms a complete ethical treatise. An earnest student of the Academy, after a few preparatory dialectical and other exercises, could very soon be referred with advantage to the *Republic* without being made to study the earlier Dialogues first. This being the case, the surprise that Glaucon is made to express when the soul is declared to be immortal is perhaps not so hard to understand as would at first sight appear. It might very well be the first occasion on which the reader had been brought face to face with the doctrine in question, at any rate as a doctrine seriously entertained by Plato; and this expression of astonishment on Glaucon's part is very likely a means which Plato chooses to adopt in order to indicate not that the theory of immortality now to be brought forward is entirely new and distinct from what we find in earlier Dialogues such as the *Crito, Phaedrus,* and *Meno,* but that it is a theory essentially differing from such popular views of immortality as the student may have previously encountered. Moreover it is natural that Plato should draw attention to this distinction in the *Republic* rather than in any other of his writings because that Dialogue contains a complete exposition of doctrine so far as it was yet formulated in his mind.

It will be necessary to return later to a more detailed consideration of the *Republic* and its bearing on Plato's theory of immortality. Meanwhile it will be well in view of what has been said above, before proceeding to determine the precise nature of Plato's own theory, to sketch very shortly the form or forms of belief in the immortality of the soul which had hitherto been presented to the Greek intelligence, and afterwards to show from the Dialogues themselves how Plato differentiates his own theory from any such previous or contemporary belief.

CHAPTER I.

PRE-PLATONIC VIEWS OF IMMORTALITY.

In the earliest times of which we have any know-ledge the Greek cherished an innate horror of the bare thought of death. Living as he did in a beautiful and smiling land, he took in the course of his daily life a child-like, if not indeed almost childish, delight in the enjoyment of the rarely failing sunshine, the shady groves, and the cool, sparkling fountains of his native Hellas. No life that he could imagine beyond the grave could be in any way worthy of comparison with that which he was accustomed to live and to see lived on earth ; after death all was misery and gloom. Nowhere is this pessimistic attitude more prominently brought before us than in the eleventh book of the *Odyssey*, the so-called Νέκυια. Elsewhere in Homer, but nowhere more emphatically than here, we are told that a man's 'soul' (ψυχή) is nothing more than a sort of wraith which informs the body during life and continues to a certain extent to resemble it outwardly after death, being hence called εἴδωλον, an 'image' or 'phantom.' This εἴδωλον, however, though it continues superficially to resemble the man, is not really the man's 'self' at all : for the word αὐτός, when it is used in speaking of a man after his death, means either the dead body or else the

man as he was when he lived on earth. Only in one
instance, that of Heracles, is the man himself said to
'dwell on high with the gods,' and the passage in which
this statement occurs is now generally recognised as
belonging to a much later period than the rest of the
book. Nowhere 'below' is any joy to be found. Even
Achilles, or rather his εἴδωλον, whose lot is ostensibly
more cheerful than that of the others, refuses to be
comforted :—

> μὴ δή μοι θάνατόν γε παραύδα, φαίδιμ' 'Οδυσσεῦ·
> βουλοίμην κ' ἐπάρουρος ἐὼν θητευέμεν ἄλλῳ,
> ἀνδρὶ παρ' ἀκλήρῳ, ᾧ μὴ βίοτος πολὺς εἴη,
> ἢ πᾶσιν νεκύεσσι καταφθιμένοισιν ἀνάσσειν.
>
> (HOM. *Od.* XI 488—491.)

Thus the realm of Hades as Homer pictures it is nothing
more than a world of shadows, so vague and shadowy in
fact as hardly to imply a belief in immortality at all.

Nor can it be seriously maintained that anything
more definite or more desirable than this dreary outlook
was anticipated by the average Greek down to the time
of Plato. He would doubtless be familiar with the
Νέκυια and would have little or nothing to add to what
his Homer taught him. Enough for him was the fact,
only too plain for all to see, that after death the body
did not live any more. Whatever the 'soul' might be,
or to whatever place it might take its flight after being
parted from the body, the cardinal fact remained that it
was parted from the body, and while that was so it could
not in any true sense be said to 'live' at all. The need
of a body was felt to be imperative, as is clear from
many passages in the poets. One instance will be sufficient here. In the *Choëphori*, when Orestes and Electra

are invoking the shade of Agamemnon, Electra, knowing
that an interview with him such as she desires cannot
take place unless he has a body to appear in, prays to
Persephone to give him one :—

> ὦ Περσέφασσα, δὸς δ᾽ ἔτ᾽ εὔμορφον κράτος.
> (AESCH. *Cho.* 490.)

And a remark of Orestes a little later (517—8),

> θανόντι δ᾽, οὐ φρονοῦντι, δειλαία χάρις
> ἐπέμπετ᾽,

shows that the description which Achilles gives of the
state of a man after death is well remembered :—

> ὦ πόποι, ἦ ῥά τις ἔστι καὶ εἰν ᾽Αΐδαο δόμοισι
> ψυχὴ καὶ εἴδωλον, ἀτὰρ φρένες οὐκ ἔνι πάμπαν.
> (HOM. *Il.* XXIII 103—4.)

With Pindar indeed the case is somewhat different.
In him we find distinct allusions to the transmigration
of souls and to an Elysium in Hades where the Blest
live a happy life after death. Even Plato himself does
not scruple to quote Pindar as an authority for the
immortality of the soul :—

> ...Πίνδαρος καὶ ἄλλοι πολλοὶ τῶν ποιητῶν, ὅσοι θεῖοί
> εἰσιν,...φασὶ...τὴν ψυχὴν τοῦ ἀνθρώπου εἶναι ἀθάνατον,
> καὶ τότε μὲν τελευτᾶν, ὃ δὴ ἀποθνήσκειν καλοῦσι, τότε δὲ
> πάλιν γίγνεσθαι, ἀπόλλυσθαι δ᾽ οὐδέποτε. (*Meno* 81 B.)

But this is no evidence that the doctrine in question
was at all widespread. On the contrary, in the passage
just quoted Socrates introduces it as a doctrine belonging to a select class of people, certain ἱερῆς and ἱέρειαι

and such poets as are θεῖοι. It is clear that Plato is here thinking of the Mysteries, and it is under their influence that Pindar writes as he does about a future life in the fragments of the Θρῆνοι and occasionally elsewhere. It was not a doctrine that appealed with much force to the ordinary man. Throughout the pre-Platonic era the body is of far greater importance to the average Greek than the soul. The body up to a certain point he could understand, the soul he could not; for the Greek mind was incapable of grasping a spiritual abstraction until we come to Anaxagoras; and even he speaks with no very certain voice.

With this Homeric belief, which so far as we can see formed with little or no variation the basis of the popular creed, Plato will have absolutely nothing to do. In the third book of the *Republic* he protests strongly against it and even denounces all allusion by poets to such a miserable outlook as is depicted in the Homeric poems as being thoroughly mischievous and likely to induce an enervating and demoralising fear of death Whatever, then, may be his own view of immortality, we may rest assured that the existence of this shadowy tradition can have had—except possibly in a negative way—nothing whatever to do with its formation.

Far more important in this connexion, and at the same time quite distinct from the popular tradition, are the Mysteries mentioned above. Both the Eleusinian and the Orphic Mysteries seem to have recognised some sort of immortality, and, as we have seen, they influenced Pindar and probably others in this respect. But, whatever their influence, it must be remembered that these Mysteries were after all nothing more than religious cults; they were not in any sense systems of philosophy,

for they could give no rational account of the doctrines
they sought to inculcate, nor did they profess to establish any sort of philosophic basis for them. It seems
that the rise of both the Eleusinian and the Orphic cults
was to a large extent due to the natural and universal
desire of mankind for continued existence, the desire to
obtain at all costs a prolongation of life, if not in the
world they know, at any rate in some other as good or
better. But their adherents did not trouble themselves
to think very profoundly what was the true nature of
this 'soul,' about whose welfare they busied themselves
so anxiously, or what was the real meaning of this 'immortality' for which they strove, how it was related to
the whole order of things in the universe. The ordinary
Greek who sought refuge in the Mysteries would be
actuated principally by a desire to escape from the
dismal prospect held out to him by the Homeric pictures
of the underworld, to endeavour to secure for himself
a better fortune after death than fell to the lot of even
the greatest heroes of old time. The man who had been
initiated into the Mysteries was considered by those
'who knew' to have a vastly more fortunate lot in store
for him than the ordinary layman. The fond hope of
the initiated was that, after faithfully devoting themselves
to the service of Demeter or Iacchus or some other of
the Chthonian divinities in this life, they would in one
shape or another receive their favours after death in that
underworld where these divinities had power to confer
or withhold benefits at their will. The Orphic creed,
however, seems to have gone further than the Eleusinian
in that it recognised the doctrine of metempsychosis,
which the testimony of Herodotus enables us to trace
back to the crude religion of the barbarous peoples of

Thrace, whence the Orphic Mysteries are supposed to have originally come.

These mystic cults were in reality little less vague, though doubtless in their higher form at least more ennobling, than the traditional popular religion of the age. Strictness and purity of life on the part of the initiated rather than any particular dogmatic creed would appear to have been their most important practical result. As regards their effect on Plato, it is obvious from several passages in his works, such as the one from the *Meno* quoted above, that he was well acquainted with the Mysteries, and it is probable that they may have served to keep before his mind such problems as the immortality of the soul; but it may be said at once that such influence as they possessed manifested itself rather in the form of his exposition, and perhaps in the asceticism of his life and precepts, than in the substance of his thought. What he cannot bring directly into line with his argument he often introduces under cover of a myth; and the fanciful imagery and general form of these myths we can easily believe to have been originally suggested to him by his acquaintance with the Orphic and Eleusinian Mysteries. But beyond this it is unlikely that he was seriously influenced by them. In fact in the tenth book of the *Laws* (905 D *sqq.*), where he is controverting the opinion of those persons who, while professing to believe in the existence of gods, imagine that they can be propitiated and turned from their deliberately determined course of action by means of judicious sacrifices and offerings, it seems most probable that he here has uppermost in his mind the debased and degenerate parody of religion to which in his time the Mysteries had in the hands of some people been de-

graded. Nevertheless in their higher forms he seems to
have regarded them with respect, and may have found
some of their traditions suggestive; for besides the
above-quoted passage from the *Meno* he is generally
held to refer to Orphic traditions in several other places,
notably *Phaedo* 62 B, 69 C, 70 C; *Crat.* 400 C; *Laws*
870 D.

Side by side with the Mysteries, and in some respects
closely allied to them, is the Pythagorean religion, if
indeed the traditions and rule of life supposed to have
been handed down by Pythagoras to his disciples and
their successors can fairly be dignified with that title.
The personality of Pythagoras must always remain to
a large extent wrapped in a veil of obscurity. It is
noticeable that Aristotle, from whom most of our scanty
knowledge of the Pythagoreans and their tenets is derived, never mentions Pythagoras himself by name; he
invariably speaks of οἱ Πυθαγόρειοι. All that we really
know of the man himself is that he founded a kind of
sect or brotherhood, the chief characteristics of which
were a careful system of education and a strict rule of
life. He had no definite philosophical system, and,
though he undoubtedly exercised a good deal of influence on the course of subsequent speculation, he
cannot himself be said to belong to the philosophic
succession. That the Pythagoreans believed in the
transmigration of souls and other mystic doctrines
seems, however, certain; but they had no reasoned
metaphysical scheme in which these beliefs could find
a place. The main purpose for which the brotherhood
was founded was the systematic provision of a liberal
education, and it seems most probable that they adopted
such doctrines as that of the transmigration of the soul

from the Orphics, with whom in the strictness of their method of life they were nearly allied. Plato was in all probability well acquainted with the sect and its doctrines ; at the same time there seems to be no doubt nowadays that the influence of Pythagoreanism on his philosophy has been greatly exaggerated. The chief cause of this is to be found in the so-called *Fragments of Philolaus*, which are now generally admitted to be the spurious compilations of an author who was much later in date than either Philolaus or Plato. It is clear that this writer, whoever he may have been, knew the *Philebus* and the *Timaeus* well, and his object seems to have been to gain for Pythagoras or the Pythagoreans the credit of having originated the elaborate system of metaphysics contained in those Dialogues. It is quite possible that Plato at an early period of his career may have first come across the doctrine of metempsychosis from his intercourse with members of the Pythagorean brotherhood. That he did know something of individual Pythagoreans is a natural inference from the fact of his introducing as interlocutors in his Dialogues historical characters such as Simmias, Cebes, and Timaeus, who were undoubtedly Pythagoreans. The first two especially are portrayed with such delicate minuteness that it is hard to believe that Plato was not acquainted with them in real life. Nevertheless it would be rash ro assert that he could not have arrived at his own philosophical adaptation of the theory of transmigration independently of Pythagorean influence. In any case the precise manner in which this doctrine first entered Plato's mind is of little importance ; the point to notice is that, whereas he found it merely a vague belief, in his hands it became a reasoned philosophical theory.

The pre-Platonic philosophers contributed nothing of importance in this connexion. It is true that Heraclitus and Empedocles held views of an existence of the soul anterior to and separate from the body; but, so far as we are in a position to judge, these views took the form of mere dogmatic assertions which they made no attempt to connect with their more distinctly philosophical theories or to adopt as an integral part of a system. The immortality of the soul was to them little more than a vague belief resting on a different plane altogether from that of their philosophical convictions, with which indeed it seems sometimes very hard to reconcile. They must have arrived at these beliefs quite independently of their physical and metaphysical speculations, and it is probable that they, like the Pythagoreans, derived them from Orphic sources. Moreover, we have always to remember that these pre-Platonic philosophers had not arrived at any clear notion of what they meant by the 'soul,' and such theories of soul as they professed were all of a materialistic nature. In Anaxagoras, it is true, we can trace the germ of something higher. He took the great step of recognising νοῦς in the abstract as the prime cause of the universe. At the same time he was unable himself to see the full value of his own principle. Both Plato and Aristotle, while admiring the originality of his genius, complain that he did not go far enough. The abstract principle, of which he was the first discoverer, was capable of very great development; but it needed the genius of Plato himself to turn it to real account.

There still remains Socrates. He, like Pythagoras, was not a philosopher in the strict sense of the term; that is to say, he did not attempt to solve the riddle of

the universe, but confined himself to the sphere of
human conduct.	Nevertheless Socrates, to a greater
extent even than Pythagoras, was a powerful factor in
determining the course to be taken by philosophy in the
future; and he must not be left out of account in any
appreciation of the contribution rendered by pre-Platonic
thought in connexion with our present subject.	What,
then, was the attitude of the historical Socrates towards
the question of the immortality of the soul? It is not
easy to give a very definite opinion on this point.
We learn from a well-known passage in Xenophon's
Memorabilia Socratis that he attached the highest importance to the possession by man of a ' soul,' which more
than anything else about him partakes of the nature of
the Divine :—

ἀλλὰ μὴν καὶ ἀνθρώπου γε ψυχή, εἴπερ τι καὶ ἄλλο
τῶν ἀνθρωπίνων, τοῦ θείου μετέχει.
(XEN. Mem. IV iii 14.)

But we nowhere hear of his making any direct state-
ment declaring a belief that the soul is immortal.	The
words on this subject which are put into his mouth at
the close of the *Apology* are very guarded, and it is
probable that they represent his customary way of
speaking on the question :—

δυοῖν γὰρ θάτερόν ἐστι τὸ τεθνάναι· ἢ γὰρ οἷον μηδὲν
εἶναι μηδ' αἴσθησιν μηδεμίαν μηδενὸς ἔχειν τὸν τεθνεῶτα,
ἢ κατὰ τὰ λεγόμενα μεταβολή τις τυγχάνει οὖσα καὶ
μετοίκησις τῇ ψυχῇ τοῦ τόπου τοῦ ἐνθένδε εἰς ἄλλον
τόπον. (PLAT. *Apol.* 40 C.)

Here the words τὰ λεγόμενα most probably refer to the
Orphic and Pythagorean traditions.	Thus, whether death

means absolute extinction, or whether, as some maintain, it is the entrance into another life, Socrates regards the prospect with equanimity. He will not give any decided opinion on the subject. And after all such an attitude is only what we should naturally expect in accordance with the general position which he takes up in regard to similar inquiries. He declines, on this subject as on all others, to arrogate to himself any special knowledge, and he delivers himself of no special dogma. All that we are entitled to say is that it is very probable that as a matter of fact he did anticipate a future life in some form or other. We can hardly help feeling that the unwavering belief in the immortality of the soul which pervades the *Phaedo* represents, in part at least, the faith of the historical Socrates as well as Plato's personal conviction. But he will not assert the belief dogmatically; and moreover he is as destitute as his predecessors of any philosophical base upon which to ground it. We may conclude, then, that for the form of his theory of immortality Plato owes no direct debt to Socrates, though it is conceivable and even likely that in this problem as in others the inspiration to follow up a particular line of thought was derived in the first instance from the suggestive discourse of his master.

We are now in a position to see clearly the sort of difference which we may naturally expect to find between Plato's doctrine of the immortality of the soul and all other such doctrines, previous or contemporary. It is a difference between vague popular or mystic beliefs resting on no philosophical basis on the one hand and a reasoned philosophical theory on the other. This is just the difference which Cicero discerns between the Pythagorean and the Platonic treatment of the question :—

rationem illi [sc. *Pythagorei*] *sententiae suae non fere reddebant, nisi quid erat numeris aut descriptionibus explicandum. Platonem ferunt, ut Pythagoreos cognosceret, in Italiam venisse et didicisse Pythagorea omnia, primumque de animorum aeternitate non solum sensisse idem quod Pythagoram, sed rationem etiam attulisse.*

(CIC. *Tusc. Disp.* I xvii.)

And this too is, I fancy, precisely the difference which Plato himself intends us to feel when we read Glaucon's remark in the passage from the tenth book of the *Republic,* which I have taken as my text. In the preceding books Socrates has given an analysis of soul far in advance of anything in the way of scientific psychology that had been achieved before. "Can you really maintain," asks Glaucon in effect, "that this ψυχή which you have been describing, the seat of the intellect, the emotions, and the passions, is immortal?" "I can," replies Socrates: and then follows a short proof of the immortality of the soul. What this theory of immortality really meant for Plato, how he arrived at it, and what modifications, if any, it underwent in his hands as his metaphysical opinions changed, let us now essay to determine.

CHAPTER II.

THE *SYMPOSIUM.*

Dr Jackson, whose general view of Plato's philosophical development I follow throughout, would on metaphysical grounds divide the Dialogues into the following five groups:—

I. The *Socratic* Dialogues: *i.e.* those in which Plato does not advance beyond the position of the historical Socrates; that is to say, he deals for the most part with *definitions.* A typical example of this group is the *Euthyphro.*

(This group will not concern us here.)

II. The *Educational* Dialogues: *i.e.* those which, however they may differ in other respects, agree in this point, that in each of them some current *educational system* is criticized. Of these there are six, *viz.* the *Protagoras, Gorgias, Phaedrus, Symposium, Euthydemus, Meno.* In the *Phaedrus*, the *Symposium*, and the *Meno* we can trace the first beginnings of the *Theory of Ideas.*

(This is how Dr Jackson would arrange this group: I should prefer to transpose the *Phaedrus* and the *Symposium*, though this change is of slight importance.)

III.   The Dialogues of the *First Metaphysical Period*: *i.e.* those in which the *Earlier Theory of Ideas* is formulated.   Of these there are three, *viz.* the

> *Republic* (Plato works out his own constructive educational system, founding it on a philosophical —*i.e.* metaphysical—basis, which is sketched dogmatically) ;
> *Phaedo* (the Theory of Ideas is further developed, though not with such confidence of tone as in the *Republic*) ;
> *Cratylus* (the Theory of Ideas is opposed to Heracliteanism).

IV.   The Dialogues of the *Second Metaphysical Period*, *i.e.* those in which the *Later Theory of Ideas* is worked out in a technical manner.   Of these there are six, *viz.* the *Parmenides, Philebus, Theaetetus, Sophist, Politicus, Timaeus.*   (Of these the *Theaetetus, Sophist,* and *Politicus* are mainly logical; the *Parmenides,Philebus,* and *Timaeus* mainly ontological.   In the *Critias*, which apparently is intended to follow the *Timaeus*, a return is already made to the earlier manner : this Dialogue, therefore, is of no metaphysical importance.)

V.   The work of Plato's old age, in which he returns from metaphysics to his former studies—ethics, politics, and sociology.   This period is represented by one Dialogue, *viz.* the *Laws.*

I propose now to comment successively on six of these Dialogues which I consider specially important for determining the character and development of Plato's theory of the immortality of the soul.   These six are the *Symposium*, the *Phaedrus*, the *Republic*, the *Phaedo*, the

Timaeus, and the *Laws*. I shall deal with them in this
order, which I believe to be also the order in which they
were written.

At the outset I find myself at issue with Mr E. S.
Thompson: for whereas I regard the *Symposium* as
prior to the *Meno* and the *Republic*, he in his edition of
the *Meno* maintains that the *Symposium* is later than
both these Dialogues and should be classed with the
Phaedo. This is a serious difference of opinion, and it
will be necessary to say a few words in justification of
the view I take in opposition to so eminent a Platonic
scholar, the more especially as he agrees in the main
with Dr Jackson's arrangement of the Dialogues. In so
far as he would put the *Meno* just before and the
Phaedo soon after the *Republic*, I cordially agree with
Mr Thompson; but I am quite unable to follow him in
coupling the *Symposium* with the *Phaedo* and therefore
placing it later than the *Meno* and the *Republic*. Apparently the chief reason which causes him to assign this
later date to the *Symposium* is to be found in the greater
development of the doctrine of δόξα and of the antithesis
between δόξα and ἐπιστήμη which he discerns in the
Symposium as compared with the *Meno* and the *Republic*.
In a note on *Meno* 97 B he says: "Another reference
to the doctrine of the *Meno* occurs in the important
passage *Symp.* 202 A:

ἢ οὐκ ᾔσθησαι ὅτι ἔστι τι μεταξὺ σοφίας καὶ
ἀμαθίας; Τί τοῦτο; Τὸ ὀρθὰ δοξάζειν καὶ ἄνευ τοῦ ἔχειν
λόγον δοῦναι οὐκ οἶσθ', ἔφη, ὅτι οὔτε ἐπίστασθαί ἐστιν·
ἄλογον γὰρ πρᾶγμα πῶς ἂν εἴη ἐπιστήμη; οὔτε ἀμαθία·
τὸ γὰρ τοῦ ὄντος τυγχάνον πῶς ἂν εἴη ἀμαθία; ἔστι δὲ
δή που τοιοῦτον ἡ ὀρθὴ δόξα, μεταξὺ φρονήσεως καὶ
ἀμαθίας."

Now this method of determining the mutual relations of two Dialogues by means of supposed 'references' in the one to the other must always, it seems to me, be unsatisfactory when unsupported by strong evidence of some other kind. A result which is arrived at by discussion in one Dialogue may of course in another be taken as being more or less familiar, and may consequently be referred to only in a cursory manner. On the other hand it can equally well happen that an opinion may be advanced and allowed to pass without full discussion in a Dialogue where it is not of very special importance, and then in a later Dialogue it may be dealt with in a more critical and elaborate manner. And in the present instance it seems to me that in this way we get at least as likely an explanation of the respective allusions to δόξα in the *Symposium* and the *Meno*. I cannot find in the *Symposium* any 'development of the doctrine of δόξα contained in the *Meno*' such as Mr Thompson supposes to exist; nor does he state anywhere, so far as I can see, in what precisely this 'development' consists; the 'development of the doctrine of δόξα' is surely to be found not in the *Symposium* but in the *Republic*. In any case it seems to me that whatever argument for the later date of the *Symposium* can be extracted from its treatment of this question must be more than counterbalanced by arguments on the other side which take for their *criteria* the Theory of Ideas and the doctrine of immortality.

The other arguments which Mr Thompson adduces in support of the view he adopts seem hardly to deserve serious refutation. In the course of the introduction to his edition of the *Meno* (p. lii) he says: "The next dialogues to be considered in relation to the *Meno* are

the *Symposium* and the *Phaedo*.   Both of these I regard
as later than the *Republic*, and *a fortiori* later than
the *Meno*.   In spite of their great difference they have
this in common, that both present an idealized picture
of Socrates more full and vivid than any to be found
elsewhere."   Is not this rather an exaggeration ?   Are
we justified in connecting the *Symposium* on this ground
with the *Phaedo* any more than with the *Apology*, the
Crito, or above all the *Phaedrus*?   And in any case
Plato is a consummate literary artist ; would he not be
capable of introducing 'an idealized picture of Socrates'
wherever he considered that the literary effect would be
thereby enhanced, even though a few years had elapsed
since he last had occasion to do so?   Mr Thompson continues : " Plato rises in them " [*sc.* the *Symposium* and
the *Phaedo*] " to what is absolutely his highest point of
poetical beauty, both in imagination and in diction."
Here we are at once tempted to ask again, What of the
Phaedrus?   Surely it is with the *Phaedrus*, not the
Phaedo, that the *Symposium* should naturally be coupled,
on these grounds as well as on the more important
ground of similarity of subject-matter and general tone.
Mr Thompson's final argument is, if anything, still more
flimsy.   "One strong reason," he says, "for thinking
them later than the *Republic* is that in assigning the
Phaedrus, *Euthydemus* and *Meno* (with the *Menexenus*
and *Clitophon*) to the years 386—383 B.C.—during all
which time Plato must have been working at his *chef
d'oeuvre*—we are sufficiently filling up his time."   That
is to say, assuming that these dates are absolutely
correct, it is natural to suppose that Plato should have
written five Dialogues during this period, but quite unreasonable to imagine that he could have written six !

Mr Thompson is aware of the fact that the position
he assigns to the *Symposium* raises a difficult question in
regard to the development of the doctrine of immortality,
and I cannot see that he anywhere succeeds in getting
over the difficulty which thus arises. The explanation
which he offers (p. liv) does not seem to me, I confess,
to explain anything at all. It is mainly on this ground
—the view taken of immortality—that I am led to place
the *Symposium* where I do, and I feel that the earlier
date is justified on general grounds of style and subject-
matter as well. As I have said above, the *Symposium*
and the *Phaedrus* must surely go together. But which
of these two Dialogues is the earlier? This is a difficult
question to answer, and the question is perhaps after all
not a very important one. The late Dr W. H. Thompson
in the introduction to his edition of the *Phaedrus* maintains (p. xvi) that that Dialogue was intended in a sense
to follow the *Gorgias*, where Plato had made a violent
attack on Rhetoric which second thoughts induced him
to modify; and Dr Thompson's arguments seem to me
to be thoroughly convincing. Internal evidence also
makes it fairly certain that the *Gorgias* is prior to the
Symposium. But are we to infer from the fact that
the *Phaedrus* is intended to follow and correct the
Gorgias that therefore it must precede the *Symposium*?
Dr Jackson is inclined to put the *Phaedrus* first for this
reason, and also because he thinks that in the *Symposium*
Plato advances further on the road towards the Theory
of Ideas than in the *Phaedrus*. But, while fully recognising the connexion between the *Phaedrus* and the
Gorgias, I do not consider it necessary to assume on
that account that the one followed *immediately* after the
other. On the contrary, it seems to me rather more

likely that there was some interval during which Plato saw that he might be liable to misrepresentation in respect of his sweeping condemnation of Rhetoric in the *Gorgias*, and therefore resolved to correct it in the *Phaedrus*. Moreover it is by no means clear to me that a nearer approach to the Theory of Ideas is made in the *Symposium* than in the *Phaedrus*. No doubt the stages by which we are to arrive at the conception of αὐτὸ τὸ κάλλος are made clearer in the *Symposium* ; but then it seems to me quite likely that Plato, as he began to see his way clearer, was emboldened to describe in the allegory of the *Phaedrus* what this vision of loveliness would be like if we ever succeeded in reaching it.

The point which I wish to insist on most strongly, then, is that the *Symposium* should not be coupled, as Mr Thompson couples it, with the *Phaedo* : it must be taken in close connexion with the *Phaedrus*. And on the whole I am inclined to go further and say that the *Symposium* comes first, followed closely by the *Phaedrus*; then at no long interval comes the *Meno*. In the *Symposium*, as it seems to me, we have the first hint of a theory of immortality—scarcely more than a 'metaphorical immortality,' to borrow Mr Thompson's expression ; then we have a direct demonstration of immortality—no longer metaphorical—in the *Phaedrus*; and afterwards in the *Meno* the doctrine is supported by an appeal to the theory of ἀνάμνησις, the natural outcome of the myth in the *Phaedrus*.

After this preliminary statement we can now proceed to consider the teaching of the *Symposium* itself.

We have seen that in all pre-Platonic thought and also in the popular imagination of Greece the only kind

of life that was felt to be worthy of the name was corporeal life, that is to say, the life which we at present
know in this world, or else some other, but essentially
similar, life elsewhere, such as was contemplated by the
devotees of the Mysteries.   It had not as yet occurred
to the Greek mind to make a definite separation between
body and soul, between mind and matter, however much
such a distinction may have been implied or foreshadowed.
It was customary to regard the soul as nothing more than
a part of the body, a part invisible, it may be, and of a
highly refined character, but still corporeal ; and a complete body was considered to be indispensable to the
exercise by the soul of its proper functions.   From this
point of view immortality, if such a thing be conceivable,
can only mean the continuance in some form or another
of corporeal existence such as that with which we are
familiar.   Such a notion of immortality seems to have
been in Plato's mind when he wrote the *Symposium*.
There is not very much of importance in this Dialogue
for the purpose of ascertaining the nature of Plato's own
theory, but it contains one or two passages perhaps
which deserve notice before we pass on to the consideration of utterances of much greater significance in
other Dialogues.   In commenting on this and other
Dialogues I shall take the passages which seem to be
of special importance and discuss them in order as they
occur.

πολλῶν πολλὰ καὶ καλὰ ἐργασαμένων εὐαριθμήτοις
δή τισιν ἔδοσαν τοῦτο γέρας οἱ θεοί, ἐξ "Αιδου ἀνεῖναι
πάλιν τὴν ψυχήν, ἀλλὰ τὴν ἐκείνης ἀνεῖσαν ἀγασθέντες
τῷ ἔργῳ. (*Symp.* 179 C.)

Plato is here citing the legend of Alcestis as an

illustration of the mighty power of love. Her love for her husband was so great that in order to win immortality for him she consented to die herself. It was considered, says Phaedrus, a proof of the highest possible self-sacrifice to submit to death on another's behalf, to be willing, that is, to enter Hades *dead*, not, like Orpheus, attempting to do so *alive*. Such self-sacrifice therefore on the part of Alcestis won the warmest approbation from the gods. And how did they show their approbation? By doing for her something that was done for very few (εὐαριθμήτοις δή τισιν), namely ἐξ Ἅιδου ἀνεῖναι πάλιν τὴν ψυχήν. The soul of Alcestis was, as a reward for the highest kind of bravery, permitted to return from Hades to earth, the reason being that the earthly life was regarded as superior: it was on earth that the soul's functions could best be exercised, for on earth she would be united with a body. In short, existence in Hades was not really life at all; and it is this fact that accounts for the distinction made between the act of Alcestis and that (at first sight similar) of Orpheus. Orpheus when he entered Hades was alive, for he had a body; Alcestis was dead, for she had left her body on earth. The soul without the body could hardly be said to live at all; it was then merely a senseless phantom flitting about among other phantoms like itself. It is not of course to be inferred that this represents Plato's own belief even at this early stage of his philosophical career; but the passage is nevertheless instructive; we could hardly have a better illustration than that which Plato here gives us of what an ordinary Athenian of his time would regard as the natural and obvious view to take of life and death. To have his days on earth prolonged was the best and most desirable thing that could happen to a man; hence it was quite consistent to represent this as the greatest blessing the gods had it in their power to bestow. Such a representation would doubtless be the most likely to commend itself to the majority of Plato's readers at this time; and it is quite possible that Plato wished to emphasize this fact before he went on to develop his own very different view of the relations subsisting between body and soul and between death and life.

ἡ θνητὴ φύσις ζητεῖ κατὰ τὸ δυνατὸν ἀεί τε εἶναι καὶ ἀθάνατος· δύναται δὲ ταύτῃ μόνον, τῇ γενέσει, ὅτι ἀεὶ καταλείπει ἕτερον νέον ἀντὶ τοῦ παλαιοῦ. (*Symp.* 207 D.)

According to the theory here expressed the passion of love is due to the overpowering desire of the mortal nature for immortality, which is just afterwards definitely called ἀθανασία. This view of immortality, if it can fairly be regarded as such, is very much the same as that of the preceding passage. What is meant by immortality (ἀθανασία) is the everlasting continuance of life upon earth, if such a thing were possible; there is no suggestion of a future life in another world and under conditions other than those existing here. What the mortal nature desires is to be (in the strict sense of the word) 'immortal,' that is to say, to be exempt from death. And there is a sort of immortality in this sense to be obtained; it is an immortality, however, not of the individual but of the species, and it consists not in the continuance of the same life but in a succession of generations. The longing for immortality impels to love, and love results in the production, so to speak, of another self; and the mortal thing preserves its identity not in the sense that it remains absolutely unchanged

(for unchangeableness is an attribute of the divine alone),
nor yet in the continued possession of unvarying bodily
or mental characteristics (for these, as we know, are
continually changing even in the same individual); the
identity consists simply in the fact that the new self
which is the offspring of love is a being of the same
nature as the old; in other words, immortality for
mortal beings means no more than the perpetuation
of the species:—

τούτῳ γὰρ τῷ τρόπῳ πᾶν τὸ θνητὸν σῴζεται, οὐ τῷ
παντάπασι τὸ αὐτὸ ἀεὶ εἶναι ὥσπερ τὸ θεῖον, ἀλλὰ τῷ τὸ
ἀπιὸν καὶ παλαιούμενον ἕτερον νέον ἐγκαταλείπειν, οἷον
αὐτὸ ἦν· ταύτῃ τῇ μηχανῇ, ὦ Σώκρατες, ἔφη, θνητὸν
ἀθανασίας μετέχει, καὶ σῶμα καὶ τἆλλα πάντα· ἀθάνατον
δὲ ἄλλῃ. (*Symp.* 208 A, B.)

According to this view, then, all that can be called
immortality so far as things essentially mortal are concerned consists in the continuance of the species on
earth; it must not be looked for in the shape of another
life or a continuation of the same life for the individual
as was contemplated in the legend of Alcestis and
Admetus. It is to be noticed, however, that there is
one expression in the passage last quoted which seems
to contain a hint that the final word has not yet been
said on the subject: ἀθάνατον δὲ ἄλλῃ (sc. ἀθανασίας
μετέχει): the immortality which is enjoyed by a being
of its own nature immortal is of another kind than that
described above. Obviously, then, if it can be shown
that there is a sense in which the soul, as distinct from
the particular living creature which is born and dies,
may be called ἀθάνατον, we shall be entitled to conclude
that after all immortality, even for beings which we

habitually regard as mortal, may mean something more
than the mere continuance of the species.

ἢ οὐκ ἐνθυμεῖ, ἔφη, ὅτι ἐνταῦθα αὐτῷ μοναχοῦ
γενήσεται, ὁρῶντι ᾧ ὁρατὸν τὸ καλόν, τίκτειν οὐκ εἴδωλα
ἀρετῆς, ἅτε οὐκ εἰδώλου ἐφαπτομένῳ, ἀλλ᾽ ἀληθῆ, ἅτε
τοῦ ἀληθοῦς ἐφαπτομένῳ; τεκόντι δὲ ἀρετὴν ἀληθῆ καὶ
θρεψαμένῳ ὑπάρχει θεοφιλεῖ γενέσθαι, καὶ εἴπερ τῳ
ἄλλῳ ἀνθρώπων, ἀθανάτῳ καὶ ἐκείνῳ. (*Symp.* 212 A.)

The nature of the immortality which was just hinted
at above is now suggested with a little more precision.
If there is such a thing as immortality for men, says
Diotima, it must surely belong in the truest sense to the
man who has beheld αὐτὸ τὸ καλόν and in consequence
of this is enabled to produce in his mind something more
than mere semblances (εἴδωλα) of virtue ; for his object
is to obtain not semblance but truth : true virtue is his
and his alone. From all this it is easy to see that Plato
is now becoming much more philosophical than he has
been before ; in fact, as the phraseology of the passage
before us shows, he is feeling his way towards the
Theory of Ideas. It is important therefore to consider
carefully the significance of the word ἀθάνατος introduced in such a connexion. Here there is clearly no
question of an immortality such as that which has been
suggested earlier in the *Symposium.* The immortality
which is here adumbrated cannot be the mere continuance of earthly life or of a similar life in another world.
The philosopher, we are told, is especially entitled to be
called immortal in virtue of his ability to see ideal truth.
But it would be quite incompatible with Plato's whole
position in this Dialogue to suppose that ability to
apprehend the immaterial could in any way tend to

secure to its possessor the continuance of a corporeal existence. On the contrary, it is only by abstracting himself from earth and earthly things as far as possible that the philosopher can behold truth as it is in itself, the real truth that is contained in the ideal world. Even those who are in love with a human object, says Diotima, would be ready,

εἴ πως οἷόν τ᾽ ἦν, μήτε ἐσθίειν μήτε πίνειν, ἀλλὰ θεᾶσθαι μόνον καὶ ξυνεῖναι· τί δῆτα, ἔφη, οἰόμεθα, εἴ τῳ γένοιτο αὐτὸ τὸ καλὸν ἰδεῖν εἰλικρινές, καθαρόν, ἄμικτον, ἀλλὰ μὴ ἀνάπλεων σαρκῶν τε ἀνθρωπίνων καὶ χρωμάτων καὶ ἄλλης πολλῆς φλυαρίας θνητῆς, ἀλλ᾽ αὐτὸ τὸ θεῖον καλὸν δύναιτο μονοειδὲς κατιδεῖν; ἆρ᾽ οἴει, ἔφη, φαῦλον βίον γίγνεσθαι ἐκεῖσε βλέποντος ἀνθρώπου κἀκεῖνο ᾧ δεῖ θεωμένου καὶ ξυνόντος αὐτῷ ; (*Symp.* 211 D–212 A.)

All this shows that for the philosopher at least corporeal existence is not the highest kind of life that he can conceive. In this passage, then, Plato's rejection of the traditional and popular view is unmistakeable. Again, the perpetuation of the species, in which sense it has been said before that θνητὸν ἀθανασίας μετέχει, would be quite irrelevant here ; for the apprehension of the self-beautiful is a personal possession and cannot be handed on from father to son simply by the process of generation. The immortality which is now in question, however 'metaphorical' it may be, must at any rate be of a personal kind.

We have seen that, whereas the lover is content with the particular beauty he sees in his beloved, the object which the philosopher seeks to attain is the continuous and unimpeded contemplation of ideal beauty. The true philosopher not only has seen but continues to see (ὁρῶντι) this vision, and the immortality which Diotima ascribes to him is bound up with his ability to see it. The ideal world is essentially the immortal world; and the more the soul can withdraw herself from the material perception of this world to the spiritual contemplation of the other, immortality is more truly hers. Even at this early stage we can see that Plato's view of immortality is very different from any that had preceded it. He has not indeed as yet elaborated anything that can fairly be called a *theory* of immortality; but we cannot help feeling even in reading the *Symposium* that he is well on the way towards it, and what he says there is enough to show us in what respects we may expect to find it differentiated from all previous doctrines of the kind. The difference amounts in effect to this : Plato's predecessors, though they might talk of ψυχή, had no clear notion of what they meant by the term ; they were divided between the vague mysticism, which regarded explanation as impossible or unnecessary, and the rank materialism which did not shrink from the assertion that the soul was a part of the body. Neither could explain what was the nature of that which they declared to be immortal. Plato on the other hand sets about to spiritualise the conception of ψυχή and at the same time to indicate to some extent its nature; consequently he is the first philosopher to have any real appreciation of how much is implied in the assertion that the *soul* is immortal, the soul which not only lives but *thinks* (φρονεῖ). And what this immortality means can be fully understood only by the man who can train himself to apprehend beauty as it is in itself, who can look beyond the ceaseless flux of phenomena to the stable reality that *truly* exists behind the world of sense,

which only *seems* to exist—in fact the true philosopher,
who studies truth for its own sake. Dissatisfied with
the materialist explanation of the universe, and dis-
daining the wholly unscientific procedure of mysticism,
Plato stands out henceforth as the inventor of Idealism.
The logical method which he had inherited from Socrates
suggested to him a means of putting new life into the
discredited philosophy of Parmenides and developing it
in a way of his own. Good Heraclitean though he was,
he restricted the application of the doctrine of flux to
the material world, and sought the ultimate nature of
reality not in Matter but in Mind; and the natural
corollary follows, that the true nature of the living being
is to be found not in the body but in the soul. Moreover, as the ideal world is in the truest sense immortal,
so we may expect to find the soul immortal too; the
principle of *similia similibus cognoscuntur* enunciated by
Empedocles would readily suggest the conclusion that
the eternity of the one involves the eternity of the other.

It is not of course suggested that at the time when
he wrote the *Symposium* Plato had thought the matter
out with the distinctness that this would imply. In the
Symposium he breaks away from old traditions and
gives a faint indication of a new system of philosophy
to be developed later. In the speech of Diotima which
we have been considering we can see the dawn of
the Theory of Ideas, and along with it the dawn of
the Theory of Immortality. Neither theory has as
yet taken definite shape; but the most important and
interesting fact to notice so far is that from the first
the two are intimately connected. The one cannot be
profitably studied apart from the other, for, as we proceed to consider the later Dialogues, we shall see that

the connexion becomes strengthened with time. Plato is now becoming a philosopher in earnest; and, as his system of philosophy develops, we may reasonably expect to find that his theory of soul grows more philosophical, with the natural result that his theory of immortality becomes more and more distinct.

CHAPTER III.

THE *PHAEDRUS.*

IN the last chapter I gave reasons for the belief that the *Symposium* was written probably before the *Phaedrus* and almost certainly before the *Meno*, the *Republic*, and the *Phaedo*. On the assumption, then, that this order of the Dialogues is correct, the *Phaedrus* possesses a special interest for us, because in it we find for the first time a definite *demonstration* of the immortality of the soul. As we might expect, this is not introduced without good reason. In the *Symposium* we are told by what steps in this life the philosopher is to pass from the perception of the beauty belonging to particular beautiful objects in this world to the cognition of the ' self-beautiful' which exists in what we may describe as the world of ideas. In the *Phaedrus* Plato proceeds to describe by means of a highly poetical allegory the nature of this ideal world, the existence of which has been suggested in the *Symposium*. Thus whereas even in the *Symposium* the epithet ἀθάνατος is felt to be not inappropriately applied to the soul of the philosopher who in this life perseveres in the search for truth, in the *Phaedrus*, where the world of truth is described, it is obviously a matter of the first importance to determine what place, if any, is occupied

in that world by the soul. Consequently in the *Phaedrus*
Plato goes deeper into psychology than he has ever gone
before, though as yet he treats the subject for the most
part in an allegorical manner. Moreover, in considering
the relation of the soul to the world of eternally abiding
truth and the real nature both of that world and of the
soul which apprehends it, the question of immortality is
obviously one which cannot be left out of account. It is
not surprising, therefore, to find the account of the nature
of soul prefaced by a proof of its immortality.

Having thus made clear the main purport of the
Dialogue so far as this question is concerned, we may
now proceed to take account of some of the details.

δεῖ οὖν πρῶτον ψυχῆς φύσεως πέρι θείας τε καὶ
ἀνθρωπίνης ἰδόντα πάθη τε καὶ ἔργα τἀληθὲς νοῆσαι.
ἀρχὴ δὲ ἀποδείξεως ἥδε. ψυχὴ πᾶσα ἀθάνατος.

(*Phaedr.* 245 C.)

These are the opening words of the directly psychological portion of the *Phaedrus*. Soul is first declared
to be immortal, and the assertion is followed at once by
a proof. It is noticeable that here the proof of immortality precedes the account of the nature of the soul, as
if Plato meant us to understand from the outset that we
are dealing with something which is essentially immortal.
Thus it seems probable that Plato had by this time come
to feel that the immortality of the soul must be established in order to make his psychological theory complete. In the passage immediately preceding that quoted
above Socrates has been saying that there is a certain
kind of madness, to wit, the madness of love, which is
sent from heaven and ordained for the benefit of mankind. We afterwards discover that this particular μανία

in its highest form is in reality the same thing as the
ἐνθουσίασις of the philosopher. It is in order to prove
that this is so that some psychological theory is felt
to be necessary ; hence the allegory which professes to
explain the nature of soul is introduced with the special
purpose of facilitating the description of this love-
madness which symbolizes philosophic 'enthusiasm.'
And as if to exhibit the importance of the subject in the
strongest light possible, Plato begins by showing that
soul is immortal.

The steps in the reasoning by which the proposition
ψυχὴ πᾶσα ἀθάνατος is proved have been made plain by
Dr Jackson in a note on the passage. In short they are
as follows :—

Let us assume that τὸ ἀεικίνητον is ἀθάνατον.

Now τὸ αὐτοκίνητον is an ἀρχὴ κινήσεως.

But an ἀρχὴ κινήσεως is ἀεικίνητον, because any
ἀρχή is ἀγένητον and ἀδιάφθορον [if the universe is to
continue].

Hence τὸ αὐτοκίνητον is ἀεικίνητον.

But τὸ ἀεικίνητον is ἀθάνατον : and therefore τὸ αὐτοκίνητον is ἀθάνατον.

Finally ψυχή and αὐτοκίνητον are identical.

Hence ψυχή is ἀθάνατον.

In this proof there are several points to be noticed.
The substance of the argument amounts in effect to this,
that in the constitution of the universe spirit, not matter,
soul, not body, is fundamental : if soul could perish, the
universe itself might cease to exist. As Dr Thompson
puts it, "organization depends on soul, not soul on
organization." It is to be observed further that in this
argument Plato makes two assumptions ; first, that τὸ

3—2

ἀεικίνητον is ἀθάνατον, and secondly, that the duration of the universe is everlasting. He cannot conceive of a world in which the sum of things is not constant, or which can at one time exist and at another not exist. This position he never abandons throughout the course of his doctrinal development; under varying forms it represents the groundwork of his metaphysical system.

So much for the details of the proof. But what after all is proved? What we want in order to make the whole passage run harmoniously is evidently a proof of the immortality of the *individual* soul as such; for it is a phenomenon which takes place in certain individual souls that gives rise to the whole psychological discussion; and it is with the character and fortunes of individual souls that the subsequent allegory has to do. But in the foregoing demonstration is it proved even on Plato's own assumptions that the individual soul is immortal? It must surely be admitted, as Dr Thompson admits, that this is not proved. What *is* proved in the passage before us is not that the *individual* soul is immortal, but that soul *in its entirety*, the vital principle of the universe, is indestructible. And this after all is what Plato ostensibly professes to prove. For the meaning of the opening sentence, ψυχὴ πᾶσα ἀθάνατος, is, as Dr Thompson says, not "every soul is immortal," but " all soul is immortal." In this form the conclusion which Plato desires to reach is stated quite definitely at the beginning; nor is there any other logical outcome of the succeeding argument. Nevertheless Plato proceeds on his way just as though the personal immortality of the soul had indeed been demonstrated; for, as we have seen, the indestructibility of the vital principle which animates the universe is by itself not strictly relevant to

the subsequent account of the true nature of the soul.
Here, then, we are confronted with a difficulty at the
outset, a difficulty which recurs in other Dialogues.

Now we cannot suppose that in this demonstration Plato really imagined that he had proved that
individual souls are immortal, especially as in the
demonstration itself he does not profess to prove any
such thing. How, then, are we to remove or explain
the difficulty which undoubtedly exists? Plato himself
has vouchsafed no explicit solution. All that we can
say, I think, amounts virtually to this. Although what
is actually proved by the argument is merely that "*all*
soul is immortal," yet it necessarily follows from this
that in a sense "*every* soul is immortal" likewise. That
is to say, at death the particular soul or portion of
universal soul which has been existing in combination
with any particular body cannot utterly perish. For
'*every* soul' must be included in '*all* soul' (πᾶσα
ψυχή), and the sum of spirit in the universe, in whatever form any portion of it may exist at any particular
time, must at any rate remain a constant quantity. This
much seems to be clearly implied in the course of the
demonstration where it is said:—

τοῦτο δὲ [SC. τὸ αὐτὸ αὑτὸ κινοῦν] οὔτ᾽ ἀπόλλυσθαι
οὔτε γίγνεσθαι δυνατόν, ἢ πάντα τε οὐρανὸν πᾶσάν τε
γένεσιν συμπεσοῦσαν στῆναι καὶ μήποτε αὖθις ἔχειν ὅθεν
κινηθέντα γενήσεται. (*Phaedr.* 245 D, E.)

For if *any* soul—or any particular portion of universal
soul: it makes no difference to the argument which way
we state it—may perish utterly, then there can be no
reason why *every* soul should not perish utterly in like
manner: for the essential nature of soul in this respect

must be universally applicable; we cannot say that, while *some* soul is immortal, *some* is mortal. And when, as on this hypothesis must in the end come to pass, *every* soul has thus ceased to exist, *all* soul must necessarily have also ceased to exist: in other words, there is no vital principle left; all life has been extinguished and no force remains whereby the continuance of the universe, which is assumed throughout, may be maintained. Hence in view of what is coming it is important to show that *all* soul is immortal. We are to understand from the beginning that psychology is not a science like chemistry; it deals not with what is merely transient, but with something which neither comes into existence nor perishes. It is not merely that the soul is composed of elements finer and more perfectly blended than those of which the body is composed, as some previous philosophers had taught. It is of a totally different nature from the body, and the elements composing it, if it can properly be said to be composed of elements at all, differ not in degree but in kind from those of the body. It is not to be regarded as if it were merely a part of the body; its nature is such that it is not, like the body, subject to the processes of generation and decay; nor is it simply the result of the harmonious blending together of bodily elements; therefore there is no reason to suppose that, when the body perishes, the soul perishes with it. Thus Plato wishes to make it perfectly clear to us here that he does not, like certain previous seekers after truth, imagine the soul to be something material, nor yet the product of the happy combination of material elements; he regards it rather as the force which combines those elements in such a way as to cause them to form the earthly tabernacle of a living thing. In any attempt to

estimate the respective positions held by body and soul
in the formation of any living being we must proceed
with the clear understanding that body is not prior to
soul ; on the contrary, a careful analysis should show us
that soul is prior to body. The empirical fact, therefore,
that any particular living creature has been taken from
our cognisance by death is no warrant for assuming that
that living creature has ceased to exist.

So much may be deduced from this demonstration that "all soul is immortal." So far as personal
immortality is concerned it supplies at most a negative
argument; that is to say, it creates a certain presump-
tion in favour of personal immortality in so far as it
tends to invalidate the popular view of the finality of
death. There is certainly a sense in which the soul
survives the death of the individual ἔμψυχον, but whether
this soul continues to exist as a conscious personality is
of course a different question, and there is nothing in the
proof of immortality which we have been considering
that can be said to furnish a direct argument in favour
of it. This Plato must have known that he could never
prove ; but in the absence of proof to the contrary it
probably seemed to him justifiable and natural to believe
that the whole quantity of soul continues to be distributed in the same personalities always. In any case,
from whatever source he may have derived his justification for believing in personal immortality, there can be
no doubt that he did believe in it, and moreover that he
considered the proof that "all soul is immortal" to give
some support to the belief. The whole tenour of this
part of the *Phaedrus* makes this clear. The allegory
which follows is obviously founded upon the belief that
all souls are individually immortal. In fact Plato has

here followed his customary method : when he wishes to
indicate his belief in a doctrine which he cannot prove
by direct argument, he embodies that doctrine in a
myth.

Having proved, then, on his own metaphysical assumptions that "all soul is immortal," and leaving it to
be assumed further that this proof renders a belief in
personal immortality at least reasonable, Plato now proceeds to psychology proper. He wishes to describe to
us the ἰδέα or general nature of the soul. In the
Phaedrus, however, he does not profess to give us a
scientific psychological analysis ; that, as he says, would
involve a θεία καὶ μακρὰ διήγησις. Plato's psychological
views are at present only in their embryonic stage ;
hence the psychology of the *Phaedrus* is given in a
poetical manner : under the form of an allegorical myth
Plato gives us a general idea of what he conceives the
nature of the soul to be. The allegorical form, however,
is not always rigidly adhered to throughout the myth.
For instance in 246 D, E the wings, which symbolize the
" upward tendencies of the soul," are said to be "fostered
by all that is wise, fair and good "; here " for the purposes
of the allegory," as Dr Thompson says, "the sign and
the thing signified are intentionally fused." And again
at 247 D θεοῦ διάνοια is spoken of as νῷ τε καὶ ἐπιστήμῃ
ἀκηράτῳ τρεφομένη, a statement which is purely metaphorical rather than allegorical. And even where the
allegorical form is maintained it is easy to see that the
description of the soul's nature in the myth is in essential
agreement with the more scientific psychology of the
Republic. For instance, all the commentators have seen
that the division of the soul in the *Republic* into τὸ
λογιστικόν, τὸ θυμοειδές, and τὸ ἐπιθυμητικόν is clearly

symbolized in the *Phaedrus* by means of the description
of the soul as a charioteer driving two horses, the one
docile and the other refractory.   But here it may be
asked : If the soul consists of these three parts, in what
sense is it immortal ?   Is only one part (the charioteer,
or τὸ λογιστικόν) immortal, or two, or even all three
parts ? Questions of this kind, however, need not disturb
us.   Though in the *Phaedrus* and in the *Republic* the
soul is undoubtedly described as being of a triple nature,
it has been conclusively shown by Mr Archer-Hind
(*Journal of Philology*, vol. X, and more shortly in the
introduction to his edition of the *Phaedo*) that the tri-
partition is in reality only metaphorical ; the three parts
are nothing more than three phases of the soul's activity
as displayed in the conjunction of soul and body, and do
not in the least affect the essential simplicity of soul as
it is in itself.   It is as a single nature that soul is
immortal, though a *human* soul in connexion with a
human body must always exhibit these three forms of
activity.

The other details of the allegory need not greatly
concern us here ; it will be sufficient to notice a few
passages which serve to illustrate the theory of soul
which is fast taking shape in Plato's mind.

πᾶσα ἡ ψυχὴ παντὸς ἐπιμελεῖται τοῦ ἀψύχου, πάντα
δὲ οὐρανὸν περιπολεῖ, ἄλλοτ᾽ ἐν ἄλλοις εἴδεσι γιγνομένη.
                                        (*Phaedr.* 246 B.)

We have in these words once more a statement of
the main argument on which the immortality of the soul
has previously been based.   From another point of view
we have in them a strong affirmation of the truth of
idealism as opposed to the ordinary materialism of the

age. In the *Phaedrus*, Plato seems first to become aware of the all-embracing nature of an idealistic explanation of the universe. His idealism has not yet crystallized into the Theory of Ideas; but we cannot help feeling that an idealistic theory of some kind is in course of development. We are here told that πᾶσα ἡ ψυχή is the 'guardian' of πᾶν τὸ ἄψυχον. This is merely an allegorical way of saying that spirit is prior to matter, which it informs and so causes the material things of this world to exist in so far as they can be said to exist at all. By πᾶσα ἡ ψυχή Plato means something more than what he has described above as ψυχὴ πᾶσα: there in saying ψυχὴ πᾶσα ἀθάνατος he is making a perfectly general statement—"all soul is immortal." Here he means something more definite than this. Πᾶσα ἡ ψυχή is 'universal soul' in the abstract; we are to understand by the expression not a personality but the sum of all spirit, which in its natural undegraded state is conceived of as directing the universe. Thus it corresponds very closely to the 'world-soul' of the *Timaeus*, which represents one of the phases of the operation of the principle ταὐτόν. The natural condition of all soul is represented in the *Phaedrus* as in the *Timaeus* as undegraded; accordingly in the myth of the *Phaedrus* each individual soul is described as being in its natural state winged, the wings, as Dr Thompson says, symbolizing its "upward tendencies"; that is to say, every soul is of its own nature pure, and aspires to rise to that divine region which is its birthright. But it also contains within it somehow (τινὶ συντυχίᾳ χρησαμένη, 248 C) a principle of evil symbolized by the ill-conditioned steed, which causes it to be degraded from its high estate and so to become the inhabitant of a mortal body. It will be best to defer

the consideration of the significance of this evil principle
until after we have examined the *Timaeus*.

ἔνθα καὶ εἰς θηρίου βίον ἀνθρωπίνη ψυχὴ ἀφικνεῖται,
καὶ ἐκ θηρίου, ὅς ποτε ἄνθρωπος ἦν, πάλιν εἰς ἄνθρωπον.
οὐ γὰρ ἥ γε μή ποτε ἰδοῦσα τὴν ἀλήθειαν εἰς τόδε ἥξει τὸ
σχῆμα. δεῖ γὰρ ἄνθρωπον ξυνιέναι κατ᾽ εἶδος λεγόμενον,
ἐκ πολλῶν ἰὸν αἰσθήσεων εἰς ἓν λογισμῷ ξυναιρούμενον.
Τοῦτο δέ ἐστιν ἀνάμνησις, ἅ ποτ᾽ εἶδεν ἡμῶν ἡ ψυχὴ συμπορευθεῖσα θεῷ καὶ ὑπεριδοῦσα ἃ νῦν εἶναί φαμεν, καὶ
ἀνακύψασα εἰς τὸ ὂν ὄντως. (*Phaedr.* 249 B, C.)

In this passage there are several points that call for
notice. In the first place the doctrine of metempsychosis
is definitely asserted for the first time. It has already
been stated that every soul on its degradation must first
inhabit a human body; we here learn that it may afterwards enter into the body of a brute, whence it may
again return into the body of a man. It is only by
means of steady application to the study of true philosophy that the soul can recover its wings and so ascend
once more to its proper abode. Thus metempsychosis
forms an element in the theory of immortality from the
very beginning. Moreover, the connexion between immortality and the Theory of Ideas, which was, as we
saw, suggested in the *Symposium*, is fully maintained in
the *Phaedrus*, as this passage clearly shows. The Theory
of Ideas, it is true, has not as yet assumed a definite
shape; but there are evident traces of it in the passage
before us. The human mind attaches a meaning to the
various phenomena in this world in virtue of the faculty
which it possesses of forming out of its particular perceptions a general notion—"a so-called form" (εἶδος)—
by which it tests and classifies the various objects pre-

sented to it. This process of forming general notions,
says Plato, is really nothing more than an act of memory;
the soul remembers as far as it is able the things which
it has seen above in its ante-natal state, and which are in
some degree suggested by the material things of earth.
These things ἅ ποτ᾽ εἶδεν ἡμῶν ἡ ψυχὴ συμπορευθεῖσα
θεῷ clearly foreshadow the transcendental 'ideas' (αὐτὰ
καθ᾽ αὑτὰ εἴδη) of the *Republic* and the *Phaedo*. And
this brings us to a third point : the connexion between
immortality and the Theory of Ideas is established by
means of the interesting theory of recollection (ἀνάμνησις), which from this time onward plays an important
part in the development of Plato's philosophy. Souls,
since they are immortal, and since they have at some
time or other before entering human bodies existed in
a different world from this, may reasonably be expected
to have some remembrance, however faint, of that other
world. Now, of the soul's faculties the one which seems
to bear least affinity to the things of this world is the
faculty of forming general notions. But since the soul
is immortal, is it not more reasonable to suppose that
these general notions are not merely formed as the result
of the contemplation of the phenomena of this world, but
rather called into remembrance by these phenomena,
which suggest something which the soul has already
known ? Yet the soul cannot have known them in this
world or in any world like this ; clearly, then, these
immaterial forms which the soul remembers must exist
in an immaterial world. Such seems to be the argument
underlying the theory. It is worth while to notice also
the special purpose which the theory is here made to
serve. In the *Phaedrus* we see that on the assumption
that the soul is immortal the theory of ἀνάμνησις makes

the existence of the ideas probable. In the *Phaedo*, on the contrary, the process is reversed ; the existence of the ideas is assumed, and then the theory of ἀνάμνησις is advanced as a proof of the ante-natal existence of the soul.

ἰχνεύοντες δὲ παρ' ἑαυτῶν ἀνευρίσκειν τὴν τοῦ σφετέρου θεοῦ φύσιν εὐποροῦσι διὰ τὸ συντόνως ἠναγκάσθαι
πρὸς τὸν θεὸν βλέπειν, καὶ ἐφαπτόμενοι αὐτοῦ τῇ μνήμῃ
ἐνθουσιῶντες ἐξ ἐκείνου λαμβάνουσι τὰ ἔθη καὶ τὰ ἐπιτηδεύματα καθ' ὅσον δυνατὸν θεοῦ ἀνθρώπῳ μετασχεῖν.

(*Phaedr.* 252 E, 253 A.)

In this passage the theory of ἀνάμνησις is introduced again, but in a slightly different connexion. It has just been made to furnish a theory of knowledge ; now an attempt is made to account by means of it for varieties of character. A man is said to "lay hold of his own god with his memory," and the particular character which he exhibits in this world is the result. What precisely is meant to be implied by this ? The meaning so far as the myth itself is concerned is of course clear enough : the varieties of human character are traced to the fact that the various souls before their first incarna- tion as human beings followed in the train of different gods and so were subjected to different influences. But behind this there seems to be a further meaning, the key to which may perhaps be found in the concluding words of the passage quoted : καθ' ὅσον δυνατὸν θεοῦ ἀνθρώπῳ μετασχεῖν. How far or in what sense can a man be said to 'partake of' a god ? It is noticeable that the ex- pression θεοῦ μετασχεῖν curiously recalls the phraseology of the earlier Theory of Ideas. As in the *Phaedo* pheno- mena are said to 'partake of' ideas, so in the *Phaedrus*

a man is said to 'partake of' a god ; and in each case
Plato is endeavouring to account for the possession of
characteristics.   It certainly looks very much as if this
passage in the *Phaedrus* contained the first beginnings
of that doctrine of μέθεξις which was destined not long
afterwards to play so important a part in the earlier
Theory of Ideas.   The origin of the distinctive qualities
which a man possesses is here mythically referred to the
god who possesses these qualities in their highest form ;
in a former existence the man's soul has been under the
influence of this god, of whom in his present life the man
continues as far as possible to 'partake.'   May we not
regard this as a foreshadowing of the time, not very far
distant, when Plato would explain the presence of any
quality in a man by saying that he 'partakes' of the
idea of that quality ?   I do not mean to say that in this
passage Plato is definitely referring to a doctrine which
was not developed till later.   But the prominence accorded to the qualities as the *immortal* part of a man—
hence the appropriateness of the word θεός—and the
somewhat peculiar use of the word μετασχεῖν certainly
seem to show the direction in which his thought was
tending.   The passage is also interesting, therefore, in
that it bears witness to the fact that the doctrine of
immortality and the Theory of Ideas are growing up
simultaneously in Plato's mind.

There is one other point which we may note in
passing.   In the passage which we have just been considering there is a distinct suggestion of an ethical use
to be made of the theory of ἀνάμνησις.   Whatever may
be symbolized by the θεός of which a man μετέχει,
it seems clear that Plato is to some extent thinking of
a standard by which a man may regulate his character

and pursuits. This standard the soul in a previous state
of existence has somehow seen realised, and by the
systematic use of the memory in this life we may
partially recall to our minds the nature of this perfection of character, and order our conduct accordingly.
We shall have occasion to return later to the question
of the ideal character of Plato's ethics.

My view, then, is that the *Phaedrus*, substantially
following along the line of thought sketched in the
Symposium, marks a distinct advance upon the conclusions of that Dialogue. In the *Symposium*, as we
saw, there is a hint of a theory of immortality closely
connected with another theory, which is developed later
into the Theory of Ideas. In the *Phaedrus* this connexion has been drawn closer by means chiefly of the
doctrine of ἀνάμνησις. Moreover it seems clear that the
question of the immortality of the soul has now acquired
a greater importance in Plato's eyes; for in the *Phaedrus*
we have for the first time a definite demonstration of
the fact that the soul *is* immortal.

CHAPTER IV.

THE *REPUBLIC*.

IF we put the *Symposium* before the *Phaedrus* and otherwise assume Dr Jackson's arrangement of the Dialogues to be correct, the interval between the writing of the *Phaedrus* and the *Republic* will be represented by two Dialogues, the *Euthydemus* and the *Meno*. Of these the *Euthydemus* does not concern us here, and the *Meno* does not call for detailed examination. It is true that in the *Meno* the question of the immortality of the soul is brought up; but it is introduced not so much for its own sake as for the elucidation of the doctrine of δόξα and ἐπιστήμη which was at this time occupying Plato's thoughts. As far as the question of immortality itself is concerned the position maintained in the *Meno* is substantially that of the *Phaedrus*. The chief interest for us lies in the development of the doctrine of ἀνάμνησις, a development which the *Phaedrus* myth would naturally suggest. Beyond this the *Meno* has no important contribution to make towards the theory of immortality, and we may therefore proceed at once to the consideration of the *Republic*.

In the *Republic*, as has been already pointed out in the Introduction, we have a careful summary and systematic co-ordination of Plato's earlier views on ethics and the allied subjects of sociology and education, together with a new metaphysical scheme of the universe on idealistic principles, the first beginnings of which may be traced in the *Symposium* and the *Phaedrus*. The metaphysical content of the Dialogue, however, is small ; the scheme is sketched in a dogmatic manner and bears evident signs of immaturity. Its ethical teaching on the other hand is no less clearly the result of long and careful thought. The system of ethics set forth in the *Republic* is made to depend primarily on a careful educational training, differing essentially from all current methods of education. In the group of Dialogues preceding the *Republic* Plato has shown up the superficiality or onesidedness of the various forms of educational training provided by the Sophists ; he now proceeds to construct his own scheme. The education on which he founds his ethics consists of a graduated course of study culminating in 'dialectic' ($\delta\iota\alpha\lambda\epsilon\kappa\tau\iota\kappa\acute{\eta}$), by which is meant the study of the Good, the source of all Being and all Knowledge—in fact, what we should now call metaphysics. Holding as he does, therefore, so high an opinion of the ethical value of education and metaphysical knowledge, Plato naturally considers it a matter of no small moment that we should have a right appreciation of the true nature of the soul, which both *is* and *knows*. It is from this point of view, then, that the theory of soul in the *Republic* is introduced. Socrates undertakes to prove " that justice is better than injustice" ($\dot{\omega}\varsigma$ $\ddot{\alpha}\mu\epsilon\iota\nu\text{o}\nu$ $\delta\iota\kappa\alpha\iota\text{o}\sigma\acute{\nu}\nu\eta$ $\dot{\alpha}\delta\iota\kappa\acute{\iota}\alpha\varsigma$), the terms $\delta\iota\kappa\alpha\iota\text{o}\sigma\acute{\nu}\nu\eta$ and $\dot{\alpha}\delta\iota\kappa\acute{\iota}\alpha$ being of course much wider in meaning than our 'justice' and 'injustice'; they stand respectively for 'morality' and 'immorality.' In the first book it is shown that 'justice' is more profitable than 'injustice'; "honesty is the best policy" may fairly be taken as the moral of the discussion at this stage in the argument. At the beginning of the second book, however, the young men, Glaucon and Adeimantus, express themselves dissatisfied with this conclusion; they want to have it proved that 'justice' is *of its own essential nature* better than 'injustice,' all consideration of rewards and punishments being left out of account. From the second book to the ninth, therefore, the main part of the Dialogue, Socrates is occupied in proving that 'justice' is *intrinsically* better than 'injustice,' and is therefore the more rational as well as the more profitable goal of human endeavour. In proof of this contention it is shown that 'justice' is the moral health, 'injustice' the moral disease, of the soul. Thus it is on the score of reason, not of profit, that morality is upheld in preference to immorality. Morality no doubt turns out in the long run to be also the more profitable course to pursue, but in accordance with the terms of the agreement made at the beginning of the second book this aspect of the question is left out of account altogether; the comparative claims of δικαιοσύνη and ἀδικία are estimated quite irrespectively of any external circumstances whatsoever.

With such a theory of morality the question of the immortality of the soul can of course have little directly to do. In the form especially in which the assertion of the soul's immortality would present itself to the ordinary Greek mind it would savour far too much of those rewards and punishments which Plato in advocating the claims of his system of ethics has determined to ignore. But we have seen that he had already decided in his own mind before he came to write the *Republic* that the soul is immortal. The subject seems to have had a peculiar

interest for him about this time, and even during the
composition of the *Republic* it must have been continually present to his imagination, the result being that in
constructing his theory of psychology he cannot help
thinking of the soul all the time as something immortal.
Accordingly it is not difficult to discern traces of the
influence of the doctrine of immortality even in the main
body of the Dialogue, where the question is not strictly
relevant ; and finally in the tenth book he cannot refrain
from giving us (in the shape of an appendix to the main
argument) a short demonstration of the doctrine itself.

At the beginning of the third book (386 A sqq.) the
question of the fate of the soul after death is glanced at;
but clearly what is said there cannot be pressed very far.
The passage cannot be taken as evidence even of a
belief in immortality ; certainly no *theory* of a future
existence can fairly be deduced from it. It is valuable
in so far as it shows us, not what Plato believes, but
what he does not believe. The subject of education is
uppermost in this part of the *Republic*. The claims of
education are felt to be paramount, and the discussion
of the question of a future life is intended to be entirely
subordinate to this end. At this point, with the subject
of education occupying the foremost place in his thoughts,
Plato feels it his duty to enter a strong protest against
the Homeric account of the underworld, its terrible
picture of gloom and despair. Such an account, he
considers, must needs exercise a pernicious influence on
the minds of the young by inducing a fear of death ; and
this would be incompatible with the true courage that
should form an element in the character of the Guardians
of the State. In order to facilitate the proper educational
development of the young, therefore, Hades must not be

described as a gloomy place; we should rather regard it as the reverse of this, and poets should be made to encourage us so to regard it :—

> τὸν δὲ ἐναντίον τύπον τούτοις λεκτέον τε καὶ ποιητέον.
> (*Rep.* 387 C.)

Thus there is no direct evidence of any belief in immortality to be gleaned from this passage. It will be observed, however, that Plato shows himself fully alive to the natural curiosity of the human mind to know what comes after death, and also to the mischievousness of the traditional manner of satisfying that curiosity. Moreover it is noticeable that, although for the purposes of the argument it would suffice to inculcate a belief that after death the individual soul as such ceases to exist, Plato, as we might expect after reading the *Phaedrus*, does not do this; he seems to feel that such a solution is not satisfactory, that the best results will be obtained by a belief that the soul does continue to exist, though not in the manner described by Homer; hence the ἐναντίος τύπος is to be recommended.

There is a more definite allusion, though it is only a passing one, to a belief in a future life in the sixth book, where Socrates says :—

> πείρας γὰρ οὐδὲν ἀνήσομεν, ἕως ἂν ἢ πείσωμεν καὶ τοῦτον [sc. Θρασύμαχον] καὶ τοὺς ἄλλους, ἢ προὔργου τι ποιήσωμεν εἰς ἐκεῖνον τὸν βίον, ὅταν αὖθις γενόμενοι τοῖς τοιούτοις ἐντύχωσι λόγοις. (*Rep.* 498 D.)

These words do undoubtedly seem to point to a distinct belief in immortality. We may perhaps find in them some hint of the nature of the ἐναντίος τύπος mentioned above. If the soul survives death at all, we are not to suppose that it then becomes a mere senseless phantom; we should rather believe that it is capable of meeting and holding converse with other souls in a state of existence more favourable than the present to the free exercise of the intellectual powers. It is quite possible that we have here a reminiscence of the historical Socrates. In the *Phaedo* Socrates is made to express with still greater definiteness this hope of meeting and conversing hereafter with the souls of the great men of the past; and in the *Apology*, where it is probable that Socrates is represented with greater historical accuracy than anywhere else in the Platonic writings, he gives utterance to the same hope, though of course he admits that it is simply a hope and nothing more : he does not profess to *know*, and therefore he will not express any opinion in a dogmatic manner. Plato, however, at this time laid himself under no such restriction; and in this matter, as in others, he may well be giving a dogmatic turn to an opinion which he believed his master to have held in all seriousness. In any case, however, what we have in this passage of the *Republic* is nothing more than a casual allusion to a doctrine which has no necessary bearing on the argument.

Before we pass on to the tenth book there is one other passage which deserves to be noticed in this connexion. It occurs in the ninth book, where the nature and faculties of the soul are more immediately under consideration. In the particular passage which concerns us here Plato is discussing the question of pleasure; and on a comparison of the various kinds of pleasure it is found that those which are allied with δόξα ἀληθής, ἐπιστήμη νοῦς, and πᾶσα ἀρετή are to be preferred to those connected with σῖτος, ποτόν, ὄψον, and ξυμπᾶσα

τροφή (585 B, C), this conclusion being based on the fact
that the former εἶδος of pleasure is τὸ τοῦ ἀεὶ ὁμοίου
ἐχόμενον καὶ ἀθανάτου καὶ ἀληθείας, καὶ αὐτὸ τοιοῦτον
ὂν καὶ ἐν τοιούτῳ γιγνόμενον, whereas the latter εἶδος
is just the reverse of this—τὸ μηδέποτε ὁμοίου [sc. ἐχό-
μενον] καὶ θνητοῦ, καὶ αὐτὸ τοιοῦτο καὶ ἐν τοιούτῳ
γιγνόμενον (585 C). And this is as much as to say that
the pleasures of the soul are to be preferred to the
pleasures of the body:—

> οὐκοῦν ὅλως τὰ περὶ τὴν τοῦ σώματος θεραπείαν γένη
> τῶν γενῶν αὖ τῶν περὶ τὴν τῆς ψυχῆς θεραπείαν ἧττον
> ἀληθείας τε καὶ οὐσίας μετέχει; Πολύ γε. Σῶμα δὲ αὐτὸ
> ψυχῆς οὐκ οἴει οὕτως; Ἔγωγε. (*Rep.* 585 C, D.)

Whence it is plain that ψυχή is to be recognised as
belonging essentially to the class of things which are
τοῦ ἀεὶ ὁμοίου ἐχόμενα καὶ ἀθανάτου καὶ ἀληθείας. The
point of view here adopted at once recalls that of the
Symposium. In the *Symposium* (212 A) we saw that
immortality may fittingly be ascribed to the man whose
soul is occupied with the production and cultivation of
ἀρετὴ ἀληθής : we now learn that this is the natural and
proper characteristic of soul as such ; hence the soul
itself may with justice be described as immortal. In the
Symposium it is the philosopher's soul to which the attribute of immortality may most appropriately be applied :
we now see that what this really means is that the
philosopher in a far higher degree than anyone else
realises the immortality of his soul. All souls alike
are immortal; but immortality is seen most clearly to
belong to the soul of the philosopher, because the
philosopher habitually applies himself to those pursuits
in which the soul exercises its own proper functions.

The greater the part played by the body and its functions in the life of a man, the less he realises his
immortality, simply because the soul, his immortal part,
is kept in the background. The agreement of the
teaching of this passage with that of the *Phaedrus* is
also clear. The body and its concerns have less ἀλή-
θεια and οὐσία than the soul; that is to say, the body
belongs merely to the phenomenal world (τὸ μηδέποτε
ὅμοιον), while the soul belongs to the ideal world which
really exists (τὸ ἀεὶ ὅμοιον). The ultimate reality of the
universe is to be found in spirit, not in matter; hence
from this point of view body is θνητόν while soul is
ἀθάνατον. Of course the question of the continued
existence of the individual soul as such is not here in
point; all that Plato is at present concerned to assert is
that the soul, as belonging to the unchanging world of
immaterial reality, is of a higher nature than the body,
and that we ought therefore to give the foremost place
in our estimation to those activities in which the soul is
least encumbered by its association with the body, and in
the exercise of which it can more effectually display its
own true nature. It is the soul, not the body, which
makes the man.

The allusions to the doctrine of the immortality
of the soul which may be discerned in the foregoing
passages are, as was only to be expected, very vague
and indefinite. Anything more precise in this direction
would have been irrelevant to the argument as it stands,
and quite out of keeping with the main purpose which
Plato had in mind in writing the *Republic.* Yet, such
as they are, they serve to show that the philosophical
conclusions with which he originally associated the
doctrine have remained substantially unaltered; and we

are left with the impression that, at the time when
Plato was engaged on the *Republic*, the subject of immortality was never very far from his thoughts and was
liable at any moment to come to the surface.

When we come to the tenth book, however, the case
is different. The intrinsic superiority of δικαιοσύνη
over ἀδικία has at the end of the ninth book been
finally established, and the restrictions under which
Socrates had placed himself in undertaking the defence
of the higher morality may now with advantage be cast
aside. The claims of δικαιοσύνη have already been
made good and established for ever on the soundest
possible basis; and having carried his main point
Socrates considers himself fairly entitled in what follows
to take into account τὰ μέγιστα ἐπίχειρα ἀρετῆς, which
in conformity with the agreement entered into at the
beginning of the second book have so far been neglected. It is not only better and nobler to be δίκαιος:
it is also in the end more profitable. The superiority of
δικαιοσύνη in this respect, however, may in many cases
not become evident during the period of this present
life on earth; in such cases the balance remains to be
readjusted in a future life or lives. Thus the μέγιστα
ἐπίχειρα ἀρετῆς of which we have heard are found to
depend directly on the fact that the soul is immortal.
For the sake of completeness, therefore, Socrates now
subjoins a short proof of the immortality of the soul.
The manner in which he proves it is as follows.

To everything in this world, he says, there is
attached a special κακόν, which as a general rule is
observed, if it goes far enough, to bring about the
destruction of that thing of which it is the κακόν. For
the purpose of illustration he takes the case of the eye.

The peculiar κακόν of the eye is ὀφθαλμία, which, if allowed to develop, finally destroys the sight of the eye; and since an eye that has lost the faculty of vision is not in the strict sense an eye any longer, it may be said to destroy the eye. Similarly blight is the special κακόν of corn, rust of iron, and so forth. Now the special κακόν of the soul has been found to be ἀδικία: the soul which is infected with ἀδικία is in a condition of mental and moral ill-health, just as the eye which is infected with ὀφθαλμία is in a condition of physical ill-health. But here the analogy ends; for whereas the eye is destroyed by ophthalmia, corn by blight, and iron by rust, we know from experience that the soul is not destroyed by 'injustice.' Life is to the soul what sight is to the eye; and though 'injustice' may injure the soul in many ways, it is not capable of destroying life. *Indirectly*, it is true, wrong-doing may cause a man to be put to death; but then so may many other things: even the practice of δικαιοσύνη itself may in a bad State bring about this result: so that is irrelevant; the point is that ἀδικία cannot *directly* destroy life. The most that can happen is that, if a man is ἄδικος, other men may be impelled to put him to death, that is to say, to cause his soul to be parted from his body. Since, then, the soul is not destroyed by its own ξύμφυτον κακόν, we may surely be justified in assuming that *nothing* can destroy it. Therefore the soul is immortal (*Rep.* 608 D—611 D).

Such is the argument. It will be convenient to defer any consideration of its merits as constituting a proof of immortality until we come to the *Phaedo*. We may, however, notice at once the sublime confidence of Socrates in offering the proof, a confidence which is characteristic of the *Republic* throughout. Οὐκ ἤσθησαι, he says to Glaucon, ὅτι ἀθάνατος ἡμῶν ἡ ψυχὴ καὶ οὐδέποτε ἀπόλλυται—as if it were a mere matter of observation. When Glaucon in surprise asks him if he can really maintain this doctrine that the soul is immortal, he is not in the least disturbed : he replies that to maintain it involves no difficulty at all ; Glaucon himself might do it. No apprehension seems to trouble him of any possible objections that might be raised against his proof ; on the contrary it seems to him to be almost self-evident. Everything goes as smoothly with this part of Plato's philosophy as with the Theory of Ideas, which he sets forth in the *Republic* with the full confidence that he is now well on his way to discover the secret of the universe.

Another point to notice is that what the argument proves, if it proves anything at all, is not the continued existence of the individual soul as a conscious personality, but simply the indestructibility of soul in general. This is the only logical outcome that we can fairly derive from the argument as it stands. We are told in effect just what we are told in the *Phaedrus*, that no soul, that is to say, no portion of the spirit which animates and informs the universe, however or wherever existing, can ever cease to exist. But although this is all that the argument goes to prove, it is evident that here, exactly as in the *Phaedrus*, what is really in question is the immortality of the individual soul. For this apparent inconsistency I have already attempted to account in the last chapter in commenting on the *Phaedrus*, and what was said there will apply here equally well. It can scarcely be doubted that personal immortality is what Plato has in mind all through the

present passage. For this is the only way of accounting
satisfactorily for the general position which he takes up,
that τὰ μέγιστα ἐπίχειρα ἀρετῆς are what they are by
reason of the fact that the soul is immortal ; they are
realised not in this life but in another life after death.
In this connexion the fact that soul as a universal
principle is indestructible would surely be quite irrelevant except in so far as it tends to make us believe that
the same personalities continue to exist independently.
Moreover the actual language used immediately after
the demonstration is concluded seems to show that it is
the doctrine of personal immortality that Socrates is
really seeking to inculcate. Having finished his proof
he goes on as follows :—

τοῦτο μὲν τοίνυν, ἦν δ᾽ ἐγώ, οὕτως ἐχέτω. εἰ δ᾽ ἔχει,
ἐννοεῖς ὅτι ἀεὶ ἂν εἶεν αἱ αὐταί. (*Rep.* 611 A.)

Mr Archer-Hind refers to this passage in the Introduction to his edition of the *Phaedo* and proceeds to
remark : " This seems at first sight like an assertion
of the continued existence of the same personalities.
A closer examination however shows that this is not
the case. Plato simply means that if the whole vital
force of the universe is distributed into a certain number
of souls, no addition to this number is possible, else the
sum total of vitality would be increased, which is inad-
missible " (p. xxviii). With the view here expressed
I cordially agree in so far that I believe that what Plato
is more immediately concerned with here is the reitera-
tion of the assertion previously made in the *Phaedrus*,
that the sum of spirit in the universe is a constant
quantity. I believe further that Mr Archer-Hind is
quite right in holding that there is nothing to justify the

supposition that Plato means us to infer from the words
quoted above that the continued existence of the same
personalities follows legitimately from the proof of
immortality which has just been brought to a close. I
do gather nevertheless that Plato deliberately intends to
leave in the reader's mind a distinct conviction of his
belief that individual souls *are* immortal as such, even
though the belief does not rest and is not intended to
rest on any strictly logical reasoning. We have seen
already that the whole purpose for which the proof of
the immortality of the soul is introduced renders this
interpretation necessary ; and the language and general
tone of the subsequent remarks seem to point irresistibly
to the same conclusion. We may notice especially the
repeated use of the plural number—ἀεὶ ἂν εἶεν αἱ αὐταί·
οὔτε γὰρ ἄν που ἐλάττους γένοιντο μηδεμιᾶς ἀπολλυμένης
οὔτε αὖ πλείους. Surely if Plato had not wished to
leave us under the impression that it was really a belief
in personal immortality that he was advocating, he
would have contrived to use other language than this to
convey his meaning. Souls, he says, must be always
the same in number. For since it has been proved that
no single soul perishes, it follows that the whole aggregate of soul can never be less ; nor can it ever be
greater ; for in that case we should be compelled to
believe that an immortal thing can be created out of
something that is mortal ; and so in the end it might
happen that all things would be immortal. I say 'the
whole aggregate of soul' because, as I have said before,
all that we can legitimately infer from the argument is
that the whole amount of soul, however it may be distributed, must always remain the same ; the fact remains,
however, that at the sacrifice of strict logical consistency

Plato says not 'soul' but 'souls.' The matter, then, stands thus : on Platonic principles the sum of spirit in the universe is constant; but Plato has chosen here to state this truth in such a form as to make it plain that he holds the belief that the universal spirit remains constant not only as being always the same in quantity, but also as being always distributed into the same conscious personalities. Nevertheless it must not be forgotten that, whereas he professes to *prove* the former, he can only *believe* the latter.

Up to this point, then, Plato considers himself to have proved the bare proposition that 'soul is immortal'; and he obviously considers himself justified in believing further that individual souls continue to exist as such throughout time. But on reflexion we cannot help feeling that after all this belief in itself does not carry us very far. It is all very well to say that the soul is immortal ; but what *is* the 'soul'? How much or how little is to be included in our conception of it from the point of view of immortality? Till we know something more about the essential nature of the soul we cannot form any adequate notion of what is meant by the assertion that it is immortal. We are somewhat in the position of Socrates when he is asked by Meno to say whether virtue can be taught before he knows what virtue is ; and we feel inclined to say with him—ὃ δὲ μὴ οἶδα τί ἐστι, πῶς ἂν ὁποῖόν γέ τι εἰδείην ; As we might expect, Plato is fully aware of the difficulty which thus arises. Consequently a little farther on we find a clear indication of a consciousness on his part that the whole question has not yet been thoroughly thought out. In 611 C, D the soul is likened to the sea-god Glaucus, whose real shape has been damaged by the sea

around him, and is still further obscured by the mass of
shells and seaweed and bits of rock that have attached
themselves to him and seem to the casual observer to be
part of the god himself. Just such a superficial view is
all that we ordinarily have of the soul. We cannot yet
know what her true nature is; for we have seen her
hitherto—as, for instance, in the rather rudimentary
psychology of the fourth book of the *Republic*, where
we have the division into τὸ ἐπιθυμητικόν, τὸ θυμοειδές,
and τὸ λογιστικόν—only when she is encumbered by
the environment of the body. The limiting conditions
under which alone she can manifest herself in this
world do not represent the true character of the soul
any more than the outer covering of shells and seaweed,
which is all that appears to the eye of the ordinary
observer, represents the true appearance of Glaucus.
What we have to do, then, is to study carefully ἡ φιλοσοφία αὐτῆς: that is to say, in order to arrive at a true
estimate of the nature of the soul as she is in herself, we
must direct our minds to that faculty in the exercise of
which she seems to have least in common with her
earthly surroundings, the faculty of abstract thought.
In so doing we may mentally strip off all the foreign
growths which are perpetually niding her true nature
from us and see her as she is in herself:—

> καὶ τότ᾽ ἄν τις ἴδοι αὐτῆς τὴν ἀληθῆ φύσιν, εἴτε
> πολυειδὴς εἴτε μονοειδής, εἴτε ὅπῃ ἔχει καὶ ὅπως. νῦν δὲ
> τὰ ἐν τῷ ἀνθρωπίνῳ βίῳ πάθη τε καὶ εἴδη, ὡς ἐγῷμαι,
> ἐπιεικῶς αὐτῆς διεληλύθαμεν. (*Rep.* 612 A.)

Here it may be noticed in passing that we have an
explicit avowal that the threefold division of the soul,
of which we have an allegorical account in the *Phaedrus*

and a plain statement in the *Republic*, is to be understood merely as a fair way of describing her nature
as it appears to us ἐν τῷ ἀνθρωπίνῳ βίῳ. Plato
does not mean that the soul is essentially tripartite
in character.

Thus the demonstration of the immortality of the
soul in the *Republic* admittedly does not achieve very
much.   Any treatment of the subject which can be
accounted satisfactory is seen to involve the consideration of other questions of a more far-reaching nature.
We know something of the soul's affections and manifestations in this present life, but that is all ; we know
nothing beyond.   Hence, when we make the assertion
that the soul is immortal, it is impossible that we should
understand the real significance of the theory which we
are asserting.   We say that the soul survives the death
of the body, but we do not by any means know what
the soul is or does when it is removed altogether from
the influence of the body.   This problem is one which
cannot now be fully and satisfactorily dealt with.   As
we have seen, the question of the immortality of the
soul does not affect the main argument of the *Republic* ;
and though Plato saw fit to say something on the
subject in an appendix to the main body of the work,
anything like an exhaustive treatment of it would be
quite out of place.   The course which further investigation of the question should follow is, however,
clearly indicated: we are directed to study the soul's
φιλοσοφία.   For the present Plato is content to adopt
his customary procedure in such cases and embody his
answer in a myth, which does not of course commit
him to any particular theory, as we are not intended

to interpret with any degree of strictness what is there
set down.

The myth itself need not be examined here in all
its details. Bearing in mind the point of view from
which it is introduced, we are not surprised to find in it
provisional solutions of metaphysical questions, such as
that of the freedom of the will and the continuance of
personality, which Plato did not see his way to solving
by direct argument. These matters are just glanced at
and summarily dismissed in that part of the myth where
the choice of another life by the disembodied souls is
described. Here it may be noted that Plato still holds
to the doctrine of metempsychosis, his belief in which
he has already asserted in the *Phaedrus*. Free will is
definitely affirmed at the end of the speech of Lachesis,
whose last words are so often quoted :—

ἀρετὴ δὲ ἀδέσποτον. ἣν τιμῶν καὶ ἀτιμάζων πλέον
καὶ ἔλαττον αὐτῆς ἕκαστος ἕξει. αἰτία ἑλομένου· θεὸς
ἀναίτιος. (*Rep.* 617 E.)

In accordance with this doctrine we are informed just
afterwards that there are far more lives to be chosen
from than there are souls to choose them :—

μετὰ δὲ τοῦτο αὖθις τὰ τῶν βίων παραδείγματα εἰς
τὸ πρόσθεν σφῶν θεῖναι ἐπὶ τὴν γῆν, πολὺ πλείω τῶν
παρόντων, εἶναι δὲ παντοδαπά. (*Rep.* 618 A.)

Moreover each soul with its many incarnations is not in
reality, as some might suppose, a series of personalities.
It is true that most of us at any rate have no recollection of former lives. This is accounted for in the
myth by the symbolical statement that all the souls,
when they have chosen their lives, are conveyed to the

plain of Lethe and are there made to drink of the river
Ameles, which causes them to forget the past. Nevertheless during the time when a new life is being chosen
each soul remembers and is consciously influenced by
the life which it has formerly led on earth. It is interesting to notice too that all the souls do not drink the
same quantity of water out of the river; some drink
more than they need:—

μέτρον μὲν οὖν τι τοῦ ὕδατος πᾶσιν ἀναγκαῖον εἶναι
πιεῖν. τοὺς δὲ φρονήσει μὴ σῳζομένους πλέον πίνειν τοῦ
μέτρου· τὸν δὲ ἀεὶ πιόντα πάντων ἐπιλανθάνεσθαι.

(*Rep.* 621 A, B.)

Though each soul forgets everything as soon as it has
drunk of the water, yet there must be some point in the
statement that the foolish souls drink more than the fixed
μέτρον. This passage should probably be read in the
light of the Platonic theory of ἀνάμνησις, and what Plato
means is that οἱ φρονήσει μὴ σῳζόμενοι, who comprise
presumably the great majority, will be able to *recollect*
very little of their former states of existence, whereas the
more circumspect, who do not drink more than is absolutely necessary, will be able to use their powers of
recollection to better purpose, and in virtue of that will
become the philosophers of the future.

I think I have now dealt with all the passages in
the *Republic* which have any important bearing on the
question of immortality. It must be confessed that it
does not contribute very much to our knowledge of
Plato's views on the subject; but taking into consideration the whole character of the Dialogue we have
no reason to expect more. The *Republic* although it is

complete in so far as it furnishes us with a reasoned system of ethics, sociology, and education, does not profess to give conclusive answers to the various metaphysical and psychological questions which must necessarily arise in the mind of the scientific student of philosophy. Plato's theory of soul is still admittedly defective. The reason for this is that he has still to set his metaphysical house in order; and not until that task is accomplished can he hope to find any suitable and permanent resting-place for the soul.

CHAPTER V.

THE *PHAEDO*.

ANYONE who, without desiring to trace the origin and growth of the doctrine of the immortality of the soul in Plato's mind, wished nevertheless to ascertain what Plato's views on the subject really were, would, I suppose, naturally turn to the *Phaedo* for his information. If he wished merely to obtain a general idea of Plato's belief, he would probably not experience much difficulty in finding what he wanted. If, however, not satisfied with this, he wished to look deeper into the details of the theory, and with this object in view proceeded further to compare the statements of the *Phaedo* with what Plato says in other Dialogues, he would almost certainly find much to perplex him. For the truth is that the *Phaedo*, though one of the most widely read of Plato's Dialogues, is at the same time one of the most difficult. There are difficulties connected with the mutual relations of the several parts of the Dialogue itself; and there are even more serious difficulties which confront us when we attempt to determine the precise relationship in which it stands to various other Dialogues. Most scholars in these days would, I imagine, agree that the *Phaedo* cannot be separated from the *Republic* by any long interval of

time; from every point of view, both in style and
subject-matter, the two seem to be intimately connected.
But here all agreement ends; for not only would some
place the *Phaedo* before the *Republic*, while others would
reverse the order, but whereas 'Platonic orthodoxy,'
which has found its ablest and most prominent ex-
ponent in Zeller,· regards the *Republic* as one of the
latest of Plato's works, 'Platonic heresy,' represented by
Dr Jackson and Mr Archer-Hind, assigns to it and to
the *Phaedo* a comparatively early date. It would be
out of place here to enter into the details of the con-
troversy: and I shall content myself, therefore, with
saying that for my own part I regard the contentions
of Dr Jackson in his series of papers in *The Journal of
Philology* on "Plato's Later Theory of Ideas," and of
Mr Archer-Hind in the Introductions to his editions of
the *Phaedo* and of the *Timaeus* as proving beyond all
reasonable doubt that, while the *Republic* and the
Phaedo undeniably belong to the same period of Plato's
doctrinal development, they do not represent his most
mature opinion on metaphysical questions.

But even supposing the truth of this view to be
provisionally accepted, it is important for the purpose of
this essay to determine further the relations subsisting
between the *Republic* and the *Phaedo* themselves. Now,
though Mr Archer-Hind's edition of the *Phaedo* touches
on almost every point that would be likely to arise in
the mind of a student of that Dialogue, it does not, so
far as I can see, contain any expression of opinion on
this point. The question nevertheless is not without
interest; and a careful consideration of it has led me
to form the conclusion that the internal evidence to
be derived from the study and comparison of the two

Dialogues tends to show that, while undoubtedly they must both be referred to substantially the same period, the *Phaedo* was intended to follow and supplement the *Republic*. I say "intended to follow" in order to allow for the possibility suggested by Dr Jackson that Plato did not necessarily finish the composition of one Dialogue before beginning to write another; but from the point of view of the *reader* it seems to me that the *Phaedo* comes next in order to the *Republic*, and in so far as there is any development of doctrine to be discerned in one as compared with the other, the advance is made in the *Phaedo* and not in the *Republic*. As the considerations on which I base this opinion are intimately connected with the subject in hand it will be well to state them without delay.

In the first place it has been remarked that there is a very noticeable difference of tone between the two Dialogues. This difference may or may not be significant; but on this ground Dr Jackson is, I believe, inclined to place the *Phaedo* after the *Republic*. In the *Republic* Plato takes up a far more confident attitude with regard to the possibility of the attainment of knowledge than he does in the *Phaedo*; and although this fact cannot be said to be incompatible with the theory that the *Phaedo* is the earlier Dialogue, yet I cannot help agreeing with Dr Jackson that on the whole it makes the opposite view the more probable. Of course it may be said that a little calm reflexion may very well have enabled Plato to rise superior to the doubts and difficulties to which the *Phaedo* gives expression, and that his triumph over them is exhibited in the buoyancy of tone with which the question of the attainment of knowledge is approached in the *Republic*.

But in view of the manner in which the same subject
is handled in Dialogues which I take to belong to a
distinctly later period, when Plato no longer regards as
possible the attainment of absolute knowledge by man,
I do not myself consider this view probable. It seems
to me much more likely that the *Phaedo* reflects the
intermediate stage : Plato is beginning to feel doubts
which he finds it difficult to set at rest ; but he cannot
yet bring himself to a frank recognition of the fact that
absolute knowledge is unattainable by man. There is
a note of disappointment, sometimes almost of despair,
in the *Phaedo*, as if Plato had once entertained hopes
the realisation of which he has now come to consider
open to grave doubt. I do not wish to lay very much
stress on this argument ; but as far as it goes it seems
to me to tell in favour of the later date of the *Phaedo*,
a contention which I hope to make good by more
conclusive arguments drawn from other considerations.

I have spoken of doctrinal development. In what
respect can the *Phaedo* be said to carry on or supplement the philosophical position of the *Republic*? I wish
to call attention to one point in which it appears to
me that it undoubtedly does so. It will be remembered
that in the tenth book of the *Republic*, after the immortality of the soul has been demonstrated, Socrates
admits that the result thus arrived at loses some of the
value it would otherwise possess, owing to the fact that
we do not yet know what the soul really is as distinct
from what it appears to be when hampered by its
corporeal environment. This problem, which is felt to
be beyond the scope of the *Republic*, is left over for
future investigation. In the *Republic* Plato has made it
his business to describe as accurately as possible the

various forms under which the soul manifests itself in
this life; more than this he does not profess to have
done. · This is clearly indicated in the words of Socrates
which I have quoted in the last chapter:—

νῦν δὲ τὰ ἐν τῷ ἀνθρωπίνῳ βίῳ πάθη τε καὶ εἴδη,
ὡς ἐγῷμαι, ἐπιεικῶς αὐτῆς διεληλύθαμεν. (*Rep.* 612 A.)

Just before this, however, he has himself pointed out in
general terms the direction in which research should
proceed:—

ἀλλὰ δεῖ, ὦ Γλαύκων, ἐκεῖσε βλέπειν. Ποῖ; ἦ δ' ὅς.
Εἰς τὴν φιλοσοφίαν αὐτῆς, καὶ ἐννοεῖν ὧν ἅπτεται καὶ
οἵων ἐφίεται ὁμιλιῶν, ὡς ξυγγενὴς οὖσα τῷ τε θείῳ καὶ
ἀθανάτῳ καὶ τῷ ἀεὶ ὄντι, καὶ οἷα ἂν γένοιτο τῷ τοιούτῳ
πᾶσα ἐπισπομένη κ.τ.λ. (*Rep.* 611 D, E.)

Now where do we meet with an investigation into the
true nature of the soul conducted on these principles?
Surely in the *Phaedo*. There, if anywhere, we are
bidden again and again, with never-failing earnestness,
to bestow unremitting attention on the φιλοσοφία of the
soul. The whole structure of the Dialogue turns upon
the point. The avowed purpose of the conversation is
to show that the wise and good man, in other words the
philosopher, will not fear death; on the contrary he will
even welcome it as a release from present evils. Why
is this attitude specially appropriate to the philosopher?
Simply because owing to his soul's φιλοσοφία, which in
his case has become habitual, he comes nearer than any
other man to a true understanding of what the soul's
nature really is. His philosophy tells him that the soul
can never find a thoroughly congenial home in this
world because by nature she does not belong to this

world at all but to the world of ideas. She will be
able to exercise her proper function of pure unimpeded
thought only when she is set free from her bodily en-
tanglement and can be, like the ideas themselves, αὐτὴ
καθ᾽ αὑτήν. This being so, it need no longer surprise us
that the philosopher will regard death not as an evil
but as a blessing. At this point I may be confronted
with my own previously uttered warning against the
attempt to settle the respective dates of two Dialogues
by means of 'references' supposed to be made in the one
to the other. It is true that a result which is reached
only after elaborate argument in one Dialogue may be
assumed without argument in another. But in the
present instance the case appears to me to be different.
The 'result' which is reached in the *Phaedo* is not
'assumed' in the *Republic*. On the contrary it seems
to be assumed that on this point no result has been
reached. The *method*, it is true, by which it is hoped
that the result may be reached is pointed out; but the
investigation itself is put off till a future occasion, much
as in the *Theaetetus* the investigation of Eleaticism is
deferred and taken up again later in the *Sophist*. I
would suggest, then, that we are meant to understand
that the investigation of the essential nature of the soul
by concentrating our attention εἰς τὴν φιλοσοφίαν αὐτῆς
is consciously deferred in the *Republic*, and that we are
to find it carried out in the *Phaedo*.

But though this reasoning seems to me to make the
later date of the *Phaedo* probable, it cannot be regarded
as absolutely conclusive. I have now, however, another
and, I hope, a stronger reason to bring forward in
support of my contention that the *Phaedo* was intended
to follow the *Republic*. And here I may remark that

this question of the mutual relations of the two Dialogues is no mere side issue. On the contrary, I hope to make clear in what follows that the discussion of it will materially assist in determining Plato's conception of immortality and the special importance which the doctrine possessed in his eyes. No one, so far as I am aware, has attempted to ascertain the relation in which the *Phaedo* stands to the *Republic* by examining and comparing the respective proofs of immortality contained in the two Dialogues, and the general attitude towards the question which Plato adopts in each of them. Such a comparison I now propose to institute, and I hope to show as a result of it that the *Phaedo* must undoubtedly be placed later than the *Republic*.

In both of these Dialogues Socrates undertakes to prove the immortality of the soul, and in both a result satisfactory to his hearers is reached ; but the spirit in which the task is undertaken and the manner in which the question is argued and finally disposed of are in each case entirely different. In the *Phaedo* the discussion of the question occupies nearly the whole of the Dialogue : in the *Republic* it is relegated to a mere appendix and there settled with the utmost despatch. In the *Phaedo* it is indispensable that the soul should be shown to be immortal in order to justify the assertion which Socrates makes at the very beginning of the Dialogue, that the truly wise and good man will meet death with cheerfulness : in the *Republic* the proof is not felt to be in any way essential, but takes the form of a supplementary discussion which is not rendered in the least degree necessary by the main argument. Finally, in the *Phaedo* the question is recognised as one of very great difficulty, and the argument is of a corre-

spondingly elaborate order; every point that arises is
dealt with in the fullest manner possible; various objections to the theory are raised and severally disposed of;
and the utmost care is taken throughout that nothing
should be slurred over and nothing left unsaid that
would tend to make the final result as conclusive and
satisfactory as possible: in the *Republic* on the other
hand the required proof is said to be quite easy, and is
entered upon in a proportionately light-hearted manner;
the argument itself is not at all of a convincing nature;
no objections are urged against it; and after it has been
concluded and accepted as satisfactory, there follows an
admission that after all the real nature of the soul has
not yet been discovered. What are we to infer from all
this? It can hardly be said that the *Republic* assumes
the results of the *Phaedo* in this matter; for, as has
been said, the arguments used in the two Dialogues
respectively are utterly dissimilar: and if in the *Republic*
Plato had meant to remind us of the result reached in
the *Phaedo*, he would surely have invoked the aid of the
Theory of Ideas, on which the final proof of immortality
in the *Phaedo* is based; more especially as the Theory
of Ideas has already been introduced into the very same
book of the *Republic* which contains the proof of the
immortality of the soul. Moreover, the proof of immortality in the *Phaedo* so far as it goes is on Platonic
principles sound, whereas the proof which the *Republic*
offers is, as I have said, far from convincing. The
argument on which that proof is based I have outlined
in the preceding chapter: it is now time to consider its
defects. It is asserted that, whereas all other things are
finally destroyed by their respective ξύμφυτα κακά, the
same is not true of the soul; we see that ἀδικία, which

is the ξύμφυτον κακόν of the soul, does not destroy it.
At the outset it may be asked : What reason have we for
assuming that ἀδικία *is* the ξύμφυτον κακόν of the soul
in this special sense? It is *a* κακόν undoubtedly, but
that it bears the same relation to the soul which
ophthalmia bears to the eye would seem to be quite an
arbitrary assumption. How can we be sure that there
is not some other ξύμφυτον κακόν hitherto undiscovered
which *does* destroy the soul as ophthalmia destroys the
eye? Even if it be urged that experience goes to
prove that *no* κακόν actually destroys the soul, this only
paves the way for a far more serious objection to the
argument. Had the clear-headed Cebes, who states his
objections so forcibly in the *Phaedo*, taken part in the
dialogue of the *Republic*, we may be quite sure that he
would never have been so well satisfied with the proof
of the immortality of the soul as Glaucon and Adeimantus are represented as being. In the light of his
criticism in the *Phaedo* we may even guess with a high
degree of probability what line his objections would
have taken. Presumably he would have said pretty
much what he does say in the *Phaedo*, namely, that
the argument such as it is merely tends to show that
the soul is very durable. It may possibly survive its
present incarnation and many others besides ; but on the
other hand the present incarnation may be its last :
and in any case no adequate ground is suggested for
concluding that it is absolutely imperishable—ὅτι ἀθάνατος ἡμῶν ἡ ψυχὴ καὶ οὐδέποτε ἀπόλλυται. The entire
argument, as we have seen, is based on the general
assumption that, whereas everything that perishes in
this world is destroyed in the last resort by its own
ξύμφυτον κακόν, we know from our own observation that

the soul is *not* destroyed by its ξύμφυτον κακόν, which is taken to be ἀδικία. Thus, like the argument from ἀνταπόδοσις in the *Phaedo*, it is an argument drawn from the supposed universal operation of a natural law. But the generalisation in this case, as in the case of ἀντα-πόδοσις, if we try to extract from either argument a proof of immortality, is unwarranted. We cannot be justified in assuming without further proof that processes which we cannot see follow the same natural laws and are subject to the same conditions as those which we can see. We are in fact attempting to generalise from an imperfect field of observation. It is indeed true that injustice *so far as we can see* does not destroy the soul; but our observation does not carry us far enough, especially as our conception of the true nature of the soul, as it might be supposed to be after death when it is no longer joined to the body, is confessedly imperfect. What grounds, then, can we have for assuming that this same natural law applies equally to the state of the soul after death, when a totally different set of conditions may be operative? The appeal to mere physical laws in a question of this kind must always be unconvincing. Moreover there is no hint in the *Republic* of any insufficiency on the part of the argument to prove what is required, whereas the similar argument in the *Phaedo*, as Mr Archer-Hind points out, is recognised as falling short of absolute proof by the addition of a qualifying phrase:—

τούτων οὕτως ἐχόντων ἆρ᾽ οὐχὶ σώματι μὲν ταχὺ διαλύεσθαι προσήκει, ψυχῇ δὲ αὖ τὸ παράπαν ἀδιαλύτῳ εἶναι ἢ ἐγγύς τι τούτου; (*Phaedo* 80 B.)

To anyone having the *Phaedo* before him the flimsi-

ness and insufficiency of the argument for immortality in
the *Republic* could not fail to be obvious. Are we to
suppose, then, that after devoting the whole force of his
intellect to the solution of the problem in the *Phaedo*
Plato almost immediately—for the two Dialogues, as I
have said, cannot in my judgment have been separated
from one another by any long interval of time—proceeded to set forth the so-called proof of the immortality
of the soul which is contained in the tenth book of the
Republic? Those who hold that there is no development
and no connected system of philosophy to be discerned in
Plato's writings would, I suppose, find no great obstacle
to believing this possible; but I confess that to me it
seems absolutely inconceivable, more especially as the
demonstration of immortality in the *Republic*, while it
supplies nothing of any importance whatever to be
added to the results of the far more elaborate treatment
of the subject in the *Phaedo*, lies quite outside the main
purpose of the Dialogue. I believe on the contrary
that a consciousness of the futility of the argument in
the *Republic* as constituting a proof of the immortality
of the soul was one of the main reasons which caused
Plato to carry the investigation deeper and settle the
question once for all on a firm basis in the *Phaedo*.

For by this time he must have come to the conclusion
that the previous demonstration of immortality in the
Phaedrus was scarcely more adequate or convincing than
that in the *Republic*. In that demonstration we saw
that Plato makes the assumption that τὸ ἀεικίνητον is
ἀθάνατον: and it is the fact that the proof that ψυχὴ
πᾶσα is ἀθάνατος is made to depend upon this assumption which constitutes its weakness as a proof of immortality in any real sense of the word. We know that

Plato began his career as a faithful adherent of Heracliteanism, and such he always remained so far as
his attitude towards the world of sense is concerned.
Aristotle makes this point quite clear :—

ἐκ νέου τε γὰρ συνήθης γενόμενος πρῶτον Κρατύλῳ
καὶ ταῖς Ἡρακλειτείοις δόξαις, ὡς ἁπάντων τῶν αἰσθητῶν
ἀεὶ ῥεόντων καὶ ἐπιστήμης περὶ αὐτῶν οὐκ οὔσης, ταῦτα
μὲν [sc. τὰ αἰσθητὰ] καὶ ὕστερον οὕτως ὑπέλαβεν.

(Ar. *Met.* A 987ᵃ 32—ᵇ 1.)

To Plato, therefore, there is a sense in which everything
in the universe, matter no less than spirit, is ἀεικίνητον.
Of course matter is not ἀεικίνητον in the same sense in
which spirit is so; but the fact remains that the epithet
ἀεικίνητον does not really differentiate spirit from matter,
and the bare proposition that τὸ ἀεικίνητον is ἀθάνατον
cannot be turned to any profitable account in proving
that soul is immortal. For on this showing the material
universe would be immortal also; and so of course in a
sense it is on Platonic principles ; that is to say, matter
as such is indestructible. But this is not the kind of
immortality which Plato wishes to claim for the soul;
he is in search of something more definite, something
that will more effectually differentiate the soul from the
body. It is not surprising, therefore, that the theory of
immortality as represented by the proof in the *Phaedrus*
should have come to be regarded by him as unsatisfactory, and in need at all events of serious modification.
In my view, then, the proof of the immortality of the
soul in the *Phaedo* is intended to correct and supersede
the proofs in the *Phaedrus* and the *Republic*, which must
by this time have been regarded by Plato as inadequate.

   If this be so, another question naturally suggests

itself for consideration. Why does Plato bestow so
much thought on the subject of immortality at all?
Why especially does he show such intense earnestness
and anxiety as he does in the *Phaedo* to make it clear
that his belief has a solid foundation in his philosophy?
If we may judge from the *Republic*, the question whether
our souls are immortal or not does not affect the validity
of his philosophical opinions from the standpoint either of
metaphysics or of ethics.   Whether the soul is immortal
or not, the ideas are more real than phenomena, and
justice is better than injustice.   Why, then, on the first
suspicion that the arguments by which he had hitherto
sought to uphold the doctrine of immortality are unsound or inconclusive, does he hasten to re-establish it
on a basis which nothing can undermine?   Our answer
to this question will depend upon the point of view from
which we consider the *Phaedo* to have been written.
What was Plato's main object in composing the Dialogue?   Mr Archer-Hind maintains that the proof of the
immortality of the soul in the *Phaedo* is intended to
be a merely subordinate issue, the chief purpose of the
Dialogue being the affirmation of the Theory of Ideas.
In the Introduction to his edition of the *Phaedo* he
says (p. xiii):—"The assertion of the Ideas as the
causes of existence and the objects of cognition ; the
affirmation that they constitute the ultimate reality
upon which all sound reasoning must be based—this is
the most significant metaphysical result of the *Phaedo*,
and this beyond doubt was Plato's dearest purpose in
composing it.   And yet, so far as form goes, this is only
subsidiary to the establishment of a doctrine which has
turned out to be necessary to the maintenance of the
primary proposition."   For my own part I cannot feel

convinced that this description of Plato's purpose in
writing the *Phaedo* quite accurately represents the truth
of the matter. I think the doctrine of immortality possesses a greater importance for Plato than Mr Archer-
Hind seems inclined to allow. Assuming that I am right
in placing the *Republic* before the *Phaedo,* the ideas have
already been asserted as the causes of existence and
the objects of cognition, and that too in a much fuller
and more precise manner than in the *Phaedo.* It may
of course be said that neither exposition of the theory
is quite complete without the other; and this may
perhaps be admitted: but in any case the additional
contribution that is made to it in the *Phaedo* does not
amount to very much, and would hardly by itself be
sufficient to justify the composition for this purpose of
such an elaborate Dialogue as the *Phaedo.* For it will
hardly be denied that the ontological exposition contained in the *Phaedo* is of a somewhat vague character
and does not add anything of very great importance
that would not naturally be inferred from the clear
statements of the *Republic.*

Let us consider once more the ostensible purpose of
the proof of immortality from the point of view of the
actual conversation. It is the knowledge that his soul is
immortal which alone will enable the philosopher to
meet death cheerfully; for only when his soul is emancipated from the fetters of the body can he hope to know
the ideas. I submit, therefore, that Plato's main object
in writing the *Phaedo* was simply to substantiate the
doctrine of the immortality of the soul, the reason being
that a belief in the truth of this doctrine affords to the
philosopher his only ground for hoping that he will
sooner or later attain direct cognition of the ideas. It

is no doubt the Theory of Ideas that is uppermost in
Plato's mind at this time, but the existence of the world
of ideas has already been confidently affirmed in the
Republic: consequently it is, I think, with the question
of their *cognition* rather than their *existence* that he
chiefly concerns himself in the *Phaedo*. This question
has now become closely connected with the question of
immortality, as will be seen when we take into account
the above-mentioned difference of tone which characterizes the *Phaedo* as compared with the *Republic*. At the
time when he wrote the *Republic* Plato thought that he
was on his way to the discovery of a higher logic by
means of which the philosopher might actually acquire
in this life direct knowledge of the ideas themselves.
The attempt, however, was foredoomed to failure, and
consequently we find in the *Phaedo* that this confidence
no longer exists. The necessary limitations of the
human intelligence, at least in so far as its operations
in this life are concerned, are now felt to be too
powerful, and what promised in the *Republic* to be a
royal road to knowledge turns out in the end to be
a *cul-de-sac* ending abruptly on the shore of an impass-
able gulf. In the *Phaedo* Plato is beginning, though
unwillingly, to recognise this fact. But he will not on
that account consent to abandon his own cherished
creation, the Theory of Ideas. The assumption of the
existence of the ideal world still remains for him the
basis of all his speculation ; and the difficulty raised by
the question of the cognition of the ideas must be met
in some other way. In these circumstances what could
be more natural than that he should look for aid to the
doctrine of the immortality of the soul, which has for
some time been in his thoughts? He turns to it now

with a new interest. In this life even the philosopher
does not know the ideas and cannot have any reasonable hope of knowing them. But though we do not
actually *know* them, we have some faint *recollection* of
their nature, and the vividness of this recollection can
be increased by the aid of philosophy. In fact, though
we do not know the ideas *now*, we *have* at some time or
other had direct knowledge of them; that is to say, if
we accept the theory of ἀνάμνησις, which is upheld in
the *Phaedo* as strongly as ever: even Simmias affirms his
unhesitating conviction of the truth of the doctrine,
although he thereby renders untenable his own theory
that soul is a harmony. And since we *have* known the
ideas, why should we not know them again? If the
Idea of Good is supreme, we must not believe that the
general process of things is from good to bad and
from bad to worse; yet this pessimistic conclusion will
become almost inevitable, if we are constrained to admit
that we have passed from the knowledge of the ideas
never to know them again. No: if, as seems only too
probable, we cannot know the ideas in this life, then the
conclusion to which we must come is obvious; the soul
with all its cognitive faculties must be immortal. Moreover the soul of the true philosopher, who has gained the
mastery over his body and its low aspirations and spent
his days in the stedfast pursuit of truth, will after his
present life pass at once into another and more perfect
existence. He will then be freed from all the limitations
imposed by the body on the exercise by his soul of her
own proper function of uninterrupted contemplation;
and in this incorporeal life he will know the ideas again
even as he knew them before his first incarnation in
human form. Such is the fair hope which is held out in

the *Phaedo* to the philosopher, a hope which will enable him to face death not merely with equanimity but with unfeigned joy. Far from deploring it as an evil he will welcome its advent as the opening of a gate leading to another life better and more real than the present, a life of pure and unimpeded thought. Thus by the philosopher at least the present life should be regarded as in a very real sense a preparation for the life to come ; and all who will listen to him will find in the hope of eventually knowing the ideas a powerful inducement to apply themselves zealously to philosophy.

But what prospect, it may reasonably be asked, is offered to the souls of less earnest and less gifted human beings? And what is the position from this point of view of the lower animals? Obviously these inferior souls are not fitted to pass immediately from this life to the philosophic state of pure contemplation of the ideas. Whatever death may have in store for the philosopher, others cannot hope to be so fortunate. Yet it would of course be extremely unphilosophical to maintain that the philosopher's soul alone is immortal. On Platonic principles indeed it would be quite impossible : the great pronouncement of the *Phaedrus*— ψυχὴ πᾶσα ἀθάνατος—can never be abandoned. In order to make the theory of immortality as complete as possible it must be shown to be of universal application ; and for this purpose the theory of metempsychosis is in the *Phaedo* distinctly re-affirmed. For all souls alike their present life is or should be a preparation for another ; but whereas for the philosopher his present life represents the final stage of preparation, for inferior beings this cannot be so. Inferior souls after death must pass into another state of existence similar to the

present ; it depends upon themselves, however, whether
the second state shall be higher or lower than the first.
An abode in the ideal world can be theirs only after
they have by dint of steady application in all their
various incarnations finally attained to the truly philosophic life in this world. Then, and not till then, will
death mean for them the final ascent to the heights
of pure philosophy and the uninterrupted contemplation
of the ideas.

Such is the philosophical use which Plato proposes
to make of his theory of the immortality of the soul.
It is a theory which, as we have seen, has long been
in his thoughts, and which it has taken some time and
trouble to elaborate. But the time and trouble have
not been wasted, for we now see that the theory has
a real philosophical value. Mr Archer-Hind is fully
aware of this value, and anyone who reads his Introduction to the *Phaedo* will see that my account of it
does not differ essentially from his. But this only
increases my surprise at his regarding the proof of immortality in the *Phaedo* as playing a merely subordinate
part to the affirmation of the ideas. I am convinced
that the reason of his doing so is that he has not given
sufficient weight to the difference in Plato's attitude in
regard to this question in the *Phaedo* as compared with
earlier Dialogues. He does not seem to see that a *new*
importance has now come to be attached to the doctrine.
That in the *Phaedo* Plato does regard immortality as a
matter of great importance must be clear to everyone who observes the deep earnestness which marks
the whole treatment of the subject. But it is an importance which has not existed before. Hitherto the
doctrine of the immortality of the soul has been merely

an interesting theory affording a field for still more
interesting speculation; and we cannot discover that
it is anything more than this until we come to the
Phaedo. Even here it may be true in a sense to say
that it forms no essential part of Plato's philosophical
system, whether we regard it from a metaphysical or an
ethical point of view. The metaphysical explanation
of the universe on the hypothesis of the Theory of
Ideas, and the system of ethics which is founded upon
that theory, have both been arrived at in the *Republic*
without any dependence whatever being placed upon
the doctrine of immortality; and in both respects the
teaching of the *Republic* remains valid. As I have
already pointed out, the question of the immortality of
the soul is left entirely out of account while Plato is
expounding the details of his scheme; it comes up
afterwards only in an appendix dealing with a subject
upon which men would naturally tend to speculate, and
in which the students of the Academy would perhaps
be specially interested : they would not, therefore, wish
to see it altogether ignored in what professed to be
a complete philosophical treatise. The *Phaedo*, however,
is dissociated from the *Republic* by an important change
in Plato's opinion. The goal of his educational scheme
is the discovery of the true nature of the ideas : and the
realisation in practice of the ideal state will become
possible when the αὐτὸ ἀγαθόν is known. The goal
remains the same, but in the *Phaedo* Plato no longer
looks forward with confidence, as he did in the *Republic*,
to the attainment of this absolute knowledge in this
world even by the philosopher. And with this despair
of the attainment of absolute knowledge, which must
have begun to force itself upon him soon after the

Republic was written, the question of the immortality of
the soul at once assumes a much more serious aspect,
inasmuch as the philosopher's sole hope of finally
understanding the true meaning of his philosophy is
inextricably bound up with his hope of immortality.
In these circumstances Plato is led to reconsider his
attitude towards this inquiry, which has now assumed an
importance before unthought of. It is a subject which
he can no longer afford, as before, to handle in a light
and superficial manner. The truth of this doctrine has
become vital to him. Accordingly, when on reflexion
he recognises the imperfections of the proof of immortality which he has given in the *Republic*, he at once
sets to work to reconstruct it and place the doctrine on
a firmer basis—on no less a basis in fact than the Theory
of Ideas itself, which has remained throughout the final
assumption of all his philosophy. The thoroughness of
treatment and earnestness of tone which are such con-
spicuous features of the *Phaedo* are thus amply accounted
for by the undeniable importance of the subject.

This, then, is the point of view from which I conceive the *Phaedo* to have been written. The Theory of
Ideas in one of its most important aspects has been im-
perilled. The *existence* indeed of the ideas Plato has never
doubted; but the possibility at least of our ever *knowing*
them has been called in question, and the doubts thus
raised, if proved to be well-founded, would in the mind of
the Plato of this period deprive the theory itself of much
of its value: for the consummation which he hoped for
could come about only as the result of exact knowledge
of the contents of the ideal world. This being so the
proof of his theory that the soul is immortal alone
remains to him as a means of preserving the full use-

fulness of a system of philosophy which nothing will persuade him to abandon. Accordingly he prepares to substantiate it with all his strength.

The details of the proof and especially the relation of the several arguments for immortality in the *Phaedo* to one another need not concern us here. These points have been admirably and exhaustively dealt with by Mr Archer-Hind in his edition of the Dialogue, and I have only to say that I unreservedly accept his conclusions. I may be permitted, however, to call special attention to the close connexion subsisting between the Theory of Ideas on the one hand and the theory of immortality on the other. As I have tried to show, there has always been a connexion more or less close between them; and now in the light of the final and most convincing argument for immortality in the *Phaedo* we see that the connexion has become so intimate that the two theories are to a large extent mutually interdependent. The assumption of the existence of eternal immutable ideas, the objects of knowledge, presupposes the immortality of the soul as an indispensable condition of the attainment of that knowledge; while the immortality of the soul can in its turn be convincingly proved on the assumption that the Theory of Ideas in its present form is true. Nevertheless it must be admitted that none of the arguments used go very far towards proving that individual souls as such are immortal. This point also is made clear by Mr Archer-Hind, and there is nothing for me to add to what he says on the subject. The most that can be said is that a certain probability is given to the doctrine of individual immortality: it certainly is not proved even on Platonic principles. What is proved is the essential indestructi-

bility and eternity of the universal soul. Plato must
surely have been aware of this, and yet it cannot
reasonably be doubted that individual immortality is
in his mind throughout. It is true that Hegel maintains
that Plato did not, and Teichmüller that on his own
principles he could not, believe in individual immortality.
Their arguments in support of this conclusion have,
I think, been sufficiently answered by Mr Archer-Hind ;
and I am in complete agreement with his view, which
is that, however much or however little may be actually
proved, the reasonableness of a belief in the doctrine
that individual souls are of their own nature immortal
is certainly the teaching of the *Phaedo*. He does not
give reasons in detail for holding this opinion, and
certainly in view of the plain language of the Dialogue
such a course hardly seems necessary. We may note,
however, the persistence with which Socrates is continually declaring his conviction that death is no mis-
fortune for the man who has used his opportunities
well in this life ; and this conviction is due solely to
his belief that death is after all only the preliminary,
the necessary preliminary, to a happier existence, in
which, may be, it will fall to his lot to converse with
the souls of the great men who have died before him.
Plato would hardly have expressed himself continually
in such terms if he did not wish to indicate a belief
in individual immortality. Moreover the doctrine of
metempsychosis is uncompromisingly asserted :—

καὶ μέχρι γε τούτου πλανῶνται [sc. αἱ τῶν φαύλων
ψυχαὶ] ἕως ἂν τῇ τοῦ ξυνεπακολουθοῦντος τοῦ σωματοειδοῦς ἐπιθυμίᾳ πάλιν ἐνδεθῶσιν εἰς σῶμα. ἐνδοῦνται
δέ, ὥσπερ εἰκός, εἰς τοιαῦτα ἤθη ὁποῖ' ἅττ' ἂν καὶ μεμε-
λετηκυῖαι τύχωσιν ἐν τῷ βίῳ. Τὰ ποῖα δὴ ταῦτα λέγεις,

ὦ Σώκρατες ; Οἷον τοὺς μὲν γαστριμαργίας τε καὶ ὕβρεις
καὶ φιλοποσίας μεμελετηκότας καὶ μὴ διευλαβημένους
εἰς τὰ τῶν ὄνων γένη καὶ τῶν τοιούτων θηρίων εἰκὸς
ἐνδύεσθαι· κ.τ.λ. (*Phaedo* 81 D, E.)

If this is the language of metaphor, it is surely metaphor very much misapplied. Plato must mean to
declare his belief in metempsychosis, and this is a
doctrine which is applicable only to individual immortality. In fact all through the Dialogue we are
continually meeting with language which is consistent
with no other hypothesis than this; and we can hardly
fail to agree with Mr Archer-Hind in saying that " certainly if Plato is not here in earnest with individual
immortality, he may fairly be charged with having
passed from mysticism to mystification." But the fact
remains that the doctrine is not *proved*. I have already
said all that occurs to me in the way of explanation
in discussing the similar difficulty which meets us in
the *Phaedrus*. Plato must be well aware that he cannot
any more than anyone else prove that each soul continues to exist as the same conscious personality. He
proves what he can, namely that soul can never· die,
and while there is no conclusive objection to be urged
against it, he bids us accept further the belief that the
universal soul is always distributed into the same separate personalities :—

παντὸς μᾶλλον ἄρα, ἔφη, ὦ Κέβης, ψυχὴ ἀθάνατον
καὶ ἀνώλεθρον, καὶ τῷ ὄντι ἔσονται ἡμῶν αἱ ψυχαὶ ἐν
῞Αιδου. (*Phaedo* 106 E, 107 A.)

Such is Plato's persuasion. Moreover there is one
passage in the Dialogue which seems to contain a suggestion that Plato recognises the discrepancy that must

be felt to exist between his arguments and his inferences, but that he would have us know nevertheless that he fervently believes more than the arguments themselves can actually be held to prove. For this, I fancy, is the true significance of the language which Socrates uses in a striking passage :—

πρῶτον μὲν τοίνυν, ἔφη, τοῦτο εὐλαβηθῶμεν, καὶ μὴ παρίωμεν εἰς τὴν ψυχήν, ὡς τῶν λόγων κινδυνεύει οὐδὲν ὑγιὲς εἶναι, ἀλλὰ πολὺ μᾶλλον ὅτι ἡμεῖς οὔπω ὑγιῶς ἔχομεν, ἀλλὰ ἀνδριστέον καὶ προθυμητέον ὑγιῶς ἔχειν, σοὶ μὲν οὖν καὶ τοῖς ἄλλοις καὶ τοῦ ἔπειτα βίου παντὸς ἕνεκα, ἐμοὶ δὲ αὐτοῦ ἕνεκα τοῦ θανάτου. ὡς κινδυνεύω ἔγωγε ἐν τῷ παρόντι περὶ αὐτοῦ τούτου οὐ φιλοσόφως ἔχειν, ἀλλ᾿ ὥσπερ οἱ πάνυ ἀπαίδευτοι φιλονείκως. καὶ γὰρ ἐκεῖνοι ὅταν περί του ἀμφισβητῶσιν, ὅπη μὲν ἔχει περὶ ὧν ἂν ὁ λόγος ᾖ οὐ φροντίζουσιν, ὅπως δὲ ἃ αὐτοὶ ἔθεντο ταῦτα δόξει τοῖς παροῦσιν, τοῦτο προθυμοῦνται. καὶ ἐγώ μοι δοκῶ ἐν τῷ παρόντι τοσοῦτον μόνον ἐκείνων διοίσειν. οὐ γὰρ ὅπως τοῖς παροῦσιν ἃ ἐγὼ λέγω δόξει ἀληθῆ εἶναι προθυμηθήσομαι, εἰ μὴ εἴη πάρεργον, ἀλλ᾿ ὅπως αὐτῷ ἐμοὶ ὅ τι μάλιστα δόξει οὕτως ἔχειν.

(*Phaedo* 90 D—91 A.)

This is as much as to say that he is more anxious to believe than to prove his doctrine. Nor can it be merely the attitude of the historical Socrates that is here presented to us ; that we have had in the *Apology*, where the position taken up is very different from that which is suggested here. In this part of the *Phaedo* Socrates is quite clearly Plato's προφήτης : this becomes still more obvious a little later on, where we have a history of the development of philosophical opinions which can stand for nothing else but the growth of

Plato's own mind. Especially significant is the distinction drawn between his own state of mind and
that of the eristics referred to above as οἱ πάνυ ἀπαίδευτοι. It is not others so much as himself that he
wishes to convince. The reason of this is, as I have
tried to show, to be found in the critical condition in
which the Theory of Ideas finds itself.

I hope I have now made clear what I take to be
Plato's general position in the *Phaedo* with regard to
the question of immortality. There still, however, remains for consideration one special aspect of it which,
I think, calls for more attention than it has at present
received. The question which I am about to raise
concerns the theory of soul as exhibited in the *Phaedo*.
One difficulty connected with it is discussed by Mr
Archer-Hind, both in his Introduction to the Dialogue
and more fully in an article in *The Journal of Philology*
(vol. x). One phase of it I noted in the chapter on
the *Phaedrus*. Plato has been declared inconsistent
because, whereas in the *Phaedo* much of the argument
turns upon the assertion that the nature of soul is
single, in the *Phaedrus*, the *Republic*, and the *Timaeus*
it is described as triple ; and further because the origin
of passions is referred in the *Phaedo* to the body, in
the *Philebus* and the *Timaeus* to the soul. I consider
that Mr Archer-Hind has shown quite satisfactorily that
there is no real inconsistency involved, and I need only
state his conclusions, which amount to this. Soul is
naturally single, though when it is joined with body we
may discern three phases of its activity : and similarly
passions really belong to the soul, the seat of consciousness, though they become active only through
the soul's association with the body. There is, how-

ever, a further question of still greater importance connected with Plato's theory of soul, and the way in which we answer it must necessarily affect our view of his conception of immortality. Does Plato in the *Phaedo* admit the possibility that souls exist in a state of complete separation from body? Mr Archer-Hind would seem to answer this question in the negative, but on this point I find myself unable to agree with him. Plato's language in a number of passages in the *Phaedo* appears to me to point quite clearly to the conclusion that he did believe that after leaving the body the soul might exist without being joined with any body whatsoever. Certain of these passages I will now offer for consideration, attempting at the same time to show that directly or indirectly they support the view which I have expressed.

Ἡγούμεθά τι τὸν θάνατον εἶναι; Πάνυ γε, ἔφη ὑπολαβὼν ὁ Σιμμίας. Ἆρα μὴ ἄλλο τι ἢ τὴν τῆς ψυχῆς ἀπὸ τοῦ σώματος ἀπαλλαγήν; καὶ εἶναι τοῦτο τὸ τεθνάναι, χωρὶς μὲν ἀπὸ τῆς ψυχῆς ἀπαλλαγὲν αὐτὸ καθ' αὑτὸ τὸ σῶμα γεγονέναι, χωρὶς δὲ τὴν ψυχὴν ἀπὸ τοῦ σώματος ἀπαλλαγεῖσαν αὐτὴν καθ' αὑτὴν εἶναι; ἆρα μὴ ἄλλο τι ὁ θάνατος ἢ τοῦτο; Οὔκ, ἀλλὰ τοῦτο, ἔφη.

(*Phaedo* 64 C.)

From this we gather that what is meant by death is the separation of soul from body. After the death of any living creature there is in existence on the one hand a body αὐτὸ καθ' αὐτό, and on the other hand a soul αὐτὴ καθ' αὑτήν.

τὸ δ' ἔσχατον πάντων ὅτι, ἐάν τις ἡμῖν καὶ σχολὴ γένηται ἀπ' αὐτοῦ [sc. τοῦ σώματος] καὶ τραπώμεθα πρὸς τὸ σκοπεῖν τι, ἐν ταῖς ζητήσεσιν αὖ πανταχοῦ παρα-

πῖπτον θόρυβον παρέχει καὶ ταραχὴν καὶ ἐκπλήττει,
ὥστε μὴ δύνασθαι ὑπ' αὐτοῦ καθορᾶν τἀληθές, ἀλλὰ τῷ
ὄντι ἡμῖν δέδεικται ὅτι, εἰ μέλλομέν ποτε καθαρῶς τι
εἴσεσθαι, ἀπαλλακτέον αὐτοῦ καὶ αὐτῇ τῇ ψυχῇ θεατέον
αὐτὰ τὰ πράγματα. καὶ τότε, ὡς ἔοικεν, ἡμῖν ἔσται οὗ
ἐπιθυμοῦμέν τε καί φαμεν ἐρασταὶ εἶναι, φρονήσεως,
ἐπειδὰν τελευτήσωμεν, ὡς ὁ λόγος σημαίνει, ζῶσιν δὲ οὔ.
εἰ γὰρ μὴ οἷόν τε μετὰ τοῦ σώματος μηδὲν καθαρῶς
γνῶναι, δυοῖν θάτερον· ἢ οὐδαμοῦ ἔστιν κτήσασθαι τὸ
εἰδέναι ἢ τελευτήσασιν. τότε γὰρ αὐτὴ· καθ' αὑτὴν ἡ
ψυχὴ ἔσται χωρὶς τοῦ σώματος, πρότερον δ' οὔ.

(*Phaedo* 66 D—67 A.)

We now learn further that it is only in this state of
separation from the body that the soul can acquire
true knowledge (φρόνησις). In this life experience has
proved that in our efforts to obtain it we can never
shake ourselves entirely free from the disturbing influences of the body ; hence we can never know things
as they are until we are dead. In the *Republic*, however,
Plato had hoped, though it was but a hope, that this
might be done. In explaining the simile of the Cave
Socrates says :—

τὴν δὲ ἄνω ἀνάβασιν καὶ θέαν τῶν ἄνω τὴν εἰς τὸν
νοητὸν τόπον τῆς ψυχῆς ἄνοδον τιθεὶς οὐχ ἁμαρτήσει
τῆς γ' ἐμῆς ἐλπίδος, ἐπειδὴ ταύτης ἐπιθυμεῖς ἀκούειν.
θεὸς δέ που οἶδεν εἰ ἀληθὴς οὖσα τυγχάνει.

(*Rep.* 517 B.)

Thus the hope entertained by Plato in the *Republic*
is that the philosopher may be able in this life to discover the αὐτὸ ἀγαθόν for himself and then apply the
results of his knowledge to the regeneration of mankind.
But this hope is now seen to be incapable of realisation.

94 THE *PHAEDO* [CH.

Before the ideas can be known the soul must be αὐτὴ καθ᾽ αὑτήν even as the ideas themselves are αὐτὰ καθ᾽ αὑτά—αὐτῇ τῇ ψυχῇ θεατέον αὐτὰ τὰ πράγματα : and the soul can be αὐτὴ καθ᾽ αὑτήν only when death has set her free from the prison-house of the body. That is to say, the ideas are immaterial and the soul in her natural state is immaterial likewise : and if the soul is to have free communion with the ideas, she must regain this natural state of immateriality.

Ἐκ τῶν τεθνεώτων ἄρα, ὦ Κέβης, τὰ ζῶντά τε καὶ οἱ ζῶντες γίγνονται. Φαίνεται, ἔφη. Εἰσὶν ἄρα, ἔφη, αἱ ψυχαὶ ἡμῶν ἐν Ἅιδου. Ἔοικεν. (*Phaedo* 71 D, E.)

Socrates is here developing the argument in favour of immortality from ἀνταπόδοσις and γένεσις ἐξ ἐναντίων. There are two opposite states between which the soul alternates, the state τεθνηκός and the state ζῶν. The state τεθνηκός is, as we have seen, that in which ψυχή and σῶμα are separate from one another; and the state ζῶν is that in which the two are combined. For the purposes of the present argument it is necessary to assume that the state τεθνηκός represents for the soul an existence in time commensurable with the corporeal state of existence, ζῶν. There is a natural process always in operation, in which the soul passes from the one state to the other and back again. In every-day life we are familiar with the process in one direction, the passing of the soul from ζῶν to τεθνηκός: and we infer from the general uniformity which we observe in nature that the complementary process also takes place. That being so, εἰσὶν αἱ ψυχαὶ ἡμῶν ἐν Ἅιδου: in other words, there is a time when each soul is not joined with a body, and during that time it is in existence some-

where. With this passage we may compare another,
where the condition of the philosopher's soul after death
is being described :—

οὐκοῦν οὕτω μὲν ἔχουσα [sc. φιλοσοφοῦσα] εἰς τὸ
ὅμοιον αὐτῇ τὸ ἀειδὲς ἀπέρχεται, τὸ θεῖόν τε καὶ ἀθάνατον
καὶ φρόνιμον, οἷ ἀφικομένῃ ὑπάρχει αὐτῇ εὐδαίμονι
εἶναι, πλάνης καὶ ἀνοίας καὶ φόβων καὶ ἀγρίων ἐρώτων
καὶ τῶν ἄλλων κακῶν τῶν ἀνθρωπείων ἀπηλλαγμένῃ,
ὥσπερ δὲ λέγεται κατὰ τῶν μεμυημένων, ὡς ἀληθῶς
τὸν λοιπὸν χρόνον μετὰ τῶν θεῶν διαγούσῃ;

(*Phaedo* 81 A.)

The use of the word ἀειδές here should especially be
noted ; it is used by Plato to denote that which not
only *is not* seen but *cannot* be seen ; that is to say, it
describes the world of νοητά as opposed to that of
ὁρατά. The philosopher's soul, therefore, passes immediately to the immaterial world. Contrast with this the
condition of the unphilosophical soul :—

Ἀλλὰ καὶ διειλημμένην γε οἶμαι ὑπὸ τοῦ σωματοειδοῦς,
ὃ αὐτῇ ἡ ὁμιλία τε καὶ συνουσία τοῦ σώματος διὰ τὸ ἀεὶ
ξυνεῖναι καὶ διὰ τὴν πολλὴν μελέτην ἐνεποίησε ξύμφυτον; Πάνυ γε. Ἐμβριθὲς δέ γε, ὦ φίλε, τοῦτο οἴεσθαι
χρὴ εἶναι καὶ βαρὺ καὶ γεῶδες καὶ ὁρατόν· ὃ δὴ καὶ
ἔχουσα ἡ τοιαύτη ψυχὴ βαρύνεταί τε καὶ ἕλκεται πάλιν
εἰς τὸν ὁρατὸν τόπον, φόβῳ τοῦ ἀειδοῦς τε καὶ "Αιδου.

(*Phaedo* 81 C.)

Such a soul after leaving the body is not αὐτὴ καθ'
αὑτήν at all ; its affinity to things earthly will not allow
it to escape altogether from the taint of matter, and
therefore it is dragged down πάλιν εἰς τὸν ὁρατὸν
τόπον, becoming in fact a visible ghost. This is as
much as to say that after death it would naturally but

for its earthly propensities not belong to the ὁρατὸς
τόπος at all, but would pass directly to the world of
ideas; yet it would still be existent as a separate soul
apart from the body. It is obvious that language of
this sort tends towards a distinctly materialistic conception of soul, the very thing that Plato is seeking
to avoid. On this point I shall have more to say later.

Ἦσαν ἄρα, ὦ Σιμμία, αἱ ψυχαὶ καὶ πρότερον, πρὶν
εἶναι ἐν ἀνθρώπου εἴδει, χωρὶς σωμάτων καὶ φρόνησιν
εἶχον.   (*Phaedo* 76 c.)

This is the conclusion which Plato draws from the
theory of ἀνάμνησις. In an ante-natal state the soul
has existed and known the ideas; and in order to know
the ideas the soul must, as we have seen, be unencumbered with a body: hence the addition of the words χωρὶς
σωμάτων. Mr Archer-Hind considers that by these
words Plato "simply means apart from the human
bodies in which they now dwell," and for confirmation
of this he refers to 114 C. This does not seem to me
the natural meaning of the expression, nor do I think
that Plato meant it to be interpreted in that sense; on
the contrary, it seems to me that he is with perfect
consistency reiterating his conviction that in order to
know the ideas the soul must, like them, not only be of
its own nature immaterial, but must actually exist in an
immaterial state. The passage referred to (114 C) has
next to be considered: it seems to me that with it my
case is brought to a satisfactory conclusion.

τούτων δὲ αὐτῶν οἱ φιλοσοφίᾳ ἱκανῶς καθηράμενοι
ἄνευ τε σωμάτων ζῶσι τὸ παράπαν εἰς τὸν ἔπειτα χρόνον,
καὶ εἰς οἰκήσεις ἔτι τούτων καλλίους ἀφικνοῦνται.
                                        (*Phaedo* 114 C.)

Here, if anywhere, we surely have a clear statement of Plato's belief that souls can exist without being attached to a body of any kind. Even after making all allowances for metaphorical or allegorical language this conclusion seems to be amply justified. There would not be much gained from an allegorical point of view in representing souls as existing without bodies; the tendency would rather be the other way. When Plato indulges in allegory, his custom is to represent the immaterial in a material guise; and the allegory of the *Phaedrus* is, therefore, in full accord with his practice in this respect. Thus we are driven to a literal interpretation of the passage before us. But what is the literal interpretation? or rather, to what extent can the passage be literally interpreted? I maintain that the words mean exactly what they say, namely, that philosophic souls live on after death "without bodies altogether." Mr Archer-Hind, however, in his note on this passage remarks: "I conceive this to mean 'without earthly bodies': for the most exalted of finite spirits, even the gods, must have body of some sort; that is, they are subject to the conditions of space and time." He compares *Phaedr.* 246 C. But the comparison seems to me hardly fair. In the passage referred to Plato is consciously allegorizing: consequently terms which are applicable properly only to material things are applied to the soul, which is immaterial. Thus the soul is described as at one time ἐπτερωμένη and at another πτεροῤῥυήσασα : and a distinction has to be drawn between her original ethereal body and the σῶμα γήϊνον which she inhabits after falling from her high estate. But putting allegory aside there seems no more reason to assume that in her natural state the

soul has a body than that she has feathers and afterwards loses them. And as far as the gods are concerned,
what does Plato say of them ?   His words are :—

    ἀλλὰ πλάττομεν οὔτε ἰδόντες οὔτε ἱκανῶς νοήσαντες
θεόν, ἀθάνατόν τι ζῷον, ἔχον μὲν ψυχήν, ἔχον δὲ σῶμα,
τὸν ἀεὶ δὲ χρόνον ταῦτα ξυμπεφυκότα.

(Phaedr. 246 C, D.)

This seems to me to be far from giving confirmation
to Mr Archer-Hind's view.   What Plato says is not
that the gods " must have body of some sort," but that,
being unable to form an adequate conception of a god,
we represent him to our minds as a being having both
soul and body—a very different thing.   Moreover,
granted that all finite spirits " are subject to the conditions of space and time," Mr Archer-Hind assumes
that this is the same thing as saying that "they must
have body of some sort."   Now I should venture to
doubt whether at this time Plato did believe that the
one statement necessarily implies the other.   One of
my chief objects in this essay is to show that there is
good reason to believe that, when he wrote the *Phaedo*,
Plato had not arrived at so clear a notion of the significance of such terms as 'soul,' 'body,' 'space,' and
'time' as Mr Archer-Hind's assumption would imply.
I hope to show on the contrary that we can discern
a distinct development of Plato's thought in this respect.
I should be the last to deny that what Mr Archer-Hind
says would be perfectly true of the mature Platonism
of the *Timaeus* ; but whether it would equally apply to
the as yet undeveloped Platonism of the *Phaedo* is,
I make bold to think, at least questionable.   I shall
deal more fully with this point in subsequent chapters.

But on reading such passages as have been cited above from the *Phaedo*, the question which it naturally occurs to one to ask is this: If what Plato meant to say was that the soul after death does indeed have some sort of a body, though not a γήϊνον σῶμα, why did he not say so in such language as to prevent what would certainly be a very natural misapprehension?

But even if we accept Mr Archer-Hind's view I am not sure that the inference which I propose to draw from a consideration of the passages quoted above will be seriously affected. The inference is this. At the time when the *Phaedo* was written Plato considered that, so far as the individual ἔμψυχον is concerned, what he calls ψυχή and what he calls σῶμα are essentially separable the one from the other: separable, that is, not merely logically in our minds but actually in space and time: and that this separation normally takes place at death. Any ψυχή may return to inhabit another σῶμα, but there is an interval of time between such death and re-incarnation, and during that interval the philosopher's soul at all events is αὐτὴ καθ' αὑτήν. If, then, with Mr Archer-Hind, we explain away the continual employment of such phrases as χωρισμὸς ψυχῆς ἀπὸ σώματος, χωρὶς σωμάτων, ἄνευ σωμάτων, and the like—though I must say that the very emphatic expression ἄνευ σωμάτων τὸ παράπαν in the last passage I quoted (114 C) and the repeated description of the soul when separated from the body as αὐτὴ καθ' αὑτήν, recalling as it does the very phraseology used in connexion with the ideas themselves, seem to me to make such an explanation an unwarrantable violation of Plato's plain statement—we are forced to believe that Plato has so formulated his conception of the

nature of the individual soul as to render it liable to
the charge of materialism. We have to admit that in
his view a soul can exist αὐτὴ καθ' αὑτήν and yet in so
existing must necessarily have attached to it some sort
of a body. That is to say, the term ψυχή as applied to
the individual denotes not pure spirit but a certain
combination of spirit with a particular kind of matter,
different indeed from the matter which forms the substance of the things we see around us, but still matter.
If this be so, there would seem to be some reason
for the fear which Socrates discerns in the minds of
Cebes and Simmias:—

ὅμως δέ μοι δοκεῖς σύ τε καὶ Σιμμίας ἡδέως ἂν καὶ
τοῦτον διαπραγματεύσασθαι τὸν λόγον ἔτι μᾶλλον, καὶ
δεδιέναι τὸ τῶν παίδων, μὴ ὡς ἀληθῶς ὁ ἄνεμος αὐτὴν
ἐκβαίνουσαν ἐκ τοῦ σώματος διαφυσᾷ καὶ διασκεδάν-
νυσιν, ἄλλως τε καὶ ὅταν τύχῃ τις μὴ ἐν νηνεμίᾳ ἀλλ'
ἐν μεγάλῳ τινὶ πνεύματι ἀποθνῄσκων.

(*Phaedo* 77 D, E.)

If on the other hand we interpret Plato's language in
what I must consider to be the natural manner, then we
can hardly refuse to admit that at the time when the
Phaedo was written he saw no reason to doubt that the
soul itself, invisible and immaterial, can exist in time in
absolute independence of any sort of body whatsoever.
For my own part I incline to the latter view for two
reasons: in the first place, because it seems to me to be
the natural deduction from Plato's own words which
I cannot see sufficient reason for explaining away;
and in the second place, because such a conception of
the nature of the soul as I have attributed to him would
seem to be, as I hope in the following chapter to show,

in perfect harmony with the metaphysical opinions held by him at this time, to be in fact the natural corollary of those opinions.

But after all I am inclined to think that the discrepancy between these two views will not be found to be so great as might at first sight appear. In the long run they both seem to point to the same conclusion, namely, that regarded from the standpoint of the individual, ψυχή is a 'thing,' which can and does exist absolutely apart from what we know as σῶμα: and the same holds good whether we imagine Plato's conception of ψυχή to be consciously materialistic or not, the fact being that in either case it really is materialistic, though Plato himself may not at the time have imagined it to be so. For the unbodied souls must exist numerically and spatially distinct from one another; and if the souls αὐταὶ καθ' αὑτάς are thus separated, they must be, as Plato saw later, essentially material. But this does not affect the validity of the view I am here advocating. Thus it would be hard to acquit Plato in the *Phaedo* of that very '*Rohheit*' from which Hegel would fain save him (see Mr Archer-Hind's Introduction to his edition of the *Phaedo*, p. xxix). To such a theory of soul no less than to the Theory of Ideas in its earlier form grave objections are to be urged, and of this Plato could not long remain in ignorance. He found himself in difficulties, and these difficulties we now pass on to consider.

CHAPTER VI.

IMMORTALITY AND THE EARLIER THEORY
OF IDEAS.

ACCORDING to Dr Jackson's theory of Plato's philosophical development the *Phaedo*, with the somewhat
doubtful exception of the *Cratylus*, is the last of the
Dialogues which represent his metaphysical opinions
in their first dogmatic form. With the *Cratylus* we are
not here concerned. At this point, therefore, it will be
well to pause for a while before passing on to a consideration in detail of the later Dialogues, in which
according to Dr Jackson Plato's more advanced metaphysical views find expression, in order that I may give
a short account of what I conceive to be the position
which has up to the present been arrived at with regard
to the question of the immortality of the soul. The
doctrine of immortality was, as we have seen, closely
connected in Plato's mind with his Theory of Ideas;
and in order that this connexion may be realised as
clearly as possible it will be necessary to trace quite
briefly the rise of that theory, and to indicate the form
which it had taken at this stage. In so doing I shall
of necessity be treading a sufficiently well-worn path, and
I have only to say that I am content to follow closely
in the footsteps of Mr Archer-Hind, whose general view

may be gathered from the admirable summary contained in the Introduction to his edition of the *Timaeus*.
Though I do not profess to have anything new to say
on the general question, I hope that by my statement
of it, or at least of particular parts of it, I may be able
to throw some light on what is more immediately important, the genesis of Plato's theory of soul.

So far as the question of immortality is concerned,
we have seen that there was virtually nothing in the
popular tradition of Greece, and very little in any
previous or contemporary speculation, that was likely
to influence Plato to any great extent in the formation
of a theory of his own on the subject.   The tradition
of a future existence, if such it can be called, which
had come down from Homer, he rejects as demoralising
and unworthy of serious consideration : and the speculations of philosophers and mystics had been of too
vague and fanciful a nature to form the basis of any
definite theory, totally unconnected as they were with
anything that could be called a system of philosophy.
Plato was of course aware of them all, and he may
have assimilated a suggestion here and there which
seemed to him to contain a germ of truth, such as the
doctrine of metempsychosis held by the Pythagoreans
and the Orphic mystics : but that is all.   Rather than
attempt to develop in the same unscientific manner with
which they had been content such vague doctrines as
came down to him from his predecessors, he chose to
form a scientific theory of immortality for himself,
founded upon a reasoned metaphysical doctrine purely
of his own creation, the Theory of Ideas.   Thus is
Plato's position clearly marked off from that of any
of his predecessors.   The Theory of Ideas and the

Theory of Immortality seem to arise almost simultaneously in the *Symposium*; they are developed side by
side in the *Phaedrus*; and though in the *Republic* the
question of the immortality of the soul is owing to
particular circumstances kept rather in the background,
it is none the less there, and it is clear that Plato is
still much interested in the subject.   Finally, in the
Phaedo the two theories re-appear in more intimate
connexion than ever before, so much so that neither
can be regarded as complete without the other.   Let
us now trace this connexion a little more closely.

In the last chapter I had occasion to point out that
Plato, as we know from Aristotle, was in his youth
instructed by his tutor Cratylus in all the characteristic
principles of the philosophy of Heraclitus; and all
through his life he remained a faithful adherent of the
theory of flux, so far at least as his attitude to the
world of phenomena was concerned.   In this region
the doctrine of πάντα ῥεῖ seemed to him undeniably
true.   But Plato was a born metaphysician, and the
onesidedness of Heracliteanism could not long content
him. He saw, what its author did not, that such a system
of philosophy could lead in the end to nothing but
scepticism and the abandonment once for all of the
pursuit of knowledge. The fact was that for the purpose
of the acquisition of knowledge too great a part was
assigned to the senses, themselves admitted to be
fallible, while too little fell to the share of reason.   The
absurdity of Heracliteanism when pushed to its logical
conclusion is amusingly illustrated by Plato in the
Theaetetus, where he describes the extravagances to
which the ῥέοντες of Ephesus were reduced by the
exigencies of their theory. So long as nothing was

recognised but the continually changing world of phenomena, there could be nothing permanent at all to
the study of which the mind could be directed ; hence
there could be no such thing as knowledge. It was
probably Plato's acquaintance with Socrates that contributed more than anything else to save him from the
absolute scepticism which Heracliteanism inevitably
brought in its train.   Socrates, it is true, was not
a metaphysician himself; the 'bettering of opinion'
was all he had to offer in compensation for knowledge,
which according to him was removed far beyond the
reach of the human mind. Nevertheless he held that
the mind could be usefully employed in the formation
of λόγοι, logical concepts or definitions·; and though
not himself a metaphysician, by means of his system
of λόγοι he was unconsciously giving a new impetus
to metaphysics, and Plato especially was encouraged
thereby to follow a new path of philosophical speculation.   Failing, then, to discover any stable object of
knowledge in the universal flux of Heraclitus, he attempted to find what he wanted in the One of Parmenides interpreted in a reasonable manner, that is to
say, without the rigorous treatment which it had received
at the hands of Zeno. Zeno had made it his business
to disprove absolutely the existence of the Many ; but
in so doing he had rendered the One all but unmeaning:
in fact his infantile logic would reduce the sum of our
knowledge of it to that which is contained in the
identical proposition ἓν ἕν.   Interpreted in this way
Eleaticism leaves us no better off than Heracliteanism.
Plato perceived this, and the task which he set himself
was to reconcile all that was essential in these two
seemingly irreconcilable systems, the πάντα ῥεῖ of

Heraclitus and the ἓν ὂν πᾶν of Parmenides, either of which taken by itself was found to be insufficient for the purpose of giving a satisfactory explanation of the universe. The key to this reconciliation he found, as Mr Archer-Hind points out, in νοῦς, the abstract causative principle of Anaxagoras, which Plato saw could be turned to far more profitable account than its original discoverer had supposed. To Anaxagoras νοῦς was merely the force—an intelligent force—which set the mechanism of the universe in motion; Plato, however, found in it not only an *intelligent* moving cause but a *good* final cause as well, a principle which supplies the universe not only with its impetus but with its whole purpose and reality. The way to idealism was now clearly marked out before him. He is seeking something stable, something that can be known, behind the unknowable flux of phenomena which was all that Heracliteanism recognised, and at the same time something about which there was more to know than could be furnished by the Eleatic One. Such a knowable reality he finds in the province of νοῦς, a world that is not αἰσθητόν but νοητόν: and its contents are certain eternal verities which he calls εἴδη or ἰδέαι, and the existence and nature of which can be discerned only by a process of abstract reasoning, though this reasoning takes its start from a careful study of the phenomena of this world. Thus we see the justice of Aristotle's account of the origin of Plato's idealism :—

τὸ μὲν οὖν τὸ ἓν καὶ τοὺς ἀριθμοὺς παρὰ τὰ πράγματα ποιῆσαι, καὶ μὴ ὥσπερ οἱ Πυθαγόρειοι, καὶ ἡ τῶν εἰδῶν εἰσαγωγὴ διὰ τὴν ἐν τοῖς λόγοις ἐγένετο σκέψιν· οἱ γὰρ πρότεροι διαλεκτικῆς οὐ μετεῖχον.

(Ar. *Met.* A 987ᵇ 29—33.)

The formulation of the Theory of Ideas, then, was the result of Plato's logical studies. He developed and converted to his own use the method pursued by Socrates in forming definitions of ethical terms: by abstraction he formed a logical concept, and by hypostatization the concept became an idea.

This account of the rise of the Theory of Ideas, though it is far from being comprehensive, will perhaps be sufficient for my present purpose, which is to show that Plato's theory of immortality, as exemplified by the *Phaedo*, arose in very much the same way. That both theories sprang up at the same time and grew in distinctness side by side has already been indicated, and this I consider was due to the fact that in each case Plato's thought was working along the same lines. I think the theory of immortality, as we have it presented to us in the *Phaedo*, was directly suggested by the Theory of Ideas, the form of the one being the natural outcome of the reasoning which led to the other. According to the earlier Theory of Ideas, as we find it formulated in the *Republic* and the *Phaedo*, the ideas exist in a world of their own separate from and independent of the things of this world; these things, however, would not be what they are but for the immanence in them of corresponding ideas, which give to them such reality as they can be said to possess. The precise relation in which ideas stand to phenomena is not yet satisfactorily worked out; but the ideas themselves are distinctly regarded as self-existent immaterial entities. Plato then proceeds to argue that, if ideas can exist in this way in complete independence of phenomena, mind can exist in the same way in complete independence of matter; and from the as-

sertion of a possible essential separation of mind from
matter it is not a far cry to the similar assertion that
the soul can exist in a state of essential separation
from the body, and after that the immortality of the
soul follows as a quite natural extension of the theory.
It is true that the exact relation subsisting between
the soul and the body in the combined state of
existence is no more clearly defined than the connexion between ideas and phenomena, of which we
are told :—

οὐκ ἄλλο τι ποιεῖ αὐτὸ καλὸν ἢ ἡ ἐκείνου τοῦ καλοῦ
εἴτε παρουσία εἴτε κοινωνία εἴτε ὅπῃ δὴ καὶ ὅπως. οὐ
γὰρ ἔτι τοῦτο διισχυρίζομαι, ἀλλ' ὅτι τῷ καλῷ τὰ καλὰ
γίγνεται καλά. (*Phaedo* 100 D.)

Thus, as Plato does not yet see his way to defining
more exactly the relation between ideas and phenomena, we could hardly expect to find at this stage of
his thought any more precise account of the relation
between soul and body; certainly we do not find it.
In each case Plato prefers to use language of a more
or less metaphorical character; the body is the δεσμω-
τήριον of the soul, and so on. It is clear, however, that
in his opinion the soul makes the living thing what it
is, just as τῷ καλῷ τὰ καλὰ γίγνεται καλά, and with the
departure of the soul the reality of the former ἔμψυχον
departs along with it. But the soul, whether at any
given moment it is inhabiting a body or not, is always
existent and always in its essence immaterial. It is in
this respect that Plato's theory of soul exhibits so great
an advance on those of all his predecessors. Their
conceptions of the nature of the soul were all confessedly
materialistic, and their notions of immortality, if they

had any, must all have been correspondingly crude.
On the other hand, when Plato comes to deal with the
question in a really philosophical spirit, he aims at
establishing the immortality of an immaterial soul
which is essentially separable from the body with its
immateriality unimpaired. And this doctrine of the
possibility of a complete and essential separation of
soul from body is, as I have endeavoured to show,
exactly the doctrine which we find insisted on in the
Phaedo. Moreover, souls which have in this world been
duly trained and purified by the study of philosophy
continue to exist after death as individual and conscious
personalities : thus corresponding to the plurality of
absolutely self-existent ideas (αὐτὰ καθ᾽ αὑτὰ εἴδη) we
have a plurality of absolutely self-existing souls (αὐταὶ
καθ᾽ αὑτὰς ψυχαί). The ideas, being essentially immaterial, are then directly apprehended by souls whose
immateriality, obscured for a while by association with
material bodies, is by such means triumphantly re-
asserted. In full agreement with this we are emphatically told in the *Phaedo* that the soul has a close
affinity with the ideas, and that it is to the immaterial
world of ideas that she naturally belongs. It is this
very immateriality, common to both, which constitutes
the affinity between them. The proper function of the
soul is to apprehend the ideas, and the true apprehension
of them as they are in themselves is impossible unless
the soul can first be entirely emancipated from the
bondage of the body, which prevents her realising her
true nature : that is to say, the affinity is not complete
until the soul is freed from all taint of materiality.
And the attainment by the individual soul of such
a future state of immaterial existence is, I am fully

persuaded, distinctly regarded by Plato at this time as
a possible consummation, whatever may have been his
view later when his philosophy had reached a maturer
stage.   In the *Phaedo* he recognises two distinct worlds,
the world of phenomena and the world of ideas, the
one material and the other immaterial; and he contemplates the possibility of the soul passing in time
straight from the one to the other.   In both worlds it
is the soul's business to study the ideas; but whereas
in this world the study is necessarily of a very imperfect
kind, in the other it is full and perfect and can be
carried on uninterruptedly without any restrictions
whatsoever.   In our present life on earth our study of
the ideas is governed by a sort of recollection, imperfect
but true so far as it goes, which we have of the content
of the ideal world; and we have this recollection because our souls have previously existed in that world
in the immaterial state which such an existence necessarily implies.   Our souls are still in essence immaterial,
though they are precluded in their corporeal existence
from the full assertion of their immaterial nature;
hence inasmuch as they are still souls, albeit degraded
by contact with the body, they cannot but preserve to
some extent their natural affinity with the ideas and
are able therefore to a corresponding extent, varying
in different individuals, still to apprehend them in virtue
of the recollection which they never entirely lose.   The
full knowledge of the ideas, however, can be regained
only when the soul has returned once more to her own
proper sphere of existence.   The affinity of the soul
with the ideas does not of course necessarily involve
the conclusion that she, like them, is immortal: Plato
recognises this: but still he believes that it is so, that

the plurality of souls, like the plurality of ideas, remains
for ever essentially unchanged.

We see, then, that the doctrine of the immortality
of the soul, in the form at least which it assumes in the
Phaedo, bears a distinct analogy to the Theory of Ideas
in the form in which that theory was at that time stated.
The two theories in fact are mutually complementary, and
each of them bears its part in the formation of a theory
of knowledge.   It was probably the doctrine of ἀνάμνησις, referred to above, that first suggested to Plato the
formulation of a scientific theory of the immortality
of the soul.   Having once admitted, as this doctrine
compelled him to admit, that in a previous existence
the soul has possessed direct knowledge of the ideas,
he felt himself unable in justice to his own principles
to believe that the fall from a high estate indicated by
the theory of ἀνάμνησις could be permanent.   It must
be possible in some way to regain the lost step, and
the way which naturally suggested itself was the pursuit
of philosophy, the attempt in fact on the part of the
soul to recover its lost knowledge of the ideas so far
as such recovery is possible in this earthly life.   In
order that the recovery of this knowledge may be
finally completed a future life becomes a necessity, and
the future life must be the same in kind as that in
which the soul previously knew the ideas.   Thus in the
Phaedo we have a development of the notion formerly
outlined in a poetical manner in the *Phaedrus*, the
notion of an actually existing immaterial world, in
which there are on the one hand souls possessing the
faculty of cognition and on the other hand ideas which
afford a field for the natural exercise of that faculty.
And when once it is allowed that the existence of the

soul neither began with nor will end with this present
life, it became natural, if not necessary, to hold that
this existence, which is properly akin to the existence
of the ideas themselves, extends infinitely in both
directions. The ideas are essentially unchangeable and
imperishable; and the souls, which are akin to them
and know them and occupy the same world with them
as conscious personalities, must surely, as such, be unchangeable and imperishable likewise. Refusal to admit
this would involve at best a needless complication in
the face of what had already been admitted; and Plato
at any rate saw nothing to prevent him from carrying
his theory to this its natural conclusion.

To sum up. Starting from the two assumptions,
first, that there are ideas, and secondly, that they can
be known, Plato cannot help seeing that the second
assumption stands in urgent need of some measure of
justification. In the *Republic*, where the Theory of
Ideas first receives definite shape, he lets it be clearly
seen that he hopes to discover a higher system of logic
by means of which the required knowledge can be here
and now obtained. In the *Phaedo* he makes it equally
clear that his hopes have been disappointed: the stern
facts of life have proved too strong for him. He sees
now, what he could not bring himself to recognise at
first, that in this life the conditions of human knowledge are necessarily of such a kind that the ideas
cannot be known as they are in themselves. The
nearest approach to knowledge of them that we can
make consists in developing to the best of our power
that faculty of recollection which gives us some conception of their nature; but the veil cannot be lifted very
far even by the highest intellect. Thus if the present

life is all that we have to look forward to, we can never know the ideas. But it is not all. There is another alternative, which Plato is quick to seize upon. If the ideas cannot be known in this life, they must be known in another. The belief that the soul is immortal is not new to him; but he feels it necessary to look carefully into the form of his belief and to bring it into closer connexion with his philosophy. Circumstances have combined to cause this belief to assume in his eyes an aspect of the highest importance, and it is his chief concern in the *Phaedo* to emphasize this importance. He cannot indeed, even with the help of the Theory of Ideas, prove incontrovertibly that the soul of the individual, as such, is immortal; but in the *Phaedo* he undoubtedly does the next best thing. He proves on his own principles that soul is necessarily indestructible; and at the same time he makes it clear that, although he cannot absolutely *prove* that the individual soul is immortal, in his opinion at all events there are strong reasons for *believing* it to be so.

CHAPTER VII.

CHANGES IN PLATO'S DOCTRINE.

THE general character of Plato's conception of immortality at the time when he composed the *Phaedo* and the particular purpose which it was at that time intended to serve have now, I hope, been made sufficiently clear. More especially I have laid stress on the theory of soul which, as it seems to me, such a conception of immortality necessarily involves. Plato himself is at great pains to establish an intimate connexion between his doctrine of immortality and his Theory of Ideas; and in particular certain peculiar features in his theory of soul become fully intelligible only when they are considered in relation to the Theory of Ideas in the form in which he has up to the present conceived it. In view, then, of the very close connexion between the two theories it is obviously important to look carefully into any modifications that may have been introduced into the Theory of Ideas at a subsequent period; for in the circumstances any changes in this theory may fairly be expected to produce corresponding changes in Plato's theory of soul; and these changes in turn will re-act upon his conception of immortality. In what follows I hope to be able to show that this is exactly what must have happened.

So far as the Theory of Ideas itself is concerned, it is maintained by Dr Jackson and Mr Archer-Hind that we do not see it in its final shape in the *Republic* and the *Phaedo*; and it seems to me that they are certainly right. I believe with them that after the *Phaedo* had been written Plato felt himself compelled to reconsider his metaphysical opinions in certain important respects, with the result that the Theory of Ideas, in the form at least in which it had hitherto been stated, was found to be open to serious objections which could be removed only by means of systematic reconstruction. Aristotle seems distinctly to recognise two stages in Plato's philosophical views; and in agreement with his statements certain Dialogues, which on this ground must be considered the later Dialogues, appear to reflect a doctrine widely differing in various ways from that to which we have become accustomed in the *Republic* and the *Phaedo*. These Dialogues are the *Parmenides*, the *Philebus*, the *Theaetetus*, the *Sophist*, the *Politicus*, and the *Timaeus*: in them, to use Dr Jackson's phraseology, we pass on from the ' Earlier' to the ' Later Theory of Ideas.'

We have now to consider whether it is possible to discover a later theory of soul in conformity with the Later Theory of Ideas. We have seen that hitherto the development of the Theory of Ideas and the doctrine of the immortality of the soul has been a simultaneous progress until finally each theory has been embodied in a well-defined shape, of which I have endeavoured to indicate the main characteristics. Since, then, we have reason to believe that Plato's maturer judgment caused him to introduce important alterations into the Theory of Ideas, we should naturally expect to see corresponding changes in the theory of soul which the

8—2

assertion of immortality presupposes; and with Dr Jackson's account of 'Plato's Later Theory of Ideas' before us I think it will be no hard matter to determine the character of these changes. What is required is to apply Dr Jackson's results in another sphere and see how they will affect a side of Plato's philosophy to which they have not hitherto been extended. It will not be inappropriate, therefore, to begin by explaining very shortly the chief points in which the later Theory of Ideas differs from the earlier, and the main reasons which induced Plato to make the change. This done, we shall be in a better position to investigate the extent to which these or similar reasons may be expected to influence in a corresponding manner the theory of soul which he at first saw fit to adopt. As is only to be expected, I follow Dr Jackson closely so far as his general position is concerned, though in certain points I have chosen to state things in a somewhat different manner in order to bring out more clearly my own particular application of his theory.

According to Plato's earlier doctrine there is beyond and apart from the visible world of phenomena an invisible world of ideas. Each of these worlds is separately existent, but they are related to one another in such a manner that, whereas the ideas are absolutely independent of phenomena, phenomena cannot do without the ideas. In fact the ideal world is all-important to the phenomenal world, for phenomena 'partake of' (μετέχει) the ideas, and it is in virtue of this 'participation' (μέθεξις) that they possess their only claim to existence; for to Plato that alone is 'real' (ὄντως ὄν) which is transcendental. The ideas cause phenomena to be what they are and also to be capable of being

known, so far as anything which is not strictly transcendental can be said to be capable of being known at
all. This complete separation of the world of ideas
from the world of phenomena owes its origin, as Aristotle informs us, to the logical studies to which Plato
devoted himself under the inspiration of his master
Socrates. It arose in the first instance from the practice
of forming logical concepts or definitions (λόγοι) of
abstract notions such as ἀγαθόν, καλόν, δίκαιον, and the
like. Socrates stopped short here; he was content to
believe that these concepts owe such existence as they
possess entirely to the mind which forms them as the
result of the comparison of particular manifestations of
the qualities in question. Plato, however, went further
than this; he 'hypostatized' the Socratic λόγοι: that is
to say, he believed that they or something like them—
for as conceived by our minds they are necessarily imperfect—have a real or transcendental existence. In
other words, the *notions* which we form represent more
or less imperfectly *ideas* which exist in nature. It is
in full accord with our expectations, therefore, when we
find that abstract notions of this sort hypostatized form
the chief part, if not the sum-total, of the contents of
the ideal world in the earliest stage of the theory. This
stage is reached in the *Symposium* and the *Phaedrus*.

As we find it presented in these Dialogues the theory
is certainly attractive; but as yet it is poetical rather
than philosophical. But having gone so far Plato was
not slow to discover that his theory was capable of very
great development. He soon recognised that he was
passing beyond the bounds of mere logic and entering
the region of metaphysics proper. The study of metaphysics at this time was practically dead and offered a

fair field to anyone who chose to undertake the task of bringing it to life again. Plato saw his opportunity and forthwith conceived the hope of founding upon the basis of his recently discovered logical method a new metaphysical theory of the universe. Much, however, still remained to be done before this could be accomplished. It must soon have become obvious to him that he could not hope to build up his universe exclusively out of qualities; there must be ideas not only of qualities but of substances as well. In fact certain logical difficulties made this necessary. So soon as the Theory of Ideas was recognised as the foundation of a definite metaphysical system, it could not but appear illogical to admit the existence of ideas of some general notions and not of others. Accordingly, when we come to the *Republic*, we find it distinctly affirmed that there is an idea corresponding to every common term. In this way the Theory of Ideas is made to serve as a theory of Being and also as a theory of Knowledge. But there was another question which was at this time sorely exercising the Greek mind. People were asking themselves not only 'What is Being?' and 'What is Knowledge?' but 'What is Predication?' Plato attempted to extract an answer to this question also from his newly created Theory of Ideas. He came to the conclusion that predication was only to be explained by supposing the immanence in the subject, concerning which predication is made, of ideas corresponding to every such predicate. Thus in the *Phaedo* we are told that, when we predicate any quality of anything, we are really asserting the immanence in that thing of the idea corresponding to the particular quality which we are predicating of it. For instance, when we say 'Socrates is short,' what we

really mean, suggests Plato, is ' Socrates partakes of the
idea of shortness' or 'has the idea of shortness immanent
in him.' The Theory of Ideas, then, in its earlier form is
intended to answer the three questions, 'What is Being?'
' What is Knowledge?' and ' What is Predication?'

But from the point of view of a theory of knowledge it was soon found to be incapable of fulfilling the
brilliant expectations that had been formed of it.   Plato
is forced to recognise that in this life at least the ideas
cannot be known.   Thus it would seem that even in
the *Phaedo* the task of self-criticism is begun.   There
is no longer the air of happy confidence which is so
striking a feature of the *Republic*: everything does not
run as smoothly as at first it had seemed to do.   Already
we seem to detect signs of dissatisfaction with the theory
as it stands.   Plato must have gradually become conscious of its shortcomings, and he therefore sets himself
the task of going carefully over the ground again, and
in the process soon discovers fatal objections underlying
his theory in its hitherto accepted form.   These objections are very forcibly stated in the earlier part of the
Parmenides.   It will not be necessary to reproduce
them here, as they have been admirably analysed by
Dr Jackson in his paper on the *Parmenides*.   The argument known as the τρίτος ἄνθρωπος is adduced to show
that the postulation of an idea for every common term
involves in the ideal world itself the multiplication of
every idea to infinity; moreover it is shown that the
assumption that particulars partake of ideas carries
with it the inevitable consequence that in the world of
particulars the idea must either be in more than one
place at the same time or else be divided into parts :
thus on all hands the boasted immaterial unity of the

idea is seen to be illusory. It may possibly be said that criticism of this sort—for instance the comparison of the immanent idea to a sail—is not fair, inasmuch as it treats the idea as if it were a material thing, whereas by assumption it is nothing of the kind. But on a closer inspection it will be seen that the point of the criticism lies in this very fact. The Theory of Ideas in its earlier form is inconsistent; at one moment the idea is declared to be absolutely self-existent and immaterial, while at another properties are attributed to it which are incompatible with the assumption of its immateriality; its unity becomes a unity of extension and nothing more. This is a point which I think Dr Jackson might have brought out more clearly than he has done. It seems to me that the whole tendency of the searching criticism which Plato passes upon himself in the *Parmenides* is to show that the very attempt to establish the existence of an absolutely immaterial world side by side, as it were, with the material world, and of an absolutely self-existent idea in which a number of particulars partake, has after all defeated its own object. The idea turns out to be a thing that either has parts divided and subdivided between the intelligible world and various places in the phenomenal world, or else is present as a whole in different places at one and the same moment. Either supposition entails the sacrifice of its unity, or if we choose to state it so, of its immateriality.

Such are the defects which make the Theory of Ideas in its earlier shape untenable. Let us now see how the theory of soul which we find in the *Phaedo* will fare in the face of similar criticism. It must, I think, become apparent at once that this theory is no more

tenable than the other; for it involves an inconsistency
precisely similar in kind to that which has necessitated
the reconstruction of the Theory of Ideas. The soul
is unhesitatingly declared to be essentially immaterial,
and yet almost in the same breath statements are made
about it which are consistent only with the supposition
that it is of a material nature. We have seen that in
the *Phaedo* the soul is emphatically asserted to be of
like nature with the ideas: it is akin to them and, like
them, belongs by nature to a world different in all respects from that with which its association with the body
makes it familiar. That world is inhabited or may be
inhabited by souls which enjoy an absolutely independent
and immaterial existence; the free exercise by them of
their intellectual faculties is entirely unrestricted, for
they are 'without bodies altogether' (ἄνευ σωμάτων τὸ
παράπαν). In other words, in that world each soul is
αὐτὴ καθ' αὑτήν in exactly the same way as each idea
is likewise αὐτὸ καθ' αὑτό: its proper function is to
know the ideas, and for that purpose its natural likeness
to them must be as complete as possible; hence only
when it is αὐτὴ καθ' αὑτήν—as it may be after death, if
its life on earth has been guided by true philosophy—can
it apprehend the true nature of the ideas, which *ex hypothesi* are always αὐτὰ καθ' αὑτά. Now it is obvious that
such a theory as this, however earnestly and emphatically
Plato may seek to avoid the dreaded charge of materialism, must nevertheless involve a materialistic conception
of the nature of the soul. In fact the theory which,
while professedly idealistic, goes on to recognise not
only a number of actually existing immaterial ideas,
but also a number of actually existing immaterial souls,
is found to be inconsistent: behind the professed idealism

there lurks an unconscious materialism. If the assumption of the actual existence of an ideal world quite apart from and yet in some sort of relation with the phenomenal world is fatal to the immateriality of the idea, it is still more clearly fatal to the immateriality of the soul. It is true that the soul is not, like the idea, conceived as existing simultaneously .in both worlds; but it is regarded as a thing which passes from the ideal world and back again, and an interval is supposed to elapse between one incarnation and the next; thus its sojourn in the world of ideas is an existence in time, and in that respect at least is similar to its bodily life on earth. Moreover it seems sometimes to belong properly to neither world but to some intermediate region; for the state of the vicious soul after death is such that it is not altogether without body but retains some of the characteristics of its earthly life, in consequence of which it is attracted back again to earth. That Plato should suppose that the soul, if it possesses such attributes as these, could be immaterial was only natural at a time when he imagined that he could consistently maintain the essential immateriality of the idea under such conditions as must as a matter of fact make it a material thing. The fact that he did so was, I think, due in great measure to his failure to appreciate fully the nature of *Time* and the place which it occupies in the universe. It is in the *Timaeus* that we first find any adequate conception of the true significance of Time. At the stage of his philosophical career when he first formulated the Theory of Ideas it probably never occurred to him that it was necessary to consider the question at all, or indeed that there was any question to consider. .He was endeavouring to look beyond Space

and was content to accept Time as it stood, never
doubting that all things, whether material or immaterial,
exist equally in Time.   Thus the notion of an immaterial and yet temporal existence for the soul would
not at first raise any difficulties in his mind.   He had
come to the conclusion that the soul is naturally immaterial, and that on leaving the body it continues to
live in a world in which there is no such thing as
matter ; and this doctrine seemed to him for a time
to be perfectly satisfactory.   The fact that he was able
to grasp the notion of immaterial existence at all and
therefore found himself in a position to maintain that
the soul is immaterial, this in itself constitutes an
immense advance over anything that his predecessors
had achieved.   We ought rather to wonder that he
was able to form a conception so far in advance of
anything that had gone before, not that the conception
was at first inadequate or even inconsistent: in such
a matter it would be unreasonable to expect absolute
consistency in a moment.   But since his intellect was
sufficiently penetrating to discover and remedy the weak
points in his Theory of Ideas, we cannot suppose that
he remained for very long ignorant of the fact that very
much the same defects were to be found in his theory
of soul, or that in these circumstances he would not
do his utmost to make good those defects.   Coincident,
then, with the reconstruction of the Theory of Ideas
we shall be justified in looking for a similar reconstruction of the theory of soul.   In the Theory of the Ideas
one of the most important points that has yet to be
cleared up is the precise relation in which ideas stand
to phenomena ; and similarly in the theory of soul
we want a more scientific account than has yet been

given of the mutual relations of soul and body. The nature of the soul is closely allied to the nature of the ideas: hence we must expect to find that Plato's conception of the subject which apprehends will change along with his conception of the object which is apprehended. The theory of Being and the theory of Knowledge must now, as ever, be mutually complementary.

The *Timaeus* is the Dialogue to which we should naturally turn in the hope of discovering such a later theory of soul as I have given reasons for believing to exist in Plato's philosophy. The chief points of difference between the later form of the theory and the earlier may, as I have said, fairly be expected *mutatis mutandis* to be similar in their general character to those which distinguish the later from the earlier Theory of Ideas. Before attempting, therefore, to examine the *Timaeus* in order to determine the nature of the theory of soul held by Plato in this later period, it will be convenient first to sketch the lines upon which the Theory of Ideas itself was modified; we shall then be in a better position to appreciate the sort of modification to be expected in the theory of soul. To this end it will be necessary merely to state Dr Jackson's general conclusions, laying stress upon such details as will be found to be specially important in their application to our present inquiry.

We have seen that the Theory of Ideas in its earlier form was intended to furnish a theory of Being, a theory of Knowledge, and a theory of Predication. It was chiefly in order to make it serve this last purpose that to the primary assumption that there are certain eternal immutable unities called ideas Plato was induced to

attach two subordinate propositions: first, that wherever
we have a number of things called by the same name
there is a corresponding idea; and secondly, that each
thing is what it is in virtue of the immanence of the
corresponding idea. These two subordinate propositions
are found to be fatal to the primary assumption of the
existence of the ideas as immaterial unities; therefore
they have to be abandoned. Ideas cannot be recognised
corresponding to every common term, and the relation
between ideas and particulars cannot be one of immanence or participation. Before the theory can be put
upon a satisfactory footing, therefore, the list of ideas
must be carefully revised and their relation to particulars
must be stated in a different way. In a word, then,
according to Dr Jackson, the Theory of Ideas becomes
in the later time a theory of natural kinds, and particulars no longer 'participate in' but only 'resemble'
the ideas to which they correspond. In this form the
Theory of Ideas still furnishes a theory of Being and
a theory of Knowledge, but it no longer supplies a theory
of Predication. We have seen that it was primarily the
endeavour to explain predication by means of the
immanence in particulars of ideas corresponding to
every predicate that involved the Theory of Ideas in
its earlier form in the serious logical and metaphysical
complications which necessitated its restatement and
reconstruction. What, then, becomes of the problem of
predication? The answer to this question is simply
this: the problem of predication, which had puzzled
all Plato's philosophical predecessors from Zeno onwards,
and which at first puzzled Plato himself, is to him a
puzzle no longer. He now sees that the fact of predication needs no such elaborate explanation as he had

attempted to find for it. From the last words of
Parmenides in the Dialogue which bears his name we
gather that Plato has at last come to realise that
whether there are ideas or not there must always be
relations between things ; and predication is merely the
statement in language of the existence of these relations.
It is inconceivable that a number of things should exist
or seem to exist and not stand or seem to stand in
relations of various kinds to one another. And since
the existence, or apparent existence, of relations has thus
been found to be a necessity in the nature of things,
there is no longer any need to attempt to explain them
by means of the Theory of Ideas. When we say that
'Socrates is short' we are not asserting that he
'participates in the idea of shortness': we are merely
putting into words the obvious fact that he stands in
a particular relation to certain other persons or to the
generality of mankind. Thus wherever there are
relations predication follows as a matter of course.
But this puzzle of predication has up to this point
made Plato the slave of language and so has led astray
the Theory of Ideas. He has found it necessary to
assume that any group of objects to which we care
to assign a class-name must have its own special idea
to account for its possession of that class-name. The
result is confusion worse confounded. But the solution
of the puzzle by other and simpler means has now
released him from his bondage and left him free to
develop the Theory of Ideas in a natural manner without
any reference to the question of predication. He now
no longer considers it inconsistent to recognise ideas
of some general notions and not of others. Consequently
he no longer admits ideas in the strict sense, that is to

say self-existent ideas (αὐτὰ καθ' αὐτὰ εἴδη or καθ' αὐτὰ
γένη, as Aristotle calls them), except of classes of things
which are determined by nature, in fact of natural kinds.

Moreover he now discards the implicit materialism
which is presupposed by the assumption that ideas,
which are *ex hypothesi* absolutely self-dependent, are
at the same time immanent in a number of particulars
which participate in them. The relation in which
particulars stand to ideas is now no longer one of
'participation' (μέθεξις) but of 'resemblance' (μίμησις)
to a type. This is more than a mere difference of
statement; it entails a very important modification
of the theory. In the earlier form of the theory the
ideas are also regarded as types; but they are types
which are also immanent in particulars: in the later
time, however, the immanent idea is no more; and with
this characteristic gone there is no longer any question
of its being divided into parts or else present as a whole
in different places at the same time. But if the ideas are
not immanent in particulars, in what way, it may be
asked, do particulars resemble the ideas? Plato is not
at a loss for a satisfactory answer to this question.
Though the ideas are not regarded any longer as
being *themselves* immanent in particulars, they are nevertheless, as we might say, *reflected* in them by means of
certain immanent forms thrown off from themselves
which inform particulars and cause them to resemble
the idea of which they are in this sense reflexions.
These reflexions or immanent forms of the ideas are
what are called in the *Timaeus* εἰσιόντα καὶ ἐξιόντα:
they 'pass in and out' of material things but of course
have no substantive existence themselves. The ideas
themselves can have no actual existence in the world of

phenomena; they are types (παραδείγματα ἑστηκότα ἐν
τῇ φύσει, as Socrates proposes to describe them in the
Parmenides), to which particulars approximate in a
greater or lesser degree. Goodness and existence are
merely two different aspects of the same thing, or at
least they are inseparable the one from the other;
hence the goodness or true existence of particular
things varies directly in proportion to the degree of their
approximation to the idea which they represent. There
are no self-existent ideas of qualities with the single
apparent exception of the αὐτὸ ἀγαθόν, the supreme Idea
of Good. This, however, is not on the same plane with
the other ideas: it is simply a special aspect of νοῦς,
the ultimate source of all Being and therefore of all
Good; for things truly exist only in so far as they are
good. Every good quality that an object possesses is
still due to the idea, but not to the idea of that quality;
it is due to the idea of the natural kind to which the
object belongs. Good qualities are thus the result of
nearness of approximation on the part of the object
to its appropriate idea; and similarly what seem to us
to be bad qualities are the result of remoteness of
approximation to the same idea. So the rose's beauty
is still, as in the earlier form of the theory, caused by
the idea: the difference is that it is now no longer an
idea of beauty but the idea of rose, if rose is a natural
kind, that causes that beauty. And after all it may
well be that this is not so sweeping a change as at first
sight might seem to be the case. Plato is not the slave
of technical terms, and he might still speak of an εἶδος
of beauty, though this εἶδος will not be an αὐτὸ καθ᾽
αὑτὸ εἶδος. Thus, properly understood, he might still
say, as he said in the *Phaedo*, τῷ καλῷ τὰ καλὰ καλά:

but we must understand that the καλόν which is the
cause of beauty is not a self-existent idea of beauty
in which the particular καλά participate, but the idea
of that natural kind to which the individual καλά belong.
Approximation to this idea necessarily carries with it
the quality of beauty together with all other good
qualities. Thus in the later form of the theory the
ideas are still the cause both of existence and of
goodness. It is true that in a sense the çentre of gravity
of the ideal world has been shifted from quality to
substance; but we have to remember that, though it is
the substance, the natural kind as we perceive it in its
individual members, that for us determines the existence
of the idea, nevertheless what the idea typifies is after
all not so much the substance as the qualities. For
instance, we have to conceive the idea of man as
representing not man-*body* but man-*life*, which manifests
itself, and indeed must manifest itself, through the
medium of man-body. The idea of man is not possessed
of an ideal pair of legs, an ideal nose, and so on; such
characteristics as these belong solely to the material
man, whose *life* or *soul*, if we like to put it so, realises
itself in this world to the best advantage through the
medium of such material characteristics. In this way
the essential immateriality of the idea is secured: for
the idea is in reality an eternal mode of the thought
of supreme Mind—a νόημα θεοῦ, as we may call it, if we
develop another suggestion made in the *Parmenides*.

But this object is gained at some sacrifice. The
eternal mode of thought which is symbolized by the idea
must manifest itself under material conditions in order
that it may be realised in actual existence. There is
no longer any suggestion of the immaterial existence of

the ideas in time and yet in a world of their own, which
was part of the earlier doctrine. In this sense the ideas
can now no more exist without the particulars which
represent them than the particulars can exist without
the ideas which give them their meaning—a conclusion
which the Plato of the *Republic* and the *Phaedo* must
have summarily rejected as being utterly subversive of
the true dignity of the ideas. But the gradual growth
of his mind has brought Plato to recognise the mutual
interdependence of ideas and particulars as a metaphysical necessity. Mind must necessarily manifest
itself under the form of matter. But here I would
draw attention to what seems to me to be at least a
misleading statement in Dr Jackson's presentment of
the later Theory of Ideas. In his paper on the *Timaeus*
he remarks that in the later time the ideas are regarded
as only *hypothetically* existent. This statement, I am
convinced, does not correctly represent Plato's position.
What is to be regarded as only hypothetically existent
is surely not the *idea* but the *perfect particular*; and
whatever may have been the case earlier, in the later
doctrine the idea is certainly not conceived as a perfect
particular. The idea must always be existent because
it is an eternal mode of absolute thought. But the
manner of its existence is now differently conceived.
Regarded simply by itself it exists not only out of space
but out of time as well, so that in this sense it is not
actually existent as it was originally supposed to be.
In other words, the ideas are eternally existent, but
they must necessarily manifest themselves in the form
of particular existence; otherwise the fact of their
existence would be quite meaningless; we should have
a sort of pluralised Eleatic ἕν incapable of being turned

to any useful account.   It is obvious, however, that this is not the same thing as saying that the idea is only hypothetically existent.   The perfect particular on the other hand may fairly be described in such terms. It can never be actually realised, although in the assumed progress of things *towards* perfection its hypothetical existence is implicitly recognised.   Imperfection necessarily inheres in matter ; thus in order to be perfect a particular would have to renounce all materiality and become merged in the idea ; that is to say, it would cease to be a particular at all.

CHAPTER VIII.

THE *TIMAEUS*.

THE summary account given in the last chapter of the general character of Plato's later Theory of Ideas will supply some indication of the modifications which we may expect to find introduced into his conception of the nature of the soul during the same period. We are now in a position to examine the *Timaeus*, the Dialogue which, more completely than any other, illustrates from the point of view of metaphysics the essential features of the later Platonism. But before proceeding to a detailed investigation of the passages which have specially to be considered in the attempt to determine the nature of the later theory of soul with particular reference to the question of immortality, it will be convenient to give a brief survey of the general metaphysical system which is set forth in the *Timaeus*.

In his Introduction to the *Phaedo* with reference to the question of Plato's belief in the immortality of the soul Mr Archer-Hind remarks very truly (p. xxviii) that the discussion of this subject "does not belong to the treatment of the *Phaedo* at all, but to that of the *Timaeus*; and we can hope to attain a satisfactory solution only after a minute investigation of the profound and difficult metaphysics of the latter Dialogue."

Fortunately Mr Archer-Hind has himself, in his edition of the *Timaeus*, carried out this investigation, though without, so far as I can see, applying his results to the elucidation of Plato's final attitude towards the question of immortality. This is the task which I have now set myself to perform ; and to this end a short preliminary account of the metaphysics of the *Timaeus* seems to be desirable. I will only premise that Mr Archer-Hind's general interpretation of the Dialogue seems to me so obviously right in its most characteristic features that I have followed it closely in my own statement of its main import.

In the earlier part of the *Timaeus* Plato sets forth his metaphysical system in the form of an elaborate myth or allegory which purports to describe in detail the creation of the world. According to Mr Archer-Hind's theory, however, with which in the main I agree, the process thus pictured does not really take place in time and space at all: the words and phrases which suggest a temporal and spatial process are necessitated by the allegorical form of the exposition. In reading this part of the *Timaeus*, therefore, we must carefully bear in mind throughout that what in the myth is represented as a series of events following one another in time is intended in the main to represent an order of logical sequence only. In fact there is not in the strict sense of the term any *creation* of the universe at all. The description of the creation of the universe in time by the δημιουργός is purely symbolical : it symbolizes the self-evolution—not in time—of absolute νοῦς, which is one aspect of the supreme Idea of Good. Thus Plato's philosophy as set forth in the *Timaeus* is seen to be a system of monistic idealism. Both we

ourselves and the multitude of things which seem to us
to constitute a material world external to ourselves are
alike nothing else than Mind or Thought engaged in
its proper function of thinking.   But it is to be observed
that this Mind is not *our* mind : it is the Mind which
Plato refers to in the *Philebus* as νοῦς βασιλεύς, the
absolute Mind, of which our individual minds are, so
to speak, fractions.   Plato's idealism is not a relative
idealism of the Berkeleian type : it is an absolute
idealism which explains both individual minds and
matter in terms of universal Mind.   All that exists is
Mind and Mind is all that exists : but Mind must think,
or else it would not be Mind in the proper sense of the
term : a Mind which is not a thinking Mind would be
worse than meaningless.   The result of the continual
thinking of Mind is on the one hand individual minds
and on the other hand matter ; and as Mind continues
to manifest itself in these two ways, our minds, which
are particular determinations of the universal Mind, are
able to perceive other determinations of it, so that to
any particular mind there appears to be an objective
world outside itself.   Pluralisation, then, is the necessary
result of Mind's thinking.   But there are different stages
to be distinguished in the course of this pluralisation.
Neither the plurality of us beings, conceived as actually
existing in this world with mortal bodies, nor the
plurality of things in the universe, which we as ἔμψυχα
perceive, is to be attributed to the direct thinking of
Mind.   Mind first determines itself into a number of
subordinate minds intermediate between itself and our
minds.   There are thus in the universe certain beings
of a super-human type which represent, in the highest
possible finite form, the result of the direct thinking

of infinite Mind. Both corporeally and mentally they
are superior to us: their power of thought is, as far
as may be, unimpeded ; and they are immortal, their
bodies or material manifestations being of such a nature
as not to be rendered liable to dissolution. Thus the
first stage of determination is symbolized in the allegory
by the creation by the δημιουργός of the so-called θεοὶ
θεῶν, who manifest themselves in the form of the fixed
stars. But of course, strictly speaking, they are not
created at all ; there was never a time in which they were
non-existent. In fact they are simply one mode of the
existence of absolute Mind. Evolution having proceeded
thus far, we at once have on the one hand plurality,
which involves matter and space, and on the other
continuity of existence, which implies time and succession.
Even the θεοὶ θεῶν, therefore, must be to some extent
subject to the conditions of space and time ; but these
conditions do not hamper them in the same degree
in which they hamper us, for their souls are united with
the same body in perpetuity. Thus their superiority
to us in the corporeal sphere is obvious ; and their
mental superiority is made no less clear. For according
to the myth the δημιουργός entrusts to them the task of
creating the inferior beings in the universe ; that is to
say, they have to supply mortal bodies for the souls
which the δημιουργός places in their care. In other
words, the θεοὶ θεῶν, whom we perceive under the form
of the fixed stars, are in reality determinations of
supreme Mind which have the power of thinking again.
Whether Plato actually thought that the stars are
conscious beings it is perhaps hopeless to inquire ; the
whole of this part of the *Timaeus* is so deeply tinged
with mysticism that it is difficult to say exactly what is

allegory and what is not. But in any case it seems
clear that he believed that somewhere in the universe
such superhuman beings exist. The θεοὶ θεῶν, then,
possess the power of thought in a very high degree,
though not in the same degree as their so-called creator,
who is pure undifferentiated Mind. They cannot by
their thinking create souls; so they cannot be directly
responsible for the originating of any new life. Life
cannot be brought into existence in time and space out
of nothing; and all the creation which is effected by the
so-called created gods must necessarily be effected in
time and space: for the mere fact of their differentiated
existence implies that their activities are temporally and
spatially conditioned. In the scheme of the universe,
therefore, what they accomplish is not the *creation* but
the *incarnation* of particular souls of a lower order. The
position occupied by the θεοὶ θεῶν is interesting and
presents several peculiar features: I shall have occasion
to speak of it in more detail later. Next come the
beings with which we are familiar in this world—souls
inhabiting mortal bodies. These souls likewise possess
and exercise the power of thought, but in a still lesser
degree: they cannot create anything objectively in the
sense in which the θεοὶ θεῶν may be said to do so.
They, as particular manifestations of supreme Mind,
can but perceive and think *about* other similar manifestations as they are presented to them under the
conditions of space and time.

This preliminary account, incomplete as it is, of the
general significance of the *Timaeus*, especially so far as
it relates to the place occupied by individual souls in
the system of the universe, will perhaps be sufficient for
the present. We now pass on to the consideration of

particular passages in the Dialogue itself which will
serve to make clear in certain important aspects Plato's
conception of the soul's nature.

ἔστιν οὖν δὴ κατ᾽ ἐμὴν δόξαν πρῶτον διαιρετέον τάδε·
τί τὸ ὂν ἀεί, γένεσιν δὲ οὐκ ἔχον, καὶ τί τὸ γιγνόμενον μὲν
ἀεί, ὂν δὲ οὐδέποτε. τὸ μὲν δὴ νοήσει μετὰ λόγου περιληπτόν, ἀεὶ κατὰ ταὐτὰ ὄν, τὸ δ᾽ αὖ δόξῃ μετ᾽ αἰσθήσεως
ἀλόγου δοξαστόν, γιγνόμενον καὶ ἀπολλύμενον, ὄντως δὲ
οὐδέποτε ὄν. (*Tim.* 27 D, 28 A.)

It will be well at the outset to notice this, the
opening pronouncement made by Timaeus in beginning
his exposition of the nature of the universe. Here no
less than in the earlier Dialogues we have to remark the
clear distinction which Plato draws between the phenomenal and the noümenal. He was the first to recognise
the full significance of this all-important distinction.
No previous thinker—not even the great Parmenides
himself, who in this respect approaches nearest to Plato
—had had any clear conception of the true nature of immaterial existence. Even Plato's own theory was not, as
we have seen, at first completely satisfactory: some of
the attributes which he assigned to the immaterial came
dangerously near to making it material. The immaterial
realm of transcendental existence, which is Plato's
reality (τὸ ὂν ἀεί, γένεσιν δὲ οὐκ ἔχον), is νοήσει μετὰ
λόγου περιληπτόν, to be reached only by the mind
exercising its power of abstract thought; the material
world on the other hand (τὸ γιγνόμενον μὲν ἀεί, ὂν δὲ
οὐδέποτε) is δόξῃ μετ᾽ αἰσθήσεως ἀλόγου δοξαστόν, the
object not of reason but of opinion. The world of
phenomena has no independent existence at all; it is
dependent for such existence as it seems to have upon

the world of ideas. So much was recognised by Plato when he wrote the *Republic* and is now merely re-affirmed in order to show that his idealistic conception of the universe is adhered to in spite of any modifications he may have been led to make in the details of his theory. But in the *Timaeus* we are to learn further that the immaterial world, the region of Mind, is in its turn dependent for its real existence upon the seeming existence of the material world, the region of Matter: that is to say, it is now recognised to be a necessary law of the existence of Mind that it should manifest itself always under the conditions of space and time. Nevertheless the essential distinction between Mind and Matter remains as valid as before: Mind is fundamental—the ultimate basis of reality; Matter is merely an inseparable accident of the self-manifestation of Mind. Similarly there is still the old antithesis between δόξα and ἐπιστήμη apparent in the passage before us, though at the time when the *Timaeus* came to be written Plato no longer considered the attainment of absolute knowledge to be possible for a finite intelligence either in this world or in any other; all that we can do is to make a continual approximation towards it.

θέμις δὲ οὔτ᾽ ἦν οὔτ᾽ ἔστι τῷ ἀρίστῳ δρᾶν ἄλλο πλὴν τὸ κάλλιστον. λογισάμενος οὖν εὕρισκεν ἐκ τῶν κατὰ φύσιν ὁρατῶν οὐδὲν ἀνόητον τοῦ νοῦν ἔχοντος ὅλον ὅλου κάλλιον ἔσεσθαί ποτε ἔργον, νοῦν δ᾽ αὖ χωρὶς ψυχῆς ἀδύνατον παραγενέσθαι τῳ. διὰ δὴ τὸν λογισμὸν τόνδε νοῦν μὲν ἐν ψυχῇ, ψυχὴν δὲ ἐν σώματι ξυνιστὰς τὸ πᾶν ξυνετεκταίνετο, ὅπως ὅ τι κάλλιστον εἴη κατὰ φύσιν ἄριστόν τε ἔργον ἀπειργασμένος.

(*Tim.* 30 A, B.)

We have now to pass in review a series of statements bearing directly upon the essential nature of soul
and the manner of its allegorical creation, by which we
must understand its evolution out of absolute Mind.
That the existence of the δημιουργός is not to be taken
literally seems clear from the language of the passage
I have just quoted. For if he is literally the creator
of the universe, what are the κατὰ φύσιν ὁρατά, the
contemplation of which he allows to influence him in
the manner of his creation? There cannot be any ὁρατά
at all until he has created them. Obviously, therefore,
this statement at least is not to be interpreted literally.
But I will not go further into this question : Mr Archer-
Hind seems to me to have made it sufficiently plain
that the creation of the universe by the δημιουργός is
a symbolical way of describing the evolution of νοῦς.
In the passage immediately before us, however, it will
be well to consider the literal statement first. Plato
says that the creator, seeing that νοῦς even as possessed
by a finite being is the noblest of all possessions, and
wishing it to be brought into actual existence, created
mind within soul and soul within body. But the word
'created' is perhaps rather misleading in this connexion
even as forming part of the literal account ; it might be
taken to suggest that the body exists before soul and
soul before mind, which is not a necessary inference
from Plato's words. What he means to say is simply
this: whereas νοῦς is pre-existent, the δημιουργός, in
order that it may pass into finite existence (παραγενέσθαι τῳ), creates ψυχή to contain νοῦς and σῶμα to
contain ψυχή. Thus νοῦς exists apart from body on the
principle that ἕν precedes πολλά and the δημιουργός
precedes his works. When pluralisation comes in, νοῦς

is invested in ψυχή and ψυχή in σῶμα: but this does
not of course imply that σῶμα has any priority to
ψυχή or ψυχή to νοῦς. Interpreting the literal words
in the metaphysical sense which they are intended to
bear, we learn that in the course of the externalisation
of the absolute Mind νοῦς leads inevitably to ψυχή and
ψυχή in its turn to σῶμα. Thus, properly speaking, we
do not arrive at ψυχή until the logical process of
pluralisation or evolution of absolute Mind has already
begun. Plato's position here is in fact just that which is
foreshadowed in the *Sophist*:—

ΞΕ. Τί δὲ πρὸς Διός; ὡς ἀληθῶς κίνησιν καὶ ζωὴν
καὶ ψυχὴν καὶ φρόνησιν ἦ ῥᾳδίως πεισθησόμεθα τῷ
παντελῶς ὄντι μὴ παρεῖναι, μηδὲ ζῆν αὐτὸ μηδὲ φρονεῖν,
ἀλλὰ σεμνὸν καὶ ἅγιον, νοῦν οὐκ ἔχον, ἀκίνητον ἑστὸς
εἶναι;

ΘΕΑΙ. Δεινὸν μέντ᾽ ἄν, ὦ ξένε, λόγον συγχωροῖμεν.

ΞΕ. Ἀλλὰ νοῦν μὲν ἔχειν, ζωὴν δὲ μή, φῶμεν;

ΘΕΑΙ. Καὶ πῶς;

ΞΕ. Ἀλλὰ ταῦτα μὲν ἀμφότερα ἐνόντ᾽ αὐτῷ λέγομεν,
οὐ μὴν ἐν ψυχῇ γε φήσομεν αὐτὸ ἔχειν αὐτά;

ΘΕΑΙ. Καὶ τίν᾽ ἂν ἕτερον ἔχοι τρόπον;

ΞΕ. Ἀλλὰ δῆτα νοῦν μὲν καὶ ζωὴν καὶ ψυχήν,
ἀκίνητον μέντοι τὸ παράπαν, ἔμψυχον ὂν ἑστάναι;

ΘΕΑΙ. Πάντα ἔμοιγε ἄλογα ταῦτ᾽ εἶναι φαίνεται.

ΞΕ. Καὶ τὸ κινούμενον δὴ καὶ κίνησιν συγχωρητέον
ὡς ὄντα;

ΘΕΑΙ. Πῶς δ᾽ οὔ; (*Soph.* 248 E—249 B.)

In this part of the *Sophist* the Eleate is occupied in
showing that the theories of those who maintain that all
existence is material (the σπαρτοί τε καὶ αὐτόχθονες)
and those who deny that the material has any existence

(the εἰδῶν φίλοι) are each of them taken by itself insufficient to explain the universe. Being must have both a material and an immaterial aspect; if it were completely material or completely immaterial, it would be nothing. Νοῦς, ψυχή, and σῶμα (which is implied in κίνησις) must coalesce to form Being. In other words, from the point of view of the *Timaeus,* so far as actual existence is concerned, νοῦς implies ψυχή and ψυχή implies σῶμα. Or starting from the other end we may analyse ἔμψυχον into σῶμα and ψυχή, though the separation, it must be remembered, is logical and not actual; and from ψυχή again we may abstract νοῦς, which is in reality nothing else than pure ψυχή conceived as in her own nature thinking; here also, however, we must remember that Plato does not call this aspect of it ψυχή: he calls it νοῦς. In a note on this passage of the *Timaeus* Mr Archer-Hind denies the validity of Plutarch's inference from Plato's words, that ψυχή can exist only in σῶμα. Plutarch, he says, "wrongly infers from this passage that, as νοῦς can only exist in ψυχή, so ψυχή can only exist in σῶμα. This of course is not so: the converse would be more correct, that σῶμα can only exist in ψυχή. The phrase νοῦν ἐν ψυχῇ is also an exoteric expression; for Plato is not here concerned to use technical language." This criticism seems to me hardly fair. I admit that Mr Archer-Hind's converse statement conveys a better expression of Plato's real meaning. But surely according to the allegorical representation it is as correct to say that ψυχή can only exist in σῶμα as that νοῦς can only exist in ψυχή: the two statements are in this respect parallel. And this being so, is not Plutarch's error merely verbal? The statement of Plutarch to which Mr Archer-Hind objects I take to be the following :—

> ἡ ἄμορφος ὕλη καὶ ἀόριστος ὑπὸ τῆς ψυχῆς ἐνούσης
> σχηματισθεῖσα μορφὴν ἔσχε τοιαύτην καὶ διάθεσιν.
> (Plut. *Quaest. Plat.* IV 1003 B.)

The word ἐνούσης apart from the context may perhaps
be somewhat misleading, but I do not think that
Plutarch's view of Plato's meaning is radically wrong.
If instead of ἐνούσης he had said συντεταγμένης or some
similar word, would there have been anything to which
exception could fairly be taken ? On the contrary,
I think Plutarch furnishes an instructive commentary on
the present passage, and his word ἐνούσης is due merely
to the comparison which he has just drawn between the
relation of the soul to the body and that of the seed to
the tree, the seed or the power of growth inherent in it
being inside the tree. What Plato means is that ψυχή
cannot actually exist apart from σῶμα : and this, it
seems to me, is just the view which Plutarch has
attributed to him a little way back :—

> ἡ μὲν γὰρ ἄνους ψυχὴ καὶ τὸ ἄμορφον σῶμα συνυ-
> πῆρχον ἀλλήλοις ἀεί, καὶ οὐδέτερον αὐτῶν γένεσιν ἔσχεν
> οὐδὲ ἀρχήν. (Plut. *Quaest. Plat.* IV 1003 A.)

This appears to me to be a very fair statement of
Plato's position, as I hope to make clear later. Σῶμα
and ψυχή are correlative terms ; they are logically but
not actually separable elements of the same thing, ἔμψυχον, which can be looked at from the point of view
of either of its two constituents, matter and mind.
Thus σῶμα is matter endued with mind, which through
it perceives ; while ψυχή is mind localised in matter,
but of its own nature thinking. We may distinguish,
then, two methods of soul's activity : there is the

superior method, thought, and the inferior method, perception; but the two forms of activity always co-exist. Thought is the faculty exercised by the soul in virtue of her own proper nature, which is derived directly from the δημιουργός or supreme νοῦς: perception is the faculty which she exercises in virtue of her connexion with the body, such connexion being a necessary law of her existence. The preponderance of the one over the other depends upon the degree to which she has asserted her natural supremacy over the body. If we begin to study the problem of existence ἀπὸ τῶν γνωριμωτέρων ἡμῖν, as Aristotle would say, in the process of analysis ψυχή comes later than σῶμα, and from this point of view σῶμα seems to contain ψυχή: hence the word ἔμψυχον used to describe animate as opposed to inanimate existence according to the popular distinction; and hence Plutarch's very natural expression ὕλη ὑπὸ τῆς ψυχῆς ἐνούσης σχηματισθεῖσα. But if after this analysis we return upon our path and examine the question ἀπὸ τῶν γνωριμωτέρων φύσει, we see at once that the logical priority in reality rests not with σῶμα but with ψυχή. From this point of view, therefore, the *natural* point of view in the Aristotelian sense, it is more correct, as Mr Archer-Hind says, to speak of σῶμα as existing in ψυχή rather than of ψυχή as existing in σῶμα. The essential priority of ψυχή to σῶμα is explicitly recognised by Plato in a subsequent passage :—

τὴν δὲ δὴ ψυχὴν οὐχ ὡς νῦν ὑστέραν ἐπιχειροῦμεν λέγειν, οὕτως ἐμηχανήσατο καὶ ὁ θεὸς νεωτέραν. οὐ γὰρ ἂν ἄρχεσθαι πρεσβύτερον ὑπὸ νεωτέρου ξυνέρξας εἴασεν. ἀλλά πως ἡμεῖς πολὺ μετέχοντες τοῦ προστυ-χόντος τε καὶ εἰκῇ ταύτῃ πῃ καὶ λέγομεν.

(*Tim.* 34 B, C.)

And, be it noted, Plutarch is fully aware of this : in fact
the apparent discrepancy is the starting-point of this
particular Ζήτημα. But even in this more correct
statement the language is, of course, allegorical : strictly
speaking, though ψυχή is not νεωτέρα σώματος, neither
is she πρεσβυτέρα, but, as Plutarch says, οὐδέτερον αὐτῶν
γένεσιν ἔσχεν οὐδὲ ἀρχήν. In no temporal sense can the
one be said to be prior to the other.

> τῆς ἀμερίστου καὶ ἀεὶ κατὰ ταὐτὰ ἐχούσης οὐσίας καὶ
> τῆς αὖ περὶ τὰ σώματα γιγνομένης μεριστῆς τρίτον ἐξ
> ἀμφοῖν ἐν μέσῳ ξυνεκεράσατο οὐσίας εἶδος, τῆς τε ταὐτοῦ
> φύσεως καὶ τῆς θατέρου, καὶ κατὰ ταῦτα ξυνέστησεν ἐν μέσῳ
> τοῦ τε ἀμεροῦς αὐτῶν καὶ τοῦ κατὰ τὰ σώματα μεριστοῦ.
> καὶ τρία λαβὼν αὐτὰ ὄντα συνεκεράσατο εἰς μίαν πάντα
> ἰδέαν, τὴν θατέρου φύσιν δύσμικτον οὖσαν εἰς ταὐτὸν
> ξυναρμόττων βίᾳ, μιγνὺς δὲ μετὰ τῆς οὐσίας.
>
> (*Tim.* 34 C, 35 A.)

In this most important passage Plato begins in
earnest to analyse the conception of what we mean
by 'soul.' When he wrote the *Republic* he had not
seriously attempted the task, as he himself admits ;
but now that his metaphysical opinions have developed
he is able to tell us what he conceives the essential
nature of the soul to be. He does so in a manner of his
own, a manner with which we are now familiar : that is
to say, he describes allegorically how soul was created
though of course there is really no creation involved.
Soul, he tells us, is composed of two contrary elements,
which he calls respectively ταὐτόν and θάτερον, together
with a third, οὐσία, which forms a connecting link
between the other two. What is the significance of
these terms ? I think we cannot do better than adopt

substantially Mr Archer-Hind's explanation of them.
To begin with, the terms ταὐτόν and θάτερον are, as
the words themselves would imply, of very general
application ; they can hardly be said to indicate any
definite theory. They are, as Mr Archer-Hind says,
"in their widest and most radical sense respectively the
principle of unity and identity and the principle of
multiplicity and difference." They can have both a
subjective and an objective application : subjective, in
so far as they denote the two modes of activity on the
part of the soul—pure thought, which deals with the
One, and perception, which concerns itself with the
Many ; objective, in so far as they may be applied to
the respective objects of these two activities. It is
with the subjective application that we are here more
especially concerned ; for ταὐτόν and θάτερον are anti-
thetic elements in the composition of the conscious soul.
Now in order that soul may be a unity, what the δημιουργός has to do is to find some means of conciliating
these two seemingly opposite principles, ταὐτόν and
θάτερον, which represent in their various forms—Same
and Other, One and Many, Rest and Motion, and so on
—the old antithesis of Parmenides and Heraclitus. This
he accomplishes by making use of a mean term derived
from both the others (ἐξ ἀμφοῖν), which Plato calls
οὐσία, that is to say actual existence. To use Hegelian
terminology, Being (*Thesis*) and Not Being (*Antithesis*)
are reconciled in Determinate Being (*Synthesis*). Thus
in the objective sphere Plato's meaning is not difficult
to understand. Neither pure Being (the παντελῶς ὄν of
the *Sophist*) nor pure Not-Being (παντελῶς μὴ ὄν) can
have any actual existence when divorced from the other:
in other words, neither Eleaticism nor Heracliteanism

alone can give an adequate explanation of the universe.

In the subjective sphere we get much the same result. Here also, as we have seen, it is fairly easy to understand the meaning of ταὐτόν and θάτερον : but what is the significance of οὐσία regarded as an element in the composition of soul ? Again Mr Archer-Hind supplies a satisfactory answer, which amounts in effect to this. As in the objective sphere οὐσία is the actual existence in which the One realises itself in the Many, or Mind realises itself in Matter—as far as Plato's philosophy is concerned it makes no difference whichever way we state it—; so in the subjective sphere οὐσία must be understood to mean the conscious essence in which ταὐτόν and θάτερον manifest themselves as parts, or rather different aspects, of one and the same personality. The soul is a single consciousness whose activity manifests itself in two different processes, thought and perception. In distinguishing these two processes Mr Archer-Hind says that "one is the simple activity of thought as such, the other the operation of thought as subjected to the conditions of time and space." This statement seems to me rather obscure. What is "the operation of thought as subjected to the conditions of time and space?" Is it, or does it include, perception? If not, what place is assigned to perception? In the individual at least perception is an activity of soul and a place must somewhere be found for it. So it seems to me to be better to say plainly that from the point of view of the soul ταὐτόν stands for thought and θάτερον for perception. In actual existence these two faculties are always united in a single consciousness.

In this way, then, Plato works into his scheme the

unifying conception of νοῦς which he received originally as a legacy from Anaxagoras and afterwards developed in a manner of his own. The One and the Many are no longer isolated from one another in the way in which he had at first attempted to isolate them : a means has been found to reconcile their rival claims, which are discovered to be after all not incompatible. Plato has widened the conceptions of what he calls ταὐτόν and θάτερον, and now regards them both as activities of the same νοῦς: they represent reason and perception, or intelligent thought and perceptive thought, if by such expressions we may be allowed to indicate that they are both faculties of the same thinking consciousness. The important points to notice are that neither ταὐτόν nor θάτερον has any independent existence apart from the other, and that οὐσία is not so much an element in a composite whole as the whole itself, two phases of which may be distinguished in actual existence. If the problem in question is approached from our finite standpoint and not from the infinite standpoint of the δημιουργός, we see that we have to start from οὐσία and then by analysis arrive at ταὐτόν and θάτερον. Neither of these conceptions could by itself be realised in actual existence ; each without the other would be a meaningless abstraction ; and so they must have something to depend upon in common, namely οὐσία or actual existence. Therefore a thinking soul must always be a percipient soul as well, inasmuch as Mind cannot exist apart from Matter ; or in other words, soul cannot exist apart from body. The bearing of this metaphysical theory on Plato's theory of soul thus becomes obvious. The conception of soul as an actually existing immaterial essence—the ψυχὴ αὐτὴ καθ' αὐτήν which we have known in the *Phaedo*—is now seen to be a mere logical abstraction : it can have nothing corresponding to it in the sphere of actual existence.

ἐπεὶ δὲ κατὰ νοῦν τῷ ξυνιστάντι πᾶσα ἡ τῆς ψυχῆς ξύστασις ἐγεγένητο, μετὰ τοῦτο πᾶν τὸ σωματοειδὲς ἐντὸς αὐτῆς ἐτεκταίνετο καὶ μέσον μέσῃ ξυναγαγὼν προσήρμοττεν· ἡ δ' ἐκ μέσου πρὸς τὸν ἔσχατον οὐρανὸν πάντῃ διαπλακεῖσα κύκλῳ τε αὐτὸν ἔξωθεν περικαλύψασα, αὐτὴ ἐν αὐτῇ στρεφομένη, θείαν ἀρχὴν ἤρξατο ἀπαύστου καὶ ἔμφρονος βίου πρὸς τὸν ξύμπαντα χρόνον.

(*Tim.* 36 D, E.)

Continuing his account of the world-soul Plato here describes its relation to the material world in such a way as to make it clear that it is more accurate to speak of body as existing within soul than of soul as existing within body, as he might at first have seemed to imply (30 B). We now see that according to the allegory soul was first created and then body was fashioned inside soul. By this time it is scarcely necessary to insist on the fact that of course the priority of soul to body, though described in terms which seem to regard it as temporal, is not really temporal at all but logical. Soul may be said to include body within it in the sense that it contains a principle or fixed law of its own nature in accordance with which it must necessarily localise itself in space, and what we know as body is the result. For the purposes of the allegory the world is regarded as a single animal consisting of soul and body inextricably intertwined ; that is to say, it is immortal : as ἔμψυχον or ζῷον it continues to exist throughout time. This means that the doctrine of the *Phaedrus* and the *Phaedo*, that all soul—here symbolized by the ψυχὴ

τοῦ κόσμου or world-soul—is immortal, is adhered to as
strongly as ever—θείαν ἀρχὴν ἤρξατο ἀπαύστου καὶ
ἔμφρονος βίου. But the σῶμα τοῦ κόσμου also exists
for ever, and is always joined with the ψυχὴ τοῦ
κόσμου : hence there is never any fraction of soul which
is not attached to a body. Soul always exists : and just
as the ψυχὴ τοῦ κόσμου is always manifested under the
form of the σῶμα τοῦ κόσμου, so every individual soul,
even the superior souls of the θεοὶ θεῶν, can never exist
except in company with body of some sort.

　　ψυχή, τῶν νοητῶν ἀεί τε ὄντων ὑπὸ τοῦ ἀρίστου
ἀρίστη γενομένη τῶν γεννηθέντων. (*Tim.* 37 A.)

Here it is to be observed that ψυχή is definitely
classed among things which are γεννηθέντα, whereas
νοῦς is not. But γεννηθέντα in the language of the
allegory does not of course mean the same thing as γιγνόμενα, a term which applies only to material things.
Plato says that ψυχή is created ὑπὸ τοῦ ἀρίστου τῶν
νοητῶν ἀεί τε ὄντων, that is to say the δημιουργός, who
symbolizes νοῦς, the 'Absolute,' from which we derive
our origin, and beyond which we cannot analyse. Thus
by interpreting the allegory we get from this passage a
confirmation of the conclusion arrived at above. Νοῦς
cannot from any point of view be described as γεννη-
θείς, but ψυχή is in a sense γεννηθεῖσα : that is to say,
logically there is no such thing as ψυχή until the *process*
of evolution from νοῦς has already begun. Pure ψυχή,
if we can imagine such a thing, would coalesce with νοῦς :
but pure ψυχή, ψυχή apart from σῶμα, cannot, as we
have seen, be actually existent ; it is only a logical
abstraction.

　　ἡ μὲν οὖν τοῦ ζῴου φύσις ἐτύγχανεν οὖσα αἰώνιος.
καὶ τοῦτο μὲν δὴ [sc. τὸ αἰώνιον εἶναι] τῷ γεννητῷ παντε-

λῶς προσάπτειν οὐκ ἦν δυνατόν· εἰκὼ δ' ἐπινοεῖ κινητόν
τινα αἰῶνος ποιῆσαι, καὶ διακοσμῶν ἅμα οὐρανὸν ποιεῖ
μένοντος αἰῶνος ἐν ἑνὶ κατ' ἀριθμὸν ἰοῦσαν αἰώνιον εἰκόνα,
τοῦτον ὃν δὴ χρόνον ὠνομάκαμεν. (*Tim.* 37 D.)

The αὐτὸ ζῷον, the ideal type of which the ὁρατὸς
κόσμος is an image, is eternal (αἰώνιον), that is to say
out of space and time, as distinct from immortal (ἀθάνατον), a term which strictly is applicable only to
determinate existence in space and time.   Mr Archer-
Hind raises, I think, an unnecessary difficulty over the
tense of ἐτύγχανεν in the above passage.   It is true of
course, as Plato says afterwards, that only the present
tense can properly be used in speaking of that which is
eternal, but surely the phrase ἐτύγχανεν οὖσα does not
require to be accounted for as being "necessitated by
the narrative form into which he has thrown his theory,"
except in so far as every theory, if it is to be expressed
in words at all, must be 'thrown into a narrative form.'
The imperfect tense, that is to say, is due not to the
particular form in which Plato has chosen to state his
theory, but to the fact that the details of the theory
have to be stated successively in some form or other.
The form, then, of the expression ἐτύγχανεν οὖσα αἰώνιος
will be amply accounted for not by the character of
the exposition, but by the progress of the argument,
and we may translate—'we found it to be eternal.'   But
this is a small point; what is really important is to
determine the exact significance of what follows, and
here Mr Archer-Hind gives most valuable assistance.
The δημιουργός, says Timaeus, could not make the
created world (that is to say νοῦς existing in the form
of πολλά) of its own nature eternal (αἰώνιος); if it were
so, the world could not be distinguished from himself

(that is to say νοῦς existing as ἕν). He therefore did the next best thing by giving it time (χρόνος) or the property of succession. In this way he could make the κόσμος *immortal* (ἀθάνατος, ἀνώλεθρος), but that of course is not the same thing as making it *eternal*. Continued existence in time may go on for ever; but however long such existence may continue, it will never be in the slightest degree nearer to eternity, the essential attribute of which is timelessness. As I have said, I do not believe Plato had recognised this fact at the time when he wrote the *Republic* and the *Phaedo*, and his metaphysical position at that period was consequently unstable. But there can be no doubt about the distinction which is drawn between time and eternity in the *Timaeus*.

Yet, though time is not the same as eternity or even a part of it, it is curiously described as 'an eternal image of eternity' (αἰῶνος αἰώνιος εἰκών). This in view of the distinction already made is a somewhat difficult expression to understand, but Mr Archer-Hind, as usual, has a satisfactory explanation. What Plato means is that time, though not of its own nature eternal, is nevertheless necessarily implied in the existence of the eternal, which is of its own nature timeless. In other words, the material and temporal world is a necessary, and so in a sense eternal, phase of existence. Time, therefore, is eternal not in virtue of its own nature but in virtue of the nature of that existence which must of necessity manifest itself under temporal conditions. We might represent another aspect of the same fundamental truth by similarly describing space or extension as 'an immaterial image of immateriality,' because it is a necessary law of the nature of the immaterial to manifest itself according to the principle

of extension under the form of material things, that is
to say things existing subject to the conditions of space
and time. Space and time, then, are necessary modes
of the existence of the spaceless and timeless. This
conclusion is only what we should expect in accordance
with what has gone before; moreover it is exactly what
is wanted to supplement the new theory of soul. Νοῦς
must exist in the form of ψυχή, primarily in the form
of the ψυχὴ τοῦ κόσμου, which, however, in actual
existence is differentiated into particular ψυχαί. Now
each particular soul as it is in itself, or rather as it would
be if it could be freed entirely from all the associations
of the body (ψυχὴ αὐτὴ καθ᾿ αὑτήν), cannot actually
exist as such. An existence of this kind can never be
anything more than hypothetical—a pure abstraction
belonging to the sphere of the timeless and spaceless,
in which ψυχή coalesces with νοῦς. But νοῦς as such
cannot be actually divided into parts corresponding to
particular ψυχαί : hence souls cannot aspire to any such
immaterial existence as this would imply, an existence
which, it is now recognised, cannot be an existence in
time at all. Ψυχή, as we have seen, comes into existence only with pluralisation, and pluralisation brings
with it time and space as conditions necessary to the
being of pluralised existence. The plurality of actually
existing souls, therefore, must be associated with bodies
in order that their existence as particular souls may be
made possible ; and the pluralised existence of ψυχή
continues throughout time. Time and space, which
involve the necessary association of soul and body,
have thus turned out to be the inevitable concomitants
of the externalisation of absolute Mind. Νοῦς must
exist not only as ἕν but also as πολλά, and its existence

as πολλά must in turn take the form of a material and temporal existence. Hence, whereas universal soul may from one point of view be conceived as not attached to body at all but as being merely one aspect of νοῦς itself, the same cannot hold good of the multiplicity of particular souls. Attachment to a body is, as it were, the price which soul has to pay for differentiation. And since soul must be differentiated, inasmuch as evolution into pluralised existence is a necessary law of the being of νοῦς, the conclusion is obvious, that there must always be a plurality of particular souls, and these souls must always as such be united with bodies. Thus Plato's ontological speculation has caused him to modify very considerably his opinions concerning the relation of universal soul to particular souls, and the true meaning of the association of soul and body.

ἐπεὶ δ᾽ οὖν πάντες, ὅσοι τε περιπολοῦσι φανερῶς καὶ ὅσοι φαίνονται καθ᾽ ὅσον ἂν ἐθέλωσιν, οἱ θεοὶ γένεσιν ἔσχον, λέγει πρὸς αὐτοὺς ὁ τόδε τὸ πᾶν γεννήσας τάδε· Θεοὶ θεῶν, ὧν ἐγὼ δημιουργὸς πατήρ τε ἔργων, ἃ δι᾽ ἐμοῦ γενόμενα ἄλυτα ἐμοῦ γε μὴ ἐθέλοντος· κ.τ.λ. (*Tim.* 41 A.)

According to the story of the creation the δημιουργός first creates the gods and having called them together first reveals to them the nature of their own immortal existence, and then assigns to them the task of bringing mortal creatures into existence. This allegorical account of the nature and functions of the θεοὶ θεῶν must obviously have a very important metaphysical significance. The created gods, their creator tells them, are immortal; but the immortality which is their inheritance belongs to them not in virtue of their own individual nature but by reason of the direct dispensation of his own sovereign will. He has created everything for the best and cannot, therefore, will deliberately the dissolution of what he has himself created; hence whatever is directly created by the δημιουργός must for that reason be immortal. This fact is explicitly stated a little further on:—

δι' ἐμοῦ δὲ ταῦτα [sc. τὰ θνητὰ γένη] γενόμενα καὶ βίου μετασχόντα θεοῖς ἰσάζοιτ' ἄν. (*Tim.* 41 C.)

The δημιουργός cannot directly create the θνητὰ γένη: if he attempted to do so, they would be immortal, not θνητὰ γένη at all. The θεοὶ θεῶν, however, *are* directly created by the δημιουργός and are consequently immortal. Absolute Mind, which is symbolized by the δημιουργός, must think, and its thinking must take the form of pluralisation. But the products of its thinking must be the best possible; hence since they cannot be eternal in themselves—for nothing that is pluralised can be eternal—, they must possess the quality which is next in perfection to eternity, namely immortality. Their individual existence never began and will never end, but extends throughout time: moreover time can never cease: for it is, as we have seen, in a sense eternal. The θεοὶ θεῶν, therefore, are immortal in a way in which no other creature can be. They alone have received not only their souls but also their bodies directly from the δημιουργός: hence they alone can retain their unity with the same body permanently. In fact they alone of actually existing beings are primary determinations of νοῦς, though even they must have bodies of some sort in consequence of their differentiation. But their bodies are of the highest possible type; they must be of a nature so refined as to interfere as little as possible

with the free exercise of their intellectual powers. They
exist, therefore, or at any rate they appear to us to exist,
in the form of stars. The idea is very poetical, but
there does not seem to be any sufficient reason for
doubting that Plato really does intend to suggest to
us the doctrine that what we see as stars are souls
united with a fiery body and exempt from death. Such,
then, is the nature of the θεοὶ θεῶν. The θνητὰ γένη,
if they are to be really θνητά, must of necessity be
differently constituted. As individual incarnate beings
(ἔμψυχα) they are the creations not of the δημιουργός
himself but of his creatures, the θεοὶ θεῶν: in other
words, they are not primary but secondary determinations of νοῦς. Consequently, whatever may be the case
with the individual soul regarded simply as a soul, each
individual incarnation is not everlasting throughout
time. All created things which in the scale of creation
rank below the θεοὶ θεῶν are subject to death, which
means the cessation of life in a particular body.

With this I shall leave this passage for the present:
but there will be some more to say about it on a future
occasion.

ταῦτ᾽ εἶπε, κ.τ.λ.   (*Tim.* 41 D—42 E, c. xiv.)

The chapter which we have now to interpret is in
some respects the most difficult in the whole of the
Timaeus. At the same time the interpretation of it
is obviously of the first importance in order to the
true understanding of the position in the universe which
Plato assigns to individual souls. To this end it will
be necessary to consider very carefully what construc-
tion we are to put upon certain statements contained
in it so that they may be brought into conformity

with the general system of metaphysics set forth in the
Dialogue. I believe that in certain important points
the inner significance of this chapter has been very
much misunderstood, if not entirely missed. The literal
statement is fairly clear; so in default of transcribing
the whole chapter in the original I here subjoin Mr
Archer-Hind's summary of it, which seems to me to
give an adequate representation of Plato's words, though
in the matter of interpretation, as will be seen, we differ
widely.

" Thus having spoken the Artificer prepared a second
blending of soul, having its proportions like to the former
but less pure. And of the soul so formed he separated
as many portions as there were stars in heaven, and set
a portion in each star, and declared to them the laws
of nature: how that every single soul should be first
embodied in human form, clothed in a frame subject
to vehement affections and passions. And whoso should
conquer these and live righteously, after fulfilling his
allotted span, he should return to the star of his affinity
and dwell in blessedness: but if he failed thereof, he
should pass at death into the form of some lower being,
and cease not from such transmigrations until, obeying
the reason rather than the passions, he should gradually
raise himself again to the first and best form. Then
God sowed the souls severally in the different planets,
and gave the task of their incarnation to the gods he
had created, to make them as fair and perfect as mortal
nature may admit."

Regarded as an account of a particular incident in
the creation of the universe, this passage runs smoothly
enough. But we have seen reason to consider this whole
story of the creation as an elaborate allegory which is in

reality intended to symbolize under the form of a temporal process the timeless evolution of infinite Mind into finite existence; and it is in connexion with the attempt to make it harmonize with this theory that the interpretation of the chapter we are now to consider is hedged about with difficulties of no common order. I do not propose to enter into a discussion of all the difficulties that might be raised; but there are some which are so intimately connected with my present subject that they cannot be ignored; and I now pass on to consider and, if possible, to remove them. As his notes show, Mr Archer-Hind is fully aware that difficulties exist, but the way in which he tries to get over them seems to me very unsatisfactory; and while admiring to the full his brilliant interpretation of the *Timaeus* as a whole, I think that in his treatment of this particular part of it his usual clear-sightedness has for once deserted him.

To begin with, the opening words of the chapter have given rise to a difference of opinion in regard to the exact nature of the composition of the lower order of souls. The words run:—

ταῦτ᾽ εἶπε, καὶ πάλιν ἐπὶ τὸν πρότερον κρατῆρα, ἐν ᾧ τὴν τοῦ παντὸς ψυχὴν κεραννὺς ἔμισγε, τὰ τῶν πρόσθεν ὑπόλοιπα κατεχεῖτο μίσγων τρόπον μέν τινα τὸν αὐτόν, ἀκήρατα δ᾽ οὐκέτι κατὰ ταὐτὰ ὡσαύτως, ἀλλὰ δεύτερα καὶ τρίτα. (*Tim.* 41 D.)

On the words τὰ τῶν πρόσθεν ὑπόλοιπα Mr Archer-Hind has the following note: "Not the remnants of the universal soul, as Stallbaum supposes; for that, we are told in 36 B, was all used up; but of the elements composing soul, ταὐτὸν θάτερον and οὐσία." This seems to me to involve a double error. Mr Archer-Hind first erroneously attributes to Stallbaum a view which I hold to be the right one, and then puts forward one of his own which, in the absence of any explanation or justification, is difficult to understand and does not appear to be warranted by Plato's language. What does Stallbaum say? His words are :—" *Reliquias superioris mixtionis, unde anima mundi composita erat, deus summus in eundem craterem dicitur infudisse.*" Thus he takes τὰ τῶν πρόσθεν ὑπόλοιπα to mean the remnants not of the universal soul (*anima mundi*) but of the original mixture of which part had been used to make the universal soul, some portion being left over to be formed into inferior souls (δεύτερα καὶ τρίτα). According to this view the whole quantity of soul is divided between the world-soul and inferior souls, a rather curious metaphysical doctrine and one which I am convinced is not Plato's. If, however, Stallbaum had said what Mr Archer-Hind would make him say (*reliquias animae mundi*, instead of *reliquias superioris mixtionis, unde anima mundi composita erat*), I believe he would have been quite right. It is true, of course, as Mr Archer-Hind points out, that the whole quantity of soul was used up in making the world-soul, and so far his criticism of Stallbaum is valid; but we have now to do not with the *creation* of new soul but with the *differentiation* of the world-soul. From this point of view there *are* remnants of the world-soul; some of it has been used up and some has not. I should have liked Stallbaum's comment to run :—*Reliquias superioris mixtionis* (or *animae mundi*), *unde animae* deorum *compositae erant.* In this way, it seems to me, we have a perfectly satisfactory explanation of τὰ τῶν πρόσθεν ὑπόλοιπα. The world-soul—here referred to as

ἡ τοῦ παντὸς ψυχή—is the sum of all individual souls,
if looked at from our point of view; if looked at from
that of the δημιουργός, it is the soul which animates the
whole universe; to bring it into actual existence, however, he has to differentiate it into individual souls.   We
have already had an account of the first stage in this
differentiation in what is described as the creation of the
θεοὶ θεῶν : we now come to the second stage.   The souls
of the gods and the souls of mortal creatures are all
alike nothing else but differentiated portions of the
universal soul; and, as Mr Archer-Hind says, " Plato's
scheme includes a regular gradation of finite existences,
from the glorious intelligence of a star down to the
humblest herb of the field : all these are manifestations
of the same eternal essence through forms more and
more remote."   According to my view, then, the souls
of the θεοὶ θεῶν are the πρῶτα in reference to which the
souls of inferior beings are called δεύτερα καὶ τρίτα—a far
more natural comparison, it seems to me, than one
between the undifferentiated world-soul and the lower
order of finite souls.   The nature of the θεοὶ θεῶν has
just been described, and while from one point of view
their souls are placed on the same footing as the souls
of mortal creatures, it is only natural that the inferiority
of the latter should in some way be contrasted with the
superiority of the former.

But there is a much more serious difficulty than this
to come.   A little further on Plato says, or seems to say,
that every one of these inferior souls after leaving the
star to whose care it has been entrusted must first enter
into the form of a man :—

ξυστήσας δὲ τὸ πᾶν διεῖλε ψυχὰς ἰσαρίθμους τοῖς
ἄστροις, ἔνειμέ θ᾽ ἑκάστην πρὸς ἕκαστον, καὶ ἐμβιβάσας

ὡς ἐς ὄχημα τὴν τοῦ παντὸς φύσιν ἔδειξε, νόμους τε τοὺς
εἱμαρμένους εἶπεν αὐταῖς, ὅτι γένεσις πρώτη μὲν ἔσοιτο
τεταγμένη μία πᾶσιν, ἵνα μή τις ἐλάττοιτο ὑπ' αὐτοῦ, δέοι
δὲ σπαρείσας αὐτὰς εἰς τὰ προσήκοντα ἑκάσταις ἕκαστα
ὄργανα χρόνου φῦναι ζῴων τὸ θεοσεβέστατον, διπλῆς δὲ
οὔσης τῆς ἀνθρωπίνης φύσεως τὸ κρεῖττον τοιοῦτον εἴη
γένος, ὃ καὶ ἔπειτα κεκλήσοιτο ἀνήρ.

(*Tim.* 41 D—42 A.)

In spite of Stallbaum I think that Mr Archer-Hind is
unquestionably right in taking the γένεσις here spoken
of to refer to the incarnation of the souls in human form.
" Here however," he goes on to remark, " a point presents
itself in which the allegory appears *prima facie* inconsistent. At 39 E Plato says there are four εἴδη of νοητὰ
ζῷα in the αὐτὸ ζῷον: yet of αἰσθητὰ ζῷα we only have
two εἴδη at the outset: how then is the sensible world
a faithful image of the intelligible world?" The passage
to which Mr Archer-Hind refers runs as follows:—

τοῦτο δὴ τὸ κατάλοιπον ἀπειργάζετο αὐτοῦ πρὸς τὴν
τοῦ παραδείγματος ἀποτυπούμενος φύσιν. ἧπερ οὖν νοῦς
ἐνούσας ἰδέας τῷ ὃ ἔστι ζῷον, οἷαί τε ἔνεισι καὶ ὅσαι,
καθορᾷ, τοιαύτας καὶ τοσαύτας διενοήθη δεῖν καὶ τόδε
σχεῖν. εἰσὶ δὴ τέτταρες, μία μὲν οὐράνιον θεῶν γένος,
ἄλλη δὲ πτηνὸν καὶ ἀεροπόρον, τρίτη δε ἔνυδρον εἶδος,
πεζὸν δὲ καὶ χερσαῖον τέταρτον. (*Tim.* 39 E, 40 A.)

Now from this we learn that the αὐτὸ ζῷον comprises
within itself all classes of ζῷα that exist in the universe.
How can this be, if at any time every soul has taken
upon itself the form of a man? At such a time it would
seem that in the stars and men we have only two kinds
represented, the οὐράνιον θεῶν γένος and part of the
πεζὸν καὶ χερσαῖον γένος. How, then, does Mr Archer-

Hind seek to remove the apparent inconsistency which
he detects? "The answer would seem to be," he says,
"that the δημιουργός foresaw that many souls must
necessarily degenerate from the πρώτη καὶ ἀρίστη ἕξις,
and therefore left the perfect assimilation of the image
to the type to be worked out and completed in the
course of nature, with which he did not choose arbitrarily
to interfere, in order that no soul might start at a disadvantage through his doing: ἵνα μή τις ἐλαττοῖτο ὑπ'
αὐτοῦ. It is remarkable, however, that the perfection
of the copy should be accomplished through a process
of degeneration." Rather than 'remarkable' it seems to
me that such a hypothesis is on Platonic principles—
principles which Mr Archer-Hind himself has done
so much to establish as Platonic—metaphysically impossible ; that is to say, if the 'process of degeneration'
be, as Mr Archer-Hind implies, a process in time. The
ὁρατὸς κόσμος must always be a perfect representation
of the νοητὸς κόσμος: it cannot at one time be so and
at another time not. That would be an inconsistency
indeed of which it is very difficult to believe Plato
capable. We should be more than justified, therefore,
in trying to find some other explanation of his meaning
which will not render him liable to any such indictment.

I believe I am right in saying that Mr Archer-Hind
no longer adheres altogether to the explanation of this
passage which is given in the note I have quoted ; but
I do not know how he would now interpret it. I propose,
therefore, to submit an explanation of my own, which
seems to me to get over the difficulty in a manner
suggested by Mr Archer-Hind's own interpretation of
the *Timaeus* as a whole ; for I cannot help thinking that
here he has not carried his own principles far enough.

But before giving my own view I would first remark
that Mr Archer-Hind's way of stating the difficulty that
is raised by this passage does not go to the root of the
matter; in fact, as he states it, I cannot see that there
is any inconsistency at all.   It may be true that at some
particular time all the classes of νοητὰ ζῷα are not
actually represented in this world by corresponding
αἰσθητὰ ζῷα: but it does not necessarily follow that at
such a time the ὁρατὸς κόσμος is not a complete copy of
the νοητὸς κόσμος.   The phenomenal universe contains
within it *potentially* animals and vegetables corresponding to the several ideas, even if at a given moment this
or that form of life be not invested in a body.   When
a soul is joined with such a combination of matter as is
appropriate to the form of life in question, that form of
life will inevitably come into being in consequence of the
eternal existence of the idea which corresponds to it.
Of course Plato had not arrived at so clear a notion
of the nature of potentiality as Aristotle achieved later;
but his general theory of matter as a ὑποδοχή shows that
he was well on his way towards it.   In any case it would
be open to him to defend himself against the charge of
inconsistency in some such way as this: and so, I understand, Dr Jackson would defend him.

The chief difficulty, however, of the present passage
really lies deeper than this.   To begin with, we have to
observe that it is not even the form of 'human being'
(ἄνθρωπος) into which according to the literal statement
all souls of the inferior order must first enter; their first
incarnation is explicitly restricted to the form of 'man'
(ἀνήρ) as opposed to 'woman,' by which limitation a
further complication is introduced.   According to the
statement of this chapter women and all the lower

animals and plants come into being only by a process
of metempsychosis, the souls—or some of them—which
first existed in the form of men having ordered their
lives in such a manner as to bring about their degradation.   This can hardly be considered a very satisfactory
theory as it stands.   How is the species propagated
when there are only men and no women in the world?
How in a world in which human beings are the only
living creatures do the lower animals and plants first
make their appearance?   What in fact is the manner
of that πρώτη γένεσις by which men are first produced?
We think inevitably of Aristotle with his ἄνθρωπος
ἄνθρωπον γεννᾷ and feel that, if Plato has failed so
utterly to appreciate the truth which that statement
presupposes, then he has failed indeed.   But is it really
so?   I think not.

I have said that in his interpretation of this chapter
of the *Timaeus* Mr Archer-Hind appears to me not to
have carried far enough the principle of interpretation
which has guided him in his treatment of the Dialogue
as a whole.   I will now explain more fully what I meant
in making that statement, as my own explanation of the
present passage consists largely in applying that principle
further.   In his edition of the *Timaeus*, both in the
Introduction and in the notes, Mr Archer-Hind is
continually warning us against interpreting statements
which are really allegorical in character as though they
were literal statements of fact.   As a basis for the
interpretation of the myth we have to assume a certain
metaphysical theory, if we are to make the details of the
myth fit in with Plato's philosophy at all.   In particular
many things which are described in the allegory as
following one another in time should be interpreted

as standing not in chronological but in logical sequence ;
they follow one another, as Stobaeus puts it, not κατὰ
χρόνον but κατ᾽ ἐπίνοιαν. If we do not admit this
principle in interpreting the *Timaeus*, we, as Mr Archer-
Hind most justly insists, "reduce Plato's philosophy to
a chaos of wild disorder." For example, we should
have to regard the δημιουργός as an external creator
creating the universe in time, to regard him in fact,
as Aristotle himself seems to do, as creating time in
time. Mr Archer-Hind, therefore, seems to me perfectly right in ruling out any such interpretation. Now
a principle which has been applied with such success
to Plato's κοσμογονία may well be applied, I fancy, to
his ψυχογονία also ; and as it removes difficulties in the
one case we may be justified in hoping that it may be
used to remove similar difficulties in the other. The
experiment is worth making, and I think it can be made
with success. I would suggest, then, that what is spoken
of here as the first incarnation of souls in human form
(πρώτη γένεσις) is not to be understood literally as
implying that there was ever a time when men had not
been created, followed by a time when men were the
only creatures existing in the world. Such a hypothesis
seems to be on Platonic principles both physically and
metaphysically untenable, and therefore I hold that
Plato did not mean to suggest it. The statement that
all souls of a lower order than those of the gods receive
their first incarnation in the form of men must, like so
many other statements in the metaphysical portion of
the *Timaeus*, be understood symbolically. It symbolizes
the fact that in the scheme of creation man ranks first
among the inferior classes of beings ; that is to say, man
ranks next in order to the θεοὶ θεῶν, and all the other

species of animals and vegetables are arranged in a
descending scale below him. Thus the 'process of
degeneration' of which Mr Archer-Hind speaks as
accomplishing the perfection of the copy is not a
temporal process at all: and the αἰσθητὸς κόσμος is
always a correct copy of the νοητὸς κόσμος.

Mr Archer-Hind, however, finds a further difficulty
in connexion with the δευτέρα γένεσις in the form of
a woman :—

καὶ ὁ μὲν εὖ τὸν προσήκοντα χρόνον βιοὺς πάλιν εἰς
τὴν τοῦ ξυννόμου πορευθεὶς οἴκησιν ἄστρου βίον εὐδαίμονα
καὶ συνήθη ἕξοι. σφαλεὶς δὲ τούτων εἰς γυναικὸς φύσιν
ἐν τῇ δευτέρᾳ γενέσει μεταβαλοῖ. (*Tim.* 42 B.)

But this δευτέρα γένεσις can, I think, be explained on
the same lines as the πρώτη γένεσις: and in any case
I do not think it is so incongruous as Mr Archer-Hind
seems to find it. He says in his note: " Here, it must
be confessed, we have a piece of questionable metaphysic.
For the distinction of sex cannot possibly stand on the
same logical footing as the generic differences between
various animals, and in the other forms of animal life
the distinction is ignored. It is somewhat curious that
Plato, who in his views about woman's position was
immeasurably in advance of his age, has here yielded to
Athenian prejudice so far as to introduce a dissonant
element into his theory." Now, as to the 'questionable
metaphysic,' I do not believe that Plato for a moment
wishes us to suppose that he places the distinction of sex
'on the same logical footing as the generic differences
between various animals.' There is no *idea* of woman
as distinct from the idea of man ; but there is nevertheless a difference between man and woman which has to

be accounted for somehow, and Plato here wishes to
mark his sense of that difference. Moreover I cannot
see that he 'has here yielded to Athenian prejudice'
in the matter. It is true that he took a much higher
view of the position of women in the world than any
of his contemporaries; but it seems clear nevertheless
that he considered that woman as such must always be
inferior to man. This may be gathered from the discussion in the fifth book of the *Republic* about the
relative capacity in various respects of men and women.
The most characteristic features of his opinion on this
point are to be found in the following passage :—

οἶσθά τι οὖν ὑπὸ ἀνθρώπων μελετώμενον, ἐν ᾧ οὐ
πάντα ταῦτα τὸ τῶν ἀνδρῶν γένος διαφερόντως ἔχει ἢ τὸ
τῶν γυναικῶν; ἢ μακρολογῶμεν τήν τε ὑφαντικὴν λέγοντες
καὶ τὴν τῶν ποπάνων τε καὶ ἐψημάτων θεραπείαν, ἐν οἷς
δή τι δοκεῖ τὸ γυναικεῖον γένος εἶναι, οὗ καὶ καταγελα-
στότατόν ἐστι πάντων ἡττώμενον; Ἀληθῆ, ἔφη, λέγεις,
ὅτι πολὺ κρατεῖται ἐν ἅπασιν, ὡς ἔπος εἰπεῖν, τὸ γένος
τοῦ γένους. γυναῖκες μέν τοι πολλαὶ πολλῶν ἀνδρῶν
βελτίους εἰς πολλά· τὸ δὲ ὅλον ἔχει ὡς σὺ λέγεις. Οὐδὲν
ἄρα ἐστίν, ὦ φίλε, ἐπιτήδευμα τῶν πόλιν διοικούντων
γυναικὸς διότι γυνή, οὐδ' ἀνδρὸς διότι ἀνήρ, ἀλλ' ὁμοίως
διεσπαρμέναι αἱ φύσεις ἐν ἀμφοῖν τοῖν ζῴοιν, καὶ πάντων
μὲν μετέχει γυνὴ ἐπιτηδευμάτων κατὰ φύσιν, πάντων δὲ
ἀνήρ, ἐπὶ πᾶσι δὲ ἀσθενέστερον γυνὴ ἀνδρός.

(Rep. 455 C—E.)

There is no difference of kind between the respective
capacities, physical and mental, of men and women;
hence in Plato's opinion boys and girls should be brought
up exactly alike as regards both physical and mental
culture, and in later life the same pursuits should be

open to women as to men.   But though there is no
difference of kind, there is a difference of degree, and
this difference of degree is and must be always present;
that is to say, though many women may be better in
various respects than many men, yet the best men will
invariably be better than the best women.   Such is the
position which Plato takes up in the *Republic*, and I see
nothing in the *Timaeus* which is inconsistent with it.
He does not mean to imply now any more than he did
then that there is any difference of kind between
men and women; he merely wishes to emphasize the
difference of degree which inevitably accompanies the
distinction of sex.   In the *Timaeus*, however, as it
seems to me, he is asserting rather from the metaphysical point of view what in the *Republic* he has
treated as a matter of experience.   Each natural kind,
we must suppose, is naturally divided into a superior
and an inferior branch, namely the male and the female,
and other things being equal the female will always
rank lower than the male.   It is true, as Mr Archer-Hind
points out, that the distinction is expressly made only
in the case of human beings; but I do not think any
stress need be laid on this; it may be due to the fact
that for us the distinction is more noticeable in man
than in any other species.   At any rate the case of man
is naturally taken first, and Plato may well have felt a
repetition of the distinction in the case of other species
to be unnecessary.   The introduction of the sexual
distinction in this particular place is perhaps rather
awkward in some respects, but I do not think it
necessarily involves 'questionable metaphysic.'   As we
shall see later, a certain amount of awkwardness was
bound to arise in consequence of the method which

Plato chooses for the exposition of his metaphysical theories.

Putting aside the question of the distinction of sex, we may observe that the interpretation of the present chapter which I have just put forward will also serve to get rid of a similar difficulty which occurs in the later portion of the *Timaeus*, where the facts of life are treated for the most part from the standpoint of physics and physiology. In the passage to which I refer Plato is describing the means adopted by the gods for the preservation of human life :—

ἐπειδὴ δὲ πάντ᾽ ἦν τὰ τοῦ θνητοῦ ζῴου ξυμπεφυκότα μέρη καὶ μέλη, τὴν δὲ ζωὴν ἐν πυρὶ καὶ πνεύματι ξυνέβαινεν ἐξ ἀνάγκης ἔχειν αὐτῷ, καὶ διὰ ταῦτα ὑπὸ τούτων τηκόμενον κενούμενόν τ᾽ ἔφθινε, βοήθειαν αὐτῷ θεοὶ μηχανῶνται. τῆς γὰρ ἀνθρωπίνης ξυγγενῆ φύσεως φύσιν ἄλλαις ἰδέαις καὶ αἰσθήσεσι κεραννύντες, ὥσθ᾽ ἕτερον ζῷον εἶναι, φυτεύουσιν· ἃ δὴ νῦν ἥμερα δένδρα καὶ φυτὰ καὶ σπέρματα παιδευθέντα ὑπὸ γεωργίας τιθασῶς πρὸς ἡμᾶς ἔσχε, πρὶν δὲ ἦν μόνα τὰ τῶν ἀγρίων γένη, πρεσβύτερα τῶν ἡμέρων ὄντα. (*Tim.* 76 E—77 B.)

Here we learn that plants are necessary for the sustenance of man ; they must, therefore, have existed in the world as long as man has existed and before any other form of life had made its appearance : this is implied in a previous remark :—

ὡς γάρ ποτε ἐξ ἀνδρῶν γυναῖκες καὶ τἄλλα θηρία γενήσοιντο, ἠπίσταντο οἱ ξυνιστάντες ἡμᾶς.
(*Tim.* 76 D, E.)

Thus, if we are to interpret Plato's language in this passage literally, we have to assume that men and wild

plants came into the world together and continued to
exist while as yet there were no intermediate forms of
life; and a serious metaphysical complication is the
result. As before, Mr Archer-Hind is sensible of the
difficulty which arises, but he seems to accept Plato's
statement in its literal meaning. "It thus appears," he
says, "that in Plato's scheme plants do not, like the
inferior animals, arise by degeneration from the human
form. For as soon as man was first created, he would
have need of plants to provide him with sustenance. It
would appear then that in the Platonic mythology the
erring soul in the course of her transmigrations does
not enter any of the forms of plant-life." And again :
" The simultaneous appearance of mankind and of plants
in the world, while all intermediate forms of animal
life are absent, is curious, and could hardly, I think, be
defended upon ontological grounds." He would no
longer, I imagine, maintain the opinion expressed here
any more than that which is contained in the note
upon which I have already commented. It seems to me
that such a theory, even if it could be defended generally
upon ontological grounds, could not possibly be upheld
consistently with the principles of Platonic ontology.
Plato does not admit any such hard and fast distinction
between animals and plants as this would imply: he
makes this clear just afterwards : and Mr Archer-Hind,
in spite of his previous note expressing the opinion that
"the erring soul in the course of her transmigrations
does not enter any of the forms of plant-life," fully
admits the fact :—" Plato in the fullest degree maintained the unity of all life. He drew no arbitrary line
between 'animal' and 'vegetable' life: all things that
live are manifestations of the same eternal essence :

only as this evolved itself through countless gradations
of existence, the lower ranks of organisms possess less
and less of the pure activity of soul operating by herself,
until in plants and the lowest forms of animal life the
vital force only manifests itself in the power of sensa-
tion and growth." This seems to me an admirable
statement of Plato's position: but how it is to be
reconciled with the previous note I do not know. It is
surely Mr Archer-Hind, not Plato, who is inconsistent,
and it comes of trying to bind Plato down too closely
to his literal statement. I would plead for Plato as
Socrates pleads for Protagoras — ἀλλ᾽, ὦ μακάριε,
φήσει, γενναιοτέρως ἐπ᾽ αὐτὸ ἐλθὼν ὃ λέγω, εἰ δύνασαι,
ἐξέλεγξον * * * τὸν δὲ λόγον αὖ μὴ τῷ ῥήματί μου
δίωκε. We must regard the evolution of plants, as of
all other living things, as taking place κατ᾽ ἐπίνοιαν
only; and then all inconsistency, so far as Plato's real
meaning is concerned, disappears.

If the interpretation of these two passages which
I am here advocating will stand the test of examination,
as I think it will, its advantages are obvious. It removes
difficulties which would otherwise be hard to get over
and rescues Plato's philosophy, if not his literal statement of it, from the charge of inconsistency. It may be
objected to it, however, that, if it removes some difficulties, it creates others. This may be admitted, but if
the new difficulties are less serious than the old, something at least will have been gained; and I hope to be
able to show that such difficulties as remain are no more
than may fairly be accounted for by the peculiar form in
which Plato states his theory. I have already referred
to the awkwardness which results from his introducing
the distinction of sex into a passage which would

naturally be expected to deal only with the distinctions
between the various species. Still it is only awkwardness and not inconsistency that arises. But there is of
course one fairly obvious objection which can be urged
against the adoption of any such interpretation as that
which I have proposed. In the *Timaeus*, it may be said,
there is nothing to show that Plato has given up his
belief in the doctrine of metempsychosis. It seems to be
asserted not only in the particular chapter which has
been engaging our attention, but in another passage at
the very end of the Dialogue, where the literal statement
cannot be explained away by the theory of a logical
sequence :—

καὶ κατὰ ταῦτα δὴ πάντα τότε καὶ νῦν διαμείβεται
τὰ ζῷα εἰς ἄλληλα, νοῦ καὶ ἀνοίας ἀποβολῇ καὶ κτήσει
μεταβαλλόμενα. (*Tim.* 92 B.)

And surely he must be maintaining the same doctrine
in the passage with which we are more immediately
concerned ; for here, as well as in the passage just
quoted, it is to be observed that the process described
is not only a process of degeneration : the transmigration of souls may proceed in an upward as well as in
a downward direction (νοῦ καὶ ἀνοίας ἀποβολῇ καὶ
κτήσει) :—

ἀλλάττων τε οὐ πρότερον πόνων λήξοι, πρὶν τῇ ταὐ-
τοῦ καὶ ὁμοίου περιόδῳ τῇ ἐν αὑτῷ ξυνεπισπόμενος τὸν
πολὺν ὄχλον καὶ ὕστερον προσφύντα ἐκ πυρὸς καὶ ὕδατος
καὶ ἀέρος καὶ γῆς, θορυβώδη καὶ ἄλογον ὄντα, λόγῳ
κρατήσας εἰς τὸ τῆς πρώτης καὶ ἀρίστης ἀφίκοιτο εἶδος
ἕξεως. (*Tim.* 42 C, D.)

Plato here certainly seems to teach that, though souls
may degenerate, yet no soul is ever irretrievably ruined ;

lost ground may always be regained and a return made
to the πρώτη καὶ ἀρίστη ἕξις. How, then, can this be
consistent with the assertion that the process described
in this chapter proceeds not κατὰ χρόνον but κατ᾽ ἐπίνοιαν? That Plato does mean to affirm his continued
belief in the truth of the doctrine of metempsychosis
I am persuaded; and that being so it must be admitted
that the above-mentioned difficulty does arise. But
I do not see that there is any reason why it should be
regarded as fatal to my interpretation of the passage as
a whole, when we take into account all the circumstances
of the case and especially the form in which this part of
the *Timaeus* is written. Plato has chosen to employ
a particular instrument for the purpose of making
intelligible to his readers the workings of a metaphysical system which at that period in the history of
human thought it would have been well-nigh impossible
to express in exact language. That instrument I have
already referred to as allegory; and Plato doubtless
expected all intelligent students of his philosophy to
bear in mind that the outstanding feature of the allegory
of the *Timaeus* is the description of a logical order
as though it were temporal. But difficulties could
not fail to arise as the result of such a mode of pre-
sentation. Until we come to the present chapter, it is
true, the instrument has done its work fairly successfully;
we have only to recognise that what is allegorically
described as creation symbolizes the logical evolution
of Mind. But when Plato proceeds to describe not only
the evolution but the nature and, as it were, the history
of individual souls, the instrument is seen to be to a
certain extent defective, and for the best of reasons:
he has tried to make it do too much work. For under

the similitude of a process taking place in time and
space he now has to describe not only what is as a
matter of fact spaceless and timeless, but also something
else in the history of souls which does really take place
under the conditions of time and space, namely metempsychosis.   In such circumstances the allegorical form
of his exposition must almost inevitably cause confusion.   The metaphysical origin of species, the natural
inferiority of the female to the male, and the actual
history of individual souls, are described almost in the
same breath.   At the same time we have to remember
that it is not to be supposed that the process of transmigration as such has any beginning in time; and that
is perhaps one of the reasons why it is introduced in this
place.   It is eternal in the same sense in which we saw
that time itself is eternal: but it constitutes nevertheless
an actual incident in the life of the individual which
takes place in time and continues throughout time.
What I think has happened, then, in this chapter is
simply that Plato has attempted to do too much at once,
and the natural defects of the allegorical method of
exposition have thus become apparent; allegory and fact
are to a certain extent fused.   Moreover we have had
occasion to notice a very similar occurrence in the
Phaedrus, where the mythical form of the narrative is
not everywhere sustained.   The myth in the *Timaeus*
is in other respects not unlike that in the *Phaedrus*: is
it matter for surprise if they resemble one another in this
respect also?

There is one other objection worthy of notice which
might perhaps be raised against my proposed interpretation.   It may possibly be said that my theory does not
sufficiently account for the words ἵνα μή τις ἐλαττοῖτο

ὑπ' αὐτοῦ (41 E). If all souls do not begin life in this
world on an equal footing, how can it be said that
no soul starts at a disadvantage as compared with other
souls which are fortunate enough to begin by entering a
human form? I think criticism of this sort is based
upon a misapprehension. Strictly speaking there is no
question of souls 'beginning life in this world' at all.
As far as individual souls are concerned, life in this
world has been going on from everlasting and will
continue to go on without ceasing: individual life is
co-extensive with time itself. As soon as we recognise
this, we see that the statement that a soul began by
entering a human form is all but unmeaning. There is
no beginning; hence there can be no initial disadvantage.
If there were no chance for a soul to better its condition,
some souls would indeed be at a perpetual disadvantage,
but this is not so: οὐδεμία ἐλαττοῦται, because the
principle of the logical sequence secures to all souls
alike their opportunity of attaining by metempsychosis
to humanity in its higher form.

τὴν δὴ πρὸ τῆς οὐρανοῦ γενέσεως πυρὸς ὕδατός τε καὶ
ἀέρος καὶ γῆς φύσιν θεατέον αὐτὴν καὶ τὰ πρὸ τούτου
πάθη. (*Tim.* 48 B.)

Plato here speaks of 'the actual nature of fire, water,
air, and earth before the generation of the world.' We
know of course that he does not mean us to suppose
that the world was created in time; the expression must,
therefore, like so many others in the *Timaeus*, be metaphorical. But while it cannot be strictly accurate to say
that anything existed *before* the generation of the world,
inasmuch as the universe is without beginning and without end, we are obviously meant to infer that matter is

somehow inherent in the nature of things. And so we find that there are ideas to account for the existence of fire, water, air, and earth as well as ideas of animal and vegetable species. Mr Archer-Hind seems loth to admit that this is so; but in the face of Plato's language here and in other passages of the *Timaeus* (especially 51 B, where he speaks of πῦρ αὐτὸ ἐφ' ἑαυτοῦ) I cannot see any good reason for doubting it. From the point of view of us finite beings matter has an objective existence of its own quite apart from our perception of it. Like spirit, it is derived directly from the δημιουργός himself; that is to say, it is a necessary result of the direct thinking of absolute Mind. I introduce this passage here merely in so far as it tends to confirm what has been said before, that matter is a necessary element of pluralised existence. There can be no justification, therefore, for supposing that the soul after death can enter into any immaterial region and still remain an individual soul. In this point more than in anything else is shown the great advance made in the teaching of the *Timaeus* concerning the nature of the soul as compared with the doctrine of the *Phaedo*.

Here it will be convenient to leave the *Timaeus* for a while, though it will be necessary to refer to it again at some length later. I have not yet said much which bears directly upon the attitude shown in it towards the question of immortality. That will be more conveniently done after I have examined certain passages in the tenth book of the *Laws* which require to be considered in connexion with the *Timaeus*.

CHAPTER IX.

THE *LAWS*.

SUNDRY considerations, upon which it would be out of place to enter here, combine to make it practically certain that the *Laws* is one of the latest, if not actually the latest, of the Platonic Dialogues; it is in fact the product of his old age. It will be worth while, therefore, to look into this Dialogue in the hope of discovering something which may enable us to determine what were Plato's final opinions concerning the nature of the soul. It must be confessed that the *Laws* does not contribute very much that tends to increase our information on this point. There is, however, nothing surprising in this; for the *Laws* is not primarily a metaphysical treatise : in fact it contains very little that can be said to have any direct metaphysical bearing. The reason for this is obvious when we take into consideration the circumstances in which it was written. Plato has already given us his final views on metaphysics in the *Timaeus* ; views which, as we have seen, his clearer metaphysical insight has caused to differ very widely from the opinions expressed in Dialogues of the earlier period, of which the *Republic* and the *Phaedo* may be regarded as typical. In particular the Theory of Ideas and, as I hope I have been able to show, his conception of the nature of the soul have been in the interval substantially altered, or at

least largely developed and grounded upon a more
scientific basis than formerly.   During this time Plato
has been working almost exclusively at metaphysics.
We notice no such reconstruction or even development
of his ethical opinions to correspond with his advance
in metaphysical theory, from which we may justly
infer that no such change took place.   In their general
character the ethical and sociological opinions advanced
in the *Republic* still hold good.   In so far as the *Republic*
gives us an ideal scheme of ethics it was never intended
to be superseded.   As evidence of this we may notice
the introductory part of the *Timaeus*, which expressly
connects that Dialogue with the *Republic*; we observe
there the significant fact that, whereas the chief results
obtained in the *Republic* so far as ethics and sociology
are concerned are recapitulated, nothing is said about
the metaphysical speculation which it contains.   But
though its general character may remain unaltered,
Plato's ethical scheme as expounded in the *Republic*
and the *Phaedo* cannot but be affected in some of its
details by the changes which have taken place in his
metaphysical opinions.   We have seen that this ethical
scheme, especially on its educational side, was distinctly
founded upon a metaphysical basis which has subsequently been discovered to be unsound.   We are told
in the *Republic* that it is the acquisition of direct knowledge of the Good which is finally to convert δημοτικὴ
καὶ πολιτικὴ ἀρετή into ἀρετὴ ἡ τοῦ φιλοσόφου.   But
Plato was not long in discovering that direct knowledge
of the Good cannot be acquired in this world.   For a
time he found refuge in the doctrine that it might
nevertheless be obtained in another world after death.
This stage of opinion is represented by the *Phaedo*,

where the doctrine of the immortality of the soul gives some reason for hoping that after death the soul may lead an absolutely immaterial existence, the necessary condition for direct apprehension of the ideas. But before writing the *Timaeus* Plato had come to recognise that a complete and actual separation of body and soul is impossible, so that direct knowledge of the Good can never be anything more than an unrealisable ideal. Such an ideal has of course its value; we may make a continual approximation towards this knowledge, though we can never hope to reach it: but this is a very different attitude from that previously adopted. Hence, though his opinions on ethical and sociological questions have remained throughout essentially unchanged, it might fairly be expected that after his metaphysical system had reached its consummation in the *Timaeus* Plato should have in some way re-embodied and re-stated these opinions so as to render them independent of a metaphysical basis now found to be unstable, and to bring them into conformity with the changed conditions. As it stands, the scheme of the *Republic* is unworkable: it must be stated anew in such a way as to admit some hope of its realisation. This is the task to which Plato addresses himself in the *Laws*, which is consequently, as we should naturally anticipate, in the main a thoroughly practical treatise unencumbered by any fresh metaphysical speculation. Yet, though this is the character of the *Laws* as a whole, there are nevertheless in the tenth book certain statements about the soul which cannot well be left out of account in any attempt to determine Plato's final opinions concerning its nature. If we cannot expect to discover anything absolutely new, it will still be helpful to observe how

Plato expresses himself on this subject at the very end
of his philosophical career. I propose, therefore, to
examine these statements in order on the same principle
which I have adopted in dealing with other Dialogues.

κινδυνεύει γὰρ ὁ λέγων ταῦτα [sc. θεοὺς εἶναι τέχνῃ,
οὐ φύσει, κ.τ.λ.—889 E] πῦρ καὶ ὕδωρ καὶ γῆν καὶ ἀέρα
πρῶτα ἡγεῖσθαι τῶν πάντων εἶναι, καὶ τὴν φύσιν ὀνομάζειν
ταῦτα αὐτά, ψυχὴν δὲ ἐκ τούτων ὕστερον. ἔοικε δὲ οὐ
κινδυνεύειν ἀλλὰ ὄντως σημαίνειν ταῦτα ἡμῖν τῷ λόγῳ.

(*Laws* 891 B, C.)

This passage is useful in so far as it shows how the
metaphysical question of the nature of the soul comes
up for discussion in a practical treatise from which we
might naturally expect metaphysics to be excluded.
In laying down the principles of his ethical system in
the *Laws* Plato finds it necessary to say something
about religion, which, he considers, has an important
influence on the general well-being of the state. This
subject is introduced in the tenth book, and with it the
question of the true nature of the soul is found to be
directly connected. In his vindication of the importance
of religion the Athenian Stranger proceeds to denounce,
and to devise appropriate punishments for, atheists and
those who hold wrong opinions about the gods and
thus exercise a bad influence upon the general morality
of the community. In the course of his investigation
of these erroneous opinions he discovers that they are
largely to be attributed to a dangerous misapprehension
of the true nature of the soul. The tendency of this
misapprehension lies chiefly in the direction of materialism. Plato has all along been no friend to materialism;
ever since he first began to think for himself his thoughts

instinctively took a contrary direction. At times he can hardly conceal his contempt for materialists; and we now see that he considers their doctrines not only contemptible but pernicious. It must be primarily the materialists whom he is attacking in this part of the *Laws*, though his language in the passage quoted might conceivably include certain Pythagoreans who, like Simmias in the *Phaedo*, regarded the soul as a species of harmony. One of the chief offences of materialism is that it lowers the natural dignity of the soul by placing it in the scheme of the universe on a level with the body or even below it. Now we have seen reason to believe that at an earlier stage in his career Plato himself had been drifting towards a conception of the nature of the soul which was in reality materialistic, although he was not at first aware that it was so. True, his procedure was the very reverse of that of the materialists he is here attacking; it was in his zeal for asserting the absolute immateriality of the soul that he had been led to say certain things about its nature which were incompatible with any such immateriality. Long before he wrote the *Laws*, however, he had succeeded in freeing his theory of soul from all taint of materialism. In the *Timaeus* he has made it clear that he rejects materialism as unworthy of a true philosopher: in the *Laws*, writing from the ethical standpoint, he goes further and asserts that it is actually dangerous to morality. In his view no system of philosophy should be entertained which endeavours to explain mind in terms of matter: it is the metaphysician's business to devise a harmonious system by which matter is explained in terms of mind. In full agreement with this position he says a little lower down :—

ΑΘ. Εἰ δὲ ἔστι ταῦτα οὕτως, ἆρ' οὐκ ἐξ ἀνάγκης τὰ ψυχῆς συγγενῆ πρότερα ἂν εἴη γεγονότα τῶν σώματι προσηκόντων, οὔσης ταύτης πρεσβυτέρας ἢ σώματος;

ΚΛ. Ἀνάγκη.

ΑΘ. Δόξα δὴ καὶ ἐπιμέλεια καὶ νοῦς καὶ τέχνη καὶ νόμος σκληρῶν καὶ μαλακῶν καὶ βαρέων καὶ κουφῶν πρότερα ἂν εἴη· καὶ δὴ καὶ τὰ μεγάλα καὶ πρῶτα ἔργα καὶ πράξεις τέχνης ἂν γίγνοιτο, ὄντα ἐν πρώτοις, τὰ δὲ φύσει καὶ φύσις, ἣν οὐκ ὀρθῶς ἐπονομάζουσιν αὐτὸ τοῦτο, ὕστερα καὶ ἀρχόμενα ἂν ἐκ τέχνης εἴη καὶ νοῦ.

(*Laws* 892 A—C.)

At an earlier period Plato would have found it difficult to justify what he says here, recognising as he did self-existent ideas of σκληρόν, μαλακόν, and the like; but he recognises such ideas no longer, and inconsistency is thus avoided. He can say with truth that ψυχή is πρεσβυτέρα σώματος, and the works of ψυχή rank metaphysically above all things that may be regarded as the result of merely material agencies. This philosophical position, which is here stated in a somewhat popular way, is the same as that which has been more scientifically expressed in the *Timaeus*. Ψυχή is now everything: ψυχή—or in this connexion perhaps we ought rather to say νοῦς, which, as we learn from the *Timaeus*, is πρεσβύτερος ψυχῆς in the same way as ψυχή is πρεσβυτέρα σώματος—pluralises itself and thus becomes the source of everything that exists, whether spiritual or material.

Ὧι δὴ ψυχὴ τοὔνομα, τίς τούτου λόγος; ἔχομεν ἄλλον πλὴν τὸν νῦν δὴ ῥηθέντα, τὴν δυναμένην αὐτὴν αὐτὴν κινεῖν κίνησιν; (*Laws* 895 E, 896 A.)

We could hardly have a more emphatic declaration

of the purely abstract quality which characterizes Plato's final conception of the nature of soul as it is in itself (ψυχὴ αὐτὴ καθ' αὑτήν) than that which is contained in the above definition. The Athenian Stranger wishes to discover the λόγος of ψυχή as distinct both from the ὄνομα and from the οὐσία to which both ὄνομα and λόγος apply; and as the result of his search he finds that what we mean by ψυχή is a particular kind of κίνησις. This supplements what we have already learnt from the *Timaeus*, where we are told that the οὐσία, or actual existence, of ψυχή is dependent on σῶμα: apart from σῶμα, ψυχή is merely a λόγος or abstract conception. In the *Phaedrus* the soul was described as τὸ αὐτὸ ἑαυτὸ κινοῦν: the analysis is now carried deeper, and we find that it is ἡ δυναμένη αὐτὴ αὑτὴν κινεῖν κίνησις. Thus there is no longer any necessity to regard ψυχή as a self-existent *thing*, a conception which when applied to separately existent individual ψυχαί inevitably leads to materialism; the self-existent *thing* is ἔμψυχον ζῷον: ψυχή itself is a *principle*, the principle of motion. In other words, ψυχή is the principle of life which animates all things and without which nothing could exist which does exist; as the Athenian Stranger goes on to say:—

εἰ δ' ἔστι τοῦτο οὕτως ἔχον; ἆρα ἔτι ποθοῦμεν μὴ ἱκανῶς δεδεῖχθαι ψυχὴν ταὐτὸν ὂν καὶ τὴν πρώτην γένεσιν καὶ κίνησιν τῶν τε ὄντων καὶ γεγονότων καὶ ἐσομένων καὶ πάντων αὖ τῶν ἐναντίων τούτοις, ἐπειδή γε ἀνεφάνη μεταβολῆς τε καὶ κινήσεως ἁπάσης αἰτία ἅπασιν; (*Laws* 896 A, B.)

In the sphere of γένεσις we analyse actually existing ἔμψυχα into σῶμα and ψυχή: and ψυχή is prior to σῶμα inasmuch as it is the principle which more immediately represents the activity of νοῦς, beyond which we cannot analyse.

ΑΘ. Ἆρ' οὖν τὸ μετὰ τοῦτο ὁμολογεῖν ἀναγκαῖον τῶν τε ἀγαθῶν αἰτίαν εἶναι ψυχὴν καὶ τῶν κακῶν καὶ καλῶν καὶ αἰσχρῶν δικαίων τε καὶ ἀδίκων καὶ πάντων τῶν ἐναντίων, εἴπερ τῶν πάντων γε αὐτὴν θήσομεν αἰτίαν;

ΚΛ. Πῶς γὰρ οὔ;

ΑΘ. Ψυχὴν δὴ διοικοῦσαν καὶ ἐνοικοῦσαν ἐν ἅπασι τοῖς πάντη κινουμένοις μῶν οὐ καὶ τὸν οὐρανὸν ἀνάγκη διοικεῖν φάναι;

ΚΛ. Τί μήν;

ΑΘ. Μίαν ἢ πλείους; πλείους· ἐγὼ ὑπὲρ σφῶν ἀποκρινοῦμαι. δυοῖν μέν γέ που ἔλαττον μηδὲν τιθῶμεν, τῆς τε εὐεργέτιδος καὶ τῆς τἀναντία δυναμένης ἐξεργάζεσθαι.

ΚΛ. Σφόδρα ὀρθῶς εἴρηκας.

ΑΘ. Εἶεν. ἄγει μὲν δὴ ψυχὴ πάντα, κ.τ.λ.

(*Laws* 896 D, E.)

This is obviously a most important passage for the right understanding of the functions of ψυχή in Plato's cosmology. Moreover to anyone who has read the *Timaeus* Plato's language here will certainly appear at first sight rather startling. Soul, we are told, is the cause not only of good things but of bad things as well. We are prepared, it is true, for some such conclusion as this; for when it has once been conceded that soul is the cause of everything in this world, it must follow that in some sense or other bad things are to be ascribed to its operation. But we are brought up sharply when, in answer to his own question whether there is one soul that governs the universe or more than one, the Athenian has no hesitation in replying, πλείους. For

this we are not prepared; and further questions inevitably suggest themselves. What, we may ask, has
become of the absolute unity, the government of the
world by a power of good and good only, which, as
readers of the *Timaeus*, we have come to regard as a
cardinal principle of Plato's philosophy? Here we are
apparently confronted with a good world-soul and a
bad world-soul, which are continually acting in opposition to each other, whereas in the *Timaeus* we have
only one ψυχὴ τοῦ κόσμου, which is one aspect of νοῦς
working continually ἐπὶ τὸ βέλτιστον. This single
world-soul comprises all the soul in the universe, which
from our finite point of view is differentiated into individual souls and so represents the actual pluralised
existence of νοῦς. There is no room for another world-
soul. Thus there is a *prima facie* inconsistency between
the doctrine of the *Laws* and that of the *Timaeus*. Is
this inconsistency capable of explanation? Or rather,
can it be shown that there is not really any inconsistency
at all? I think that on a more careful examination the
apparent discrepancy will be seen to amount to no
more than a difference of statement which may be
accounted for by the fact that Plato is looking at things
from a different standpoint in each of the two Dialogues.
With this passage from the *Laws* we may compare
another, in some respects similar, from the *Theaetetus*.
In the course of a comparison between the philosopher
and the man of the world, who despises righteousness,
Socrates remarks in reference to the latter:—

παραδειγμάτων, ὦ φίλε, ἐν τῷ ὄντι ἑστώτων, τοῦ μὲν
θείου εὐδαιμονεστάτου, τοῦ δὲ ἀθέου ἀθλιωτάτου, οὐχ
ὁρῶντες ὅτι οὕτως ἔχει, ὑπὸ ἠλιθιότητός τε καὶ τῆς

ἐσχάτης ἀνοίας λανθάνουσι τῷ μὲν ὁμοιούμενοι διὰ τὰς
ἀδίκους πράξεις, τῷ δὲ ἀνομοιούμενοι.
(*Theaet.* 176 E, 177 A.)

In the *Laws*, as in the *Theaetetus*, we have the philosophically more accurate statement of the *Timaeus* put
in rather more popular language, just as a modern
philosopher might in certain circumstances speak of
God and the devil. The two ψυχαί, then, must be
understood metaphorically; they personify two opposite
principles which seem to be working against one another
in the world. And here we may note that in the
Philebus Protarchus, speaking from the same popular
point of view, wishes Socrates to find a place for an
αἰτία διακρίσεως as well as an αἰτία μίξεως in the world,
which so far has been divided into πέρας, ἄπειρον, and
μικτόν :—

ΣΩ. Τῆς ξυμμίξεως τούτων πρὸς ἄλληλα τὴν αἰτίαν
ὅρα, καὶ τίθει μοι πρὸς τρισὶν ἐκείνοις τέταρτον τοῦτο.

ΠΡ. Μῶν οὖν σοι καὶ πέμπτου προσδεήσει διάκρισίν
τινος δυναμένου ;

ΣΩ. Τάχ᾽ ἄν· οὐ μὴν οἶμαί γε ἐν τῷ νῦν· ἐὰν δέ τι
δέῃ, συγγνώσει πού μοι σὺ μεταδιώκοντι πέμπτον.
(*Phil.* 23 D, E.)

The αἰτία διακρίσεως, the recognition of which Protarchus demands, would be something very similar to
the bad world-soul of the *Laws*. Socrates has no use
for it in the *Philebus*, but he distinctly recognises that
it may be found useful on some other occasion; and
accordingly it finds a place in the *Theaetetus* and the
Laws, where the course of the argument calls for the
separate recognition of a principle of evil. But here

again another question arises. Are we to suppose that, since νοῦς is a unity, this one νοῦς acts in two different ways, as a principle of evil as well as a principle of good? In so far as it is νοῦς surely it cannot be evil. That is true, and therein lies the solution of the difficulty. For in the *Laws* Plato, it should be observed, speaks of the world as directed not by two νοῖ but by two ψυχαί, a statement not inconsistent with the absolute monism of the *Timaeus*. As I have already pointed out, we do not logically arrive at ψυχή until the process of evolution symbolically described in the *Timaeus* has begun. Νοῦς as such is ultimate and can work only in one way; but there is no reason why ψυχή, that is to say νοῦς *pluralised*, should not act in two ways. There are in the world things that we regard as good and things that we regard as bad, and both classes of things are caused by ψυχή, the principle of motion and life; but for the purposes of the argument Plato in the *Laws* chooses to represent the two aspects of the operation of ψυχή as two different processes caused by two distinct powers or ψυχαί, which can really be distinguished only in logical analysis. In fact the two παραδείγματα of the *Theaetetus*, the two αἰτίαι of the *Philebus*, and the two ψυχαί of the *Laws*, may be compared respectively, from different points of view, on the one hand with the ταὐτόν and θάτερον, and on the other with the νοῦς and ἀνάγκη of the *Timaeus*.

Some light may be thrown on the passage now under consideration by comparing it with the immediate sequel. After enumerating the various physical and mental processes and qualities, good and bad, which are due to the operation of soul, the Stranger sums up the position in the following words :—

καὶ πᾶσιν οἷς ψυχὴ χρωμένη νοῦν μὲν προσλαβοῦσα
ἀεὶ θεῖον ὀρθῶς θεὸς οὖσα ὀρθὰ καὶ εὐδαίμονα παιδαγωγεῖ
πάντα, ἀνοίᾳ δὲ ξυγγενομένη πάντα αὖ τἀναντία τούτοις
ἀπεργάζεται. (*Laws* 897 B.)

Here we seem to have a hint that the two ψυχαί mentioned above are not to be understood literally as two
actually and separately existing world-souls, but as two
logically separable *aspects* of soul.　From the *Timaeus*
we gather that it is the material principle, the distinguishing mark of pluralisation, in which the evil resides,
not in soul as such.　So here we find that good is
caused by ψυχή in so far as it is νοῦν προσλαβοῦσα,
and evil in so far as it is ἀνοίᾳ ξυγγενομένη.　The distinction is significant.　So far as ψυχή represents νοῦς
in its true nature—and no farther—its works are good ;
in proportion as it recedes from νοῦς they are bad.
Ψυχή is in a sense intermediate between νοῦς and σῶμα,
as we have seen in the *Timaeus*; hence remoteness from
νοῦς means a proportionate approximation to σῶμα.　We
may infer, then, that it is the σῶμα element as opposed to
the νοῦς element in ψυχή that is really the cause of evil;
but inasmuch as ψυχή cannot actually coalesce either
with νοῦς or with σῶμα but must always contain both
elements, though in ever varying proportions, it is true to
say that ψυχή is the cause of good and evil alike.　If we
could have ψυχή absolutely pure and uncontaminated
by σῶμα, that is, if ψυχή could have the characteristics
of νοῦς alone, it would be absolutely good : there would
be no evil.　But in our world of pluralised existence
this can never be ; for as soon as we have pluralisation,
evil for some reason of necessity follows.　The plurality
of separately existing ψυχαί of which the world is

composed must needs be united with σώματα, and
hence their works can never be perfectly good. Moreover just as in the *Timaeus* we see that ταὐτόν and
θάτερον are elements both of the world-soul and of
individual souls, so from the standpoint of the *Laws*
it may be said that the individual personality, no less
than the world as a whole, contains within it two ψυχαί
or two aspects of ψυχή. So far as the individual is
concerned, ἡ εὐεργέτις ψυχή will be his soul as it would
be in itself, uncontaminated by association with the
body—the ψυχὴ αὐτὴ καθ᾽ αὑτήν of the *Phaedo*; while
ἡ τἀναντία δυναμένη ἀπεργάζεσθαι ψυχή will be his soul
as it may be conceived merely as representing the
principle of pluralisation, and therefore necessarily manifesting itself in the form of body. In effect, then, the
two souls are no more than two aspects of the same
soul. The good soul is the soul as it is or would be
in itself, the true ψυχή which, as such, is πρεσβυτέρα
σώματος: the bad soul is a sort of personification of
the material principle which is necessarily involved in
the pluralisation of νοῦς.

It will thus be seen that from one point of view the
bad soul is really σῶμα masquerading as ψυχή: θάτερον
for the moment assumes the characteristics of eternity,
which properly belong to ταὐτόν. It may be worth
while here just to glance at the significance of this in
a more general aspect. We have already had occasion
to notice an instance of the same thing in the *Timaeus*,
where time is described as αἰῶνος αἰώνιος εἰκών: that
which is not in itself eternal nevertheless is in a sense
eternal, inasmuch as it represents a principle eternally
present in the nature of things. With this we may
compare another passage in the *Timaeus*:—

ἐν ᾧ δὲ ἐγγιγνόμενα ἀεὶ ἕκαστα αὐτῶν φαντάζεται καὶ
πάλιν ἐκεῖθεν ἀπόλλυται, μόνον ἐκεῖνο αὖ προσαγορεύειν
τῷ τε τοῦτο καὶ τῷ τόδε προσχρωμένους ὀνόματι, τὸ δὲ
ὁποιονοῦν τι, θερμὸν ἢ λευκὸν ἢ καὶ ὁτιοῦν τῶν ἐναντίων,
καὶ πάνθ᾽ ὅσα ἐκ τούτων, μηδὲν ἐκεῖνο αὖ τούτων καλεῖν.

(*Tim.* 49 E, 50 A.)

We are here told that, strictly speaking, the continually
changing phenomena of this world have no right to the
appellations τοῦτο and τόδε, which can properly be used
only to designate that which is unchanging and eternal.
Nevertheless we are justified in using such expressions
when we are speaking of 'that in which things severally
become and appear,' that is to say the ὑποδοχή or space,
although space really represents θάτερον in one of its
aspects. Space, however, which we usually tend to
associate only with the world of Becoming, in a sense
belongs also to the eternal world of Being; for it
represents the eternally existing law of nature which
ordains that the unextended must necessarily manifest
itself in the form of the extended. This is entirely in
accord with the description of time as αἰῶνος αἰώνιος
εἰκών. Θάτερον operates both as time and as matter,
which in the last resort is the same thing as space, and
in each case it is in a sense ταὐτόν. What Plato means
is that, though θάτερον is the principle in accordance
with which things are differentiated, it remains itself as
a principle immutable : it is, as it were, ταὐτόν with
itself. This may serve to illustrate my meaning in
saying that the bad soul of the *Laws* is a sort of
personification of the material principle. It is called
in this connexion ψυχή because it appears to us as
a power continually active in the universe and, as such,

continually thwarting the beneficent activity of ψυχή proper.

The chief lesson to be learnt from a comparison of the two ψυχαί of the *Laws* with the two παραδείγματα of the *Theaetetus*, the two αἰτίαι of the *Philebus*, and the ταὐτόν and θάτερον or νοῦς and ἀνάγκη of the *Timaeus*, is this, that Plato makes no attempt to explain material phenomena in terms of finite mind. All things, whether spiritual or material, coalesce in the ultimate unity of absolute Mind; but so far as we and our finite perceptions are concerned, Plato frankly adopts a dualistic position. From our point of view mind and matter are two different things, and matter is not merely part of the content of our minds, but something distinct from them and external to them. It seems to me that this is a better statement of Plato's views than that of Mr Archer-Hind, who shrinks from admitting that Plato can in any sense be called a dualist, and therefore tries to explain away what seems to be a distinct recognition in the *Timaeus* of ideas corresponding to the four elements. I on the other hand think that the two ψυχαί of the *Laws* certainly reflect a dualistic system; but we must always bear in mind that this system is very far removed from the crude dualism of previous philosophers. It is a kind of relative dualism, a dualism which is founded upon a carefully reasoned system of idealistic monism. The mind and the matter of our world, though external to one another, coalesce in the unity of the absolute Mind.

ἐπεὶ δὲ ἀεὶ ψυχὴ συντεταγμένη σώματι τότε μὲν ἄλλῳ, τότε δὲ ἄλλῳ, μεταβάλλει παντοίας μεταβολὰς δι' ἑαυτὴν ἢ δι' ἑτέραν ψυχήν, οὐδὲν ἄλλο ἔργον τῷ πεττευτῇ

λείπεται πλὴν μετατιθέναι τὸ μὲν ἄμεινον γιγνόμενον
ἦθος εἰς βελτίω τόπον, χεῖρον δὲ εἰς τὸν χείρονα, κατὰ
τὸ πρέπον αὐτῶν ἕκαστον, ἵνα τῆς προσηκούσης μοίρας
λαγχάνῃ. (*Laws* 903 D, E.)

This passage is interesting as showing that Plato
maintains the doctrine of metempsychosis up to the last.
It is introduced here from the moral point of view.
Everything that we do in this world is of importance,
because the character of our next life is in every case
conditioned by our conduct in this. But though the
application of the doctrine in this place is primarily
ethical, it is still not without its metaphysical significance.
In this connexion the description of ψυχή as ἀεὶ συντεταγμένη σώματι is especially noteworthy. Soul is
'always constitutionally joined with body'; there is no
state in which ψυχαί are ἄνευ σωμάτων τὸ παράπαν,
a state which was contemplated in the *Phaedo*. Divine
Providence or natural law, here referred to under the
figure of the πεττευτής, ensures that individual souls
continually migrate from one body to another; but
there can never be a time during which they are left
without any bodies at all. Such a thing would be
contrary to the law of nature, which must always work
in a certain way: this truth is here expressed in the
form of a *limitation* of the power or function of the
supreme controller of human destiny—οὐδὲν ἄλλο ἔργον
τῷ πεττευτῇ λείπεται πλὴν μετατιθέναι.

A consideration of the foregoing passages is enough
to show that so far as the theory of soul is concerned
the *Laws* is in all respects in agreement with the
Timaeus, though things are not always stated in exactly
the same way in the two Dialogues. The apparent

differences between them are in fact no less instructive
than their obvious points of agreement; as we have seen
in discussing the question of the two ψυχαί which are
said to direct the universe, the *Laws* in this respect
furnishes a useful commentary on the *Timaeus*. Thus
from the *Laws* we are enabled to supplement the
teaching of the *Timaeus* by seeing the same questions
treated from a somewhat different standpoint. The
purpose of the *Timaeus* is primarily metaphysical; and
regarded as a statement of Plato's metaphysical opinions
it is to be considered as representing them in their final
form. On the other hand the philosophy of the *Laws*
is in its general character not metaphysical but ethical,
and even in this sphere the *Laws* is not a strictly
philosophical treatise, but a treatise on popular and
practical ethics. The ideal state which is contemplated
in the *Republic* has been shown by Plato's metaphysical
researches to be incapable of earthly realisation; he
therefore worked out his metaphysical scheme afresh,
and then returning once more to his former ethical
and sociological studies he gives us the *Laws* as his
δεύτερος πλοῦς. In these circumstances it would be
unreasonable to look in the *Laws* for any new metaphysical doctrine or even for any important development
of the doctrine with which we are by this time familiar.
But though the *Laws* is not primarily metaphysical and
makes no essential addition to what we already know of
Plato's metaphysics, it nevertheless possesses an interest
and importance of its own even from a metaphysical
point of view. On reading the tenth book we cannot
help feeling that there is all the time a metaphysical
system in the background, and that this metaphysical
system is that which has been elaborated in the *Timaeus*.

In certain passages it is not difficult to discover a re-statement in a new and more popular form of some of the old doctrines contained in that Dialogue ; and from a comparison of the statements on the same subject in the two Dialogues a good deal is to be learnt in so far as the one throws light on the other. What is important to notice is that they are not inconsistent but supplement one another. In particular we have to observe that Plato's conception of the nature of the soul is the same in the *Laws* as it is in the *Timaeus* : in the *Laws*, however, his theory is to a certain extent popularised and made use of for the purpose of supporting a system of morality in the essential truth of which his confidence has remained throughout unshaken.

CHAPTER X.

IMMORTALITY AND THE LATER PLATONISM.

In reviewing the *Timaeus* and the *Laws* my main object has been to bring out the chief features of what I have called Plato's later theory of soul. In the course of this investigation the question of immortality has inevitably been left rather in the background. It remains, then, to consider how far, if at all, the immortality of the soul—that is to say, not merely the essential indestructibility of soul as a universal principle, but the everlasting continuance of the same personalities—is implied in Plato's philosophy as finally reconstituted. In order that this might be done satisfactorily it was obviously important first to determine the general character of his conception of the nature of the soul in this later period. We have seen reason to believe that this conception differs materially from that which was the natural outcome of the earlier Theory of Ideas. It is now time to indicate more clearly than has yet been done the main lines of difference between the earlier and later phases of Plato's theory of soul with special reference to the question of immortality.

So far as the theory of soul is concerned I have

throughout taken the *Phaedo* as typical of the earlier Platonism and the *Timaeus* of the later; and if we wish to compare the later theory in its most finished form with the earlier, the natural course to pursue is to contrast the statements which bear on this subject in the one Dialogue with those in the other. But Plato was doubtless well on his way towards a reconstruction of his theory of soul some time before he embodied his final metaphysical opinions in the *Timaeus*. He must have become conscious of the defects inherent in his earlier theory very soon after he had begun to see reason to doubt the soundness of the Theory of Ideas in the form in which it was first stated; for the two were bound to stand or fall together. If this is so, we should naturally expect to see some indication of this consciousness before the later theory takes definite shape, just as we are prepared for changes in the Theory of Ideas before we are made acquainted with the actual details of the new theory. The stages in the development of the theory of soul are of course not so clearly marked as the process of change in the Theory of Ideas: to expect this would be to expect too much: for ontology, not psychology, is Plato's first object at this period. But we are not left altogether unprepared for the form which the later theory of soul takes in the *Timaeus*.

The first clear signs of the impending change may, I think, be seen in a Dialogue which in all probability is intermediate between the *Phaedo* and the *Timaeus*, I mean the *Philebus*. In the *Philebus* we read:—

ΣΩ. Τὴν ἄρα ἐπάγουσαν ἐπὶ τὰ ἐπιθυμούμενα ἀποδείξας μνήμην ὁ λόγος ψυχῆς ξύμπασαν τήν τε ὁρμὴν καὶ ἐπιθυμίαν καὶ τὴν ἀρχὴν τοῦ ζῴου παντὸς ἀπέφηνεν.

ΠΡ. Ὀρθότατα.

ΣΩ. Διψῆν ἄρα ἡμῶν τὸ σῶμα ἢ πεινῆν ἤ τι τῶν
τοιούτων πάσχειν οὐδαμῆ ὁ λόγος αἱρεῖ.

ΠΡ. Ἀληθέστατα. (*Phil.* 35 D.)

Now in the *Phaedo* Plato makes a number of statements
which, superficially at any rate, are not in agreement
with this passage. As an instance we may take the
following:—

μυρίας μὲν γὰρ ἡμῖν ἀσχολίας παρέχει τὸ σῶμα διὰ
τὴν ἀναγκαίαν τροφήν· ἔτι δὲ ἄν τινες νόσοι προσπέσωσιν,
ἐμποδίζουσιν ἡμῶν τὴν τοῦ ὄντος θήραν. ἐρώτων δὲ καὶ
ἐπιθυμιῶν καὶ φόβων καὶ εἰδώλων παντοδαπῶν καὶ
φλυαρίας ἐμπίπλησιν ἡμᾶς πολλῆς, ὥστε τὸ λεγόμενον
ὡς ἀληθῶς τῷ ὄντι ὑπ' αὐτοῦ οὐδὲ φρονῆσαι ἡμῖν ἐγγίγνεται οὐδέποτε οὐδέν. καὶ γὰρ πολέμους καὶ στάσεις
καὶ μάχας οὐδὲν ἄλλο παρέχει ἢ τὸ σῶμα καὶ αἱ τούτου
ἐπιθυμίαι. (*Phaedo* 66 B, C.)

Thus in the *Phaedo* we see that the origin of the passions
is traced to the body, while in the *Philebus* it is traced
to the soul. The apparent discrepancy between the two
Dialogues which these two passages exhibit is noticed
by Mr Archer-Hind in the Introduction of his edition
of the *Phaedo*, and there is no need to go into the whole
question here. Mr Archer-Hind points out that in
reality no inconsistency is involved. The more correct
statement is that of the *Philebus*. Passions ought
strictly to be regarded as belonging to the soul : at the
same time they belong to her not in virtue of her own
nature but only in virtue of her association with the
body : that is to say, from one point of view they may
be regarded as belonging to the body, while from

another they are seen to belong more properly to the
soul. This is no doubt true: but may we not also trace
a deeper underlying significance in these two divergent
accounts of the source of the passions, something that
would make it more natural in the Plato of the *Philebus*
to ascribe their origin unequivocally to the soul and
stigmatize as inaccurate any theory that would refer them
to the body? In the *Phaedo*, as we have seen, body and
soul are considered to be absolutely and essentially
separable; such separation is effected by death, which
leaves them αὐτὸ καθ᾽ αὑτό and αὐτὴ καθ᾽ αὑτήν respectively. In such circumstances, therefore, it would
be quite natural to distinguish body and soul in such
a way as to assign to them perfectly distinct spheres
of influence. Of course there are certain pleasures which
belong to the soul quite apart from her association with
the body; but there are others which are, so to speak,
foisted upon her by the body, and from which she may
be entirely freed by death. Soul is the immortal part
of us, and in the attempt to realise her own nature she
would fain be continually striving after higher things
than can in this life be achieved : body, on the other
hand, is the mortal and worldly part, perpetually en-
cumbering the soul in her endeavour to escape from the
uncongenial environment of this world of degrading
passions. This attitude is consistently maintained all
through the *Phaedo*; and such being the case it would
of course be unnatural not to attribute exclusively to
the agency of the body those passions and desires which
are the very means which it employs in its continual
attempt to encumber the soul and drag her down from
her high estate. But by the time Plato came to write the
Philebus he was already beginning to take up a position

totally different from that of the *Phaedo* so far as the mutual relations of body and soul are concerned. He does not any longer regard body and soul as two quite separate entities existing now together and now apart; he is beginning to see that the one necessarily implies the other as a condition of what we may call actual existence. He would now no longer recognise for the individual a state τεθνηκός, in which body and soul exist absolutely apart from one another. Θάνατος may indeed still be defined, as it is defined in the *Phaedo*, as χωρισμὸς ψυχῆς ἀπὸ σώματος: but if we so define it, we must clearly understand that the particular χωρισμός which is involved in death is the separation of *this* soul from *this* body, and that is all. We must cast away all expectation that souls may exist individually after death ἄνευ σωμάτων τὸ παράπαν: for souls can exist *actually*, as distinct from *logically*, only by manifesting themselves in the form of ἔμψυχα σώματα. In accordance with such a theory of soul, which must by this time have formed implicitly if not explicitly an integral part of Plato's philosophy, it is not surprising to find that such desires and passions as were formerly held to originate in the body are in the *Philebus* definitely referred to the soul. For soul is the only reality: body is merely the form under which soul necessarily manifests herself.

Against this view, however, it may possibly be objected that, so far as desires and passions are concerned, the *Republic*, a Dialogue belonging to the same period as the *Phaedo*, reflects a theory of the nature of the soul similar to that which we find in the *Philebus*. In the ninth book of the *Republic* in the course of the discussion concerning the nature of pleasure and pain we have the following passage:—

Οὐκ ἐναντίον φαμὲν λύπην ἡδονῇ; Καὶ μάλα. Οὐκοῦν
καὶ τὸ μήτε χαίρειν μήτε λυπεῖσθαι εἶναί τι; Εἶναι
μέντοι. Μεταξὺ τούτοιν ἀμφοῖν ἐν μέσῳ ὄν, ἡσυχίαν
τινὰ περὶ ταῦτα τῆς ψυχῆς; ἢ οὐχ οὕτως αὐτὸ λέγεις;
Οὕτως. (*Rep.* 583 C.)

I do not think, however, that the somewhat vague expression ἡσυχία περὶ ταῦτα τῆς ψυχῆς can be held to imply
that all λυπαί and ἡδοναί are referred exclusively to ψυχή
as their *origin*. All that can legitimately be deduced
from it is that pleasure and pain *affect* the soul; when
they do not do so, the soul is in a state of ἡσυχία in
regard to them. Such a statement is perfectly consistent
with the hypothesis that the passions in question
originate in the body and end by affecting the soul.
And in fact such a theory certainly seems to be implied
a little further on :—

ἀλλὰ μέντοι, εἶπον, αἵ γε διὰ τοῦ σώματος ἐπὶ τὴν
ψυχὴν τείνουσαι καὶ λεγόμεναι ἡδοναὶ σχεδὸν αἱ πλεῖσταί
τε καὶ μέγισται τούτου τοῦ εἴδους εἰσί, λυπῶν τινὲς ἀπαλ-
λαγαί. (*Rep.* 584 C.)

Here there is an implied distinction between the
pleasures of the body and the pleasures of the soul,
and the bodily pleasures pass through the body to
affect the soul (ἐπὶ τὴν ψυχὴν τείνουσαι). Of course
I do not mean to say that expressions of this kind are
incompatible with Plato's later views; as a matter of
fact we have the same distinction of pleasures expressed
in much the same way in the *Philebus*. What I mean is
that the necessarily metaphorical character of this way
of speaking was more clearly recognised by Plato in his
later Dialogues; and in this connexion the emphatic

way in which even such sensations as hunger and thirst
are definitely said in the *Philebus* not to originate in
the body seems to me to be not without significance.
We find no such clear pronouncement in any earlier
Dialogue; on the contrary such sensations as hunger
and thirst would at an earlier period inevitably be
referred to the body as their origin.

The process of logical reasoning which caused Plato
to modify his theory of soul and suggested to him the
lines on which it should be modified may perhaps be
best understood by reference to the *Parmenides*, the
Dialogue in which he seems first to have taken himself
to task for the faultiness of the logical method which
had conduced to the formation of his earlier Theory of
Ideas. Plato's position as regards immortality was, as
we have seen, largely determined by the manner in
which the Theory of Ideas grew up in his mind. The
possibility of the complete separation of soul from body
was suggested to him by his own earlier metaphysical
theory, which recognised the real existence of the ideas
as being quite independent of the apparent existence
of phenomena. In his conversation with the youthful
Socrates Parmenides lays great stress on this absolute
separation of ideas from the phenomena which nevertheless partake of them:—

καί μοι εἰπέ, αὐτὸς σὺ οὕτω διῄρησαι ὡς λέγεις,
χωρὶς μὲν εἴδη αὐτὰ ἄττα, χωρὶς δὲ τὰ τούτων αὖ μετέ-
χοντα; (*Parm.* 130 B.)

The essential χωρισμός between soul and body in the
Phaedo is, as we have seen, of a character very similar
to this. Thus the two doctrines were developed con-
currently. But Plato gradually came to perceive that

this course of development was after all leading him in a
direction which he was least of all disposed to follow ; he
was in fact involving himself in a materialistic conception
on the one hand of the idea, and on the other hand of
the soul. So far as the ideas are concerned, this is made
clear in the earlier part of the *Parmenides*. The latter
part of the same Dialogue indicates to some extent the
way in which the Theory of Ideas is to be remodelled ;
and also it helps, I think, incidentally to elucidate the
form which the modified theory of soul is assuming.
Dr Jackson has shown (*Journal of Philology*, vol. XI)
that the second hypothesis (εἰ ἓν ἔστιν) discussed by
Parmenides in the Dialogue bearing his name investi-
gates a ἕν which answers in every respect to the later
Platonic ἕν, which we know sometimes as νοῦς, sometimes as ἀγαθόν. This is a ἕν which is divisible primarily
into πολλά (a definite number of kinds) and secondarily
into ἄπειρα (an indefinite number of particulars grouped
according to these kinds). We notice also that this ἕν
has an existence in time :—

Εἶναι μέν που αὐτῷ ὑπάρχει, εἴπερ ἓν ἔστιν. Ναί. Τὸ
δὲ εἶναι ἄλλο τί ἐστιν ἢ μέθεξις οὐσίας μετὰ χρόνου τοῦ
παρόντος, ὥσπερ τὸ ἦν μετὰ τοῦ παρεληλυθότος καὶ αὖ τὸ
ἔσται μετὰ τοῦ μέλλοντος οὐσίας κοινωνία ; Ἔστι γάρ.
Μετέχει μὲν ἄρα χρόνου, εἴπερ καὶ τοῦ εἶναι. Πάνυ γε.
Οὐκοῦν πορευομένου τοῦ χρόνου ; Ναί.

(Parm. 151 E, 152 A.)

Not till we come to the *Timaeus* do we see the full
significance of the conclusion that ἕν, as properly understood, μετέχει χρόνου, εἴπερ καὶ τοῦ εἶναι. To this
hypothesis is added a sort of appendix beginning as
follows :—

ἔτι δὴ τὸ τρίτον λέγωμεν. τὸ ἓν εἰ ἔστιν οἷον διεληλύθαμεν, ἆρ' οὐκ ἀνάγκη αὐτό, ἕν τε ὂν καὶ πολλὰ
καὶ μήτε ἓν μήτε πολλὰ καὶ μετέχον χρόνου, ὅτι μὲν
ἔστιν ἕν, οὐσίας μετέχειν ποτέ, ὅτι δ' οὐκ ἔστι, μὴ μετέχειν αὖ ποτὲ οὐσίας; (*Parm.* 155 E.)

This ἕν, therefore, being both 'one' and 'not-one,' as
'one' μετέχει οὐσίας and as 'not-one' οὐ μετέχει
οὐσίας. But it cannot at the same time and in the
same sense be both μετέχον οὐσίας and οὐ μετέχον
οὐσίας: hence in order to account for its passing from
the one state to the other we must suppose a moment of
transition (τὸ ἐξαίφνης), which is thus described :—

τὸ γὰρ ἐξαίφνης τοιόνδε τι ἔοικε σημαίνειν, ὡς ἐξ
ἐκείνου μεταβάλλον εἰς ἑκάτερον. οὐ γὰρ ἔκ γε τοῦ
ἑστάναι ἑστῶτος ἔτι μεταβάλλει, οὐδ' ἐκ τῆς κινήσεως
κινουμένης ἔτι μεταβάλλει· ἀλλ' ἡ ἐξαίφνης αὕτη φύσις
ἄτοπός τις ἐγκάθηται μεταξὺ τῆς κινήσεώς τε καὶ στά-
σεως, ἐν χρόνῳ οὐδενὶ οὖσα, καὶ εἰς ταύτην δὴ καὶ ἐκ
ταύτης τό τε κινούμενον μεταβάλλει ἐπὶ τὸ ἑστάναι
καὶ τὸ ἑστὸς ἐπὶ τὸ κινεῖσθαι. κ.τ.λ.

(*Parm.* 156 D, E.)

Thus the moment in which change is effected from
one condition of existence to another is not in time at
all. Now it is a characteristic of the particular ἕν which
is examined in the second hypothesis that each member
of the antitheses ὅμοιον—ἀνόμοιον, ἴσον—ἄνισον, and
the like can be predicated of it. But at the actual moment
of transition from the one state to the other it cannot
bear the predication of either member of such antitheses.
In other words, at such moments the ἕν is not in
relations at all ; consequently there can be no predication

about it. The ἕν which is here being discussed is a pluralised ἕν, and it is susceptible of predication only in so far as its parts stand in relations to one another. At the moment of transition from one relation to another nothing can be predicated of it, because at such moments it is not in time at all, and for the purposes of this hypothesis, as we have seen, real existence necessarily implies existence in time. Thus we arrive at the conclusion that at such moments of transition the ἕν is not actually existent: in so far as it may be conceived as having quitted one relation and not yet entered another, it is merely an abstraction. This mode of reasoning may, it seems to me, be applied quite legitimately to the particular form of relation subsisting between soul and body. In the Dialogues of the earlier period as well as in those of the later the doctrine of metempsychosis is continually coming to the front. Individual souls after informing one body pass on to inform another. Now these migrating souls may from one point of view be regarded as furnishing an instance of ἕν (in this case existing in the form of ἄπειρα) changing its relations, changing, that is, from *this*—a state of union with a particular body—to something which is *not-this*—a similar state of union with another particular body. For the soul is throughout assumed to be something immaterial; but Plato is now beginning to realise, what he had failed to realise when writing the *Phaedo*, that that which is absolutely immaterial as such οὐ μετέχει χρόνου: and that which οὐ μετέχει χρόνου also οὐ μετέχει οὐσίας. Thus an individual soul on ceasing to inform a particular body must at once inform another particular body; if it retains its individuality there can be no interval of time

between one incarnation and the next. If there were
any such interval, during that period a portion of soul
would have ceased temporarily to exist; and such a
hypothesis would be incompatible with Plato's great
principle which he consistently maintains, that the sum
of all things is constant. Transmigration, then, is
momentary; it is an instance of τὸ ἐξαίφνης. We have
to regard an individual soul as the universal Mind
informing or partially manifesting itself under the form
of a particular portion and combination of matter. The
individual soul is that which informs a particular body
and causes it to approximate to the idea of some natural
kind. Apart from such informing the individual soul
would be nothing. Plato, it is true, nowhere states his
theory in exactly this way; but that such a theory of
soul is implied in his philosophy certainly seems to be
a natural inference from a comparison of the logic of the
Parmenides with the metaphysics of the *Timaeus*. We
do not find a trace of any such logic or any such
abstract conception of the nature of the soul in the
Phaedo or in any other of the earlier Dialogues; it is
the product of Plato's maturest thought.

I hope I have now made sufficiently clear what
I take to be the most important change in Plato's
theory of soul which worked itself out in the interval
that elapsed between the writing of the *Phaedo* and the
Timaeus. If such a change did really take place, which
I cannot bring myself to doubt, it is obvious that it
must seriously affect the conception of immortality
which we find in the *Phaedo*. In his earlier period,
Plato, as I understand him, regards the individual soul
as being in her own nature not an abstraction merely
but a *thing*, though an immaterial thing. The soul

according to this view is simply one partner in the combination ζῶν and essentially separable from body, the other partner in the combination; and in virtue of her immortality she may thus enjoy a purely immaterial existence. It is true that metempsychosis is at this period a recognised doctrine, but an interval of time is supposed to occur between one incarnation and the next, during which the bodiless soul has an independent existence *somewhere*; and the great hope which the belief in immortality inspires in the mind of the philosopher is that his soul may never have to enter another body and may thus be free to contemplate the ideas. According to the later theory of soul which Plato's more thorough grasp of the problems of metaphysics has caused him to adopt, immortality can have no such prospect as this to offer.

Since, then, the doctrine of the immortality of the soul has been found to be incapable of playing the part which it had been hoped it would play in his philosophy, it is not unreasonable to ask whether Plato continued to the end to believe in the truth of this doctrine. If we answer this question in the affirmative, we have then to determine the form in which the belief presented itself to his mind and the place which it occupies in his philosophical system. In order to decide how far the new theory of soul is compatible with a theory of immortality we shall have to return once more to the consideration of certain passages in the *Timaeus*. Before doing so, however, we may remark that all that Plato has hitherto *proved* in this connexion on his own principles remains valid still. But this, as we have seen, does not amount to very much. All that he has shown in the *Phaedrus*, the *Republic*, and the *Phaedo* is that

soul, the universal life-giving principle, is indestructible ;
that is to say, nowhere and at no time in the universe
can there be any absolute extinction of soul or life.
The sum of all things, spirit as well as matter, must
ever remain constant; and soul having had no beginning
can have no end. At the same time it is true that in
all these Dialogues the general tone of the discussion
and the inferences that are drawn from the proof that
soul is immortal seem to show beyond all question that
Plato did as a matter of fact believe in the immortality
of the individual. But he has not proved even on his
own premisses that individual souls, as such, are immortal,
nor can he have thought that he had really proved any
such thing. What, then, is his attitude towards the
question of personal immortality in the *Timaeus*, the
Dialogue in which he has set forth in the greatest detail
the results of his latest and most finished metaphysical
thought ?

According to the fundamental metaphysical doctrine
of the *Timaeus* what we know as a plurality of individual
souls really represents the absolute unity of the universal
Mind existing—as true unity, if it is to have any meaning beyond that of the Eleatic ἕν as interpreted by
Zeno, must always exist—in the form of multiplicity.
No finite mind can directly apprehend the essential
unity of the universal Mind as it is in itself, because
every finite mind is itself a fraction of the same universal
Mind. Such notion as we may have of the ultimate
unity can come to us only through the medium of
pluralised existence. Νοῦς, as we apprehend it, is
differentiated first into classes (πολλά) and then further
into individuals (ἄπειρα) arranged in groups representing
those classes. Now it is a fixed law inherent in the

essential nature of νοῦς that besides existing as ἕν it
must exist also both as πολλά and as ἄπειρα: but this
of course does not imply that either the πολλά or the
ἄπειρα must necessarily remain from our point of view
permanently the same in content and character. It is
true that according to Plato's theory of the universe
nature seems to be 'careful of the type'; for in his
scheme there is an idea permanently existing which
accounts for the existence of each of the πολλά or
natural kinds, whatever they may be. Even the existence of this permanent idea, however, would not, so far
as we can see, prevent any particular type, as we
apprehend it, from dying out; for the εἰσιόντα καὶ
ἐξιόντα in question, that is to say, the immanent forms
which in the world of phenomena represent the idea of
this type, cannot do their work unless they find the
appropriate material conditions present; then only can
they give rise to actual material representations of the
idea. The idea itself is permanent, but its manifestation
in the same form is not necessarily so. In fact Plato
himself tells us that the γένος as well as the particular
ζῷον is liable to change :—

πᾶσα γὰρ ξύστασις νόσων τρόπον τινὰ τῇ τῶν ζῴων
φύσει προσέοικε. καὶ γὰρ ἡ τούτων ξύνοδος ἔχουσα
τεταγμένους τοῦ βίου γίγνεται χρόνους τοῦ τε γένους
ξύμπαντος καὶ κατ᾽ αὐτὸ τὸ ζῷον εἱμαρμένον ἕκαστον
ἔχον τὸν βίον φύεται, χωρὶς τῶν ἐξ ἀνάγκης παθη-
μάτων. (*Tim.* 89 B, C.)

The coupling together of the species and the individual
in this connexion is interesting. It would seem that
the theory of natural kinds which forms so important
an element in the Platonic ontology is strangely modern
in that it can readily be connected with the Darwinian

theory of evolution. Mr Archer-Hind has noticed the
approximation of Plato's physical theories to Darwinism
in another passage of the *Timaeus* (76 D). It is as if
a sort of metempsychosis were provided for the species
as well as for the individual soul. The universal type
may be represented at different times by different particulars, just as the individual soul may at different times
be localised in different bodies. Plato does not commit
himself so far as to assert definitely what are the
natural kinds or species. They may be narrower or
they may be wider than we suppose. A particular idea
may at a given period be represented or partially represented by wolves: but wolves may die out and the
idea be represented by dogs or foxes. Each idea
is the absolute νοῦς manifesting itself according to a
fixed law in a particular way; as such it must be eternal:
but it need not be so in so far as it is represented by the
members of a particular species as we at a given time
apprehend the characteristics of that species. The ideas
themselves must be permanent; for, as has been hinted
in the *Parmenides*, they are παραδείγματα ἑστηκότα ἐν
τῇ φύσει: that is to say, they are laws of nature, in
accordance with which the particular members of a given
species strive to approximate to a hypothetically existing perfect particular of that species. In other words,
they typify special forms of life which may be differentiated from one another according to a graduated scale.

So much for Plato's carefulness of the type: and
now what has he to say about the single life? In order
to understand this part of his theory we must go back
for a moment to the account of the creation of the world
as it is represented in the mythical narrative of the
Timaeus. In particular we must turn to the thirteenth
and fourteenth chapters (41 A sqq.) on which I have

already commented at some length in my examination of the *Timaeus*. In this part of the Dialogue the myth purports to describe the creation of the souls of mortal creatures ; and if we wish to discover whether Plato's metaphysical system recognises individual immortality or not, it is here that we shall be most likely to find what we want. The δημιουργός, we are told, first created those beings whom he addresses as θεοὶ θεῶν ; they are gods who in the physical universe manifest themselves to us in the form of fixed stars. He creates both their souls and their bodies, and also by his own will effects the union of these souls and bodies. Metaphysically this means that as separately existing beings they are the product of the direct thinking of νοῦς, and the essential nature of this thinking ensures that they of necessity manifest themselves in the form of fixed stars. That is to say, not only as ψυχαί but as ἔμψυχα ζῷα they are the direct thoughts of νοῦς, and as such they represent the highest form of finite existence. Dr Jackson would, I believe, express this truth by say-ing that there is a distinct idea for each one of them, an idea which is represented in perpetuity by a single particular : though for my own part I should not state it in this way. But in any case what we have to notice is that the permanence of their souls is of a different kind from the permanence of their bodies. Their souls as being direct determinations of the absolute Mind are of their own nature immortal and therefore pre-serve their individuality permanently. Not so their bodies. Their bodies too are in a sense immortal ; that is to say, they are not subject to that form of dissolution which we know as death. But they are not, like the souls which inform them, essentially indestructible. According to the myth the θεοὶ θεῶν are distinctly told that in this sense they are not of their own nature immortal: their immortality is dependent upon the will of their creator, which, however, the creator tells them, is a more powerful guarantee than any merely physical law. The θεοὶ θεῶν, therefore, unlike the inferior creatures which compose the θνητὰ γένη, retain their unity with the same body permanently. Here, then, at any rate we have an instance of immortality in the κόσμος as Plato conceived it. It does not, it is true, involve an absolutely immaterial existence for individuals such as was contemplated in the *Phaedo*; but it is nevertheless a case of individual immortality about which there can hardly be any question.

At this point, however, another question presents itself. What, it may be asked, is the exact meaning of this 'will of God' which is more powerful than the natural law which governs material phenomena? In what way does it assure to the θεοὶ θεῶν a form of immortality to which other finite beings cannot aspire? I take it that what Plato means is something of this kind. We know, as I have had occasion to remark before, that so far as the material world is concerned Plato remained to the last a thorough-going Heraclitean. All material things in so far as they are merely material are governed by the universally operative principle of πάντα ῥεῖ. This physical theory, therefore, would compel him to admit that no body of any kind whatsoever can be exempt from the law of universal flux. Everything that is σωματοειδές must always be ἐπίρρυτον καὶ ἀπόρρυτον. As a result, then, of the universal working of this natural law, even the θεοὶ θεῶν will not have permanently bodies that remain identically the same.

Some of the particles which compose their bodies will
be continually flying off, and fresh particles will be
continually arriving to supply their place. The will of
the creator does not interfere with this natural law:
that would be impossible: for the will of the creator
itself after all symbolizes a natural law. But what it does
is this: it ensures that the bodies of the θεοὶ θεῶν shall
not be weakened by this perpetual flux and shall therefore not suffer dissolution and death. Such appears to be
the natural interpretation of the creator's statement:—

> τὸ μὲν οὖν δή δεθὲν πᾶν λυτόν, τό γε μὴν καλῶς
> ἁρμοσθὲν καὶ ἔχον εὖ λύειν ἐθέλειν κακοῦ. δι᾽ ἃ καὶ
> ἐπείπερ γεγένησθε, ἀθάνατοι μὲν οὐκ ἐστὲ οὐδ᾽ ἄλυτοι
> τὸ πάμπαν, οὔ τι μὲν δὴ λυθήσεσθέ γε οὐδὲ τεύξεσθε
> θανάτου μοίρας, τῆς ἐμῆς βουλήσεως μείζονος ἔτι δεσμοῦ
> καὶ κυριωτέρου λαχόντες ἐκείνων οἷς, ὅτ᾽ ἐγίγνεσθε, ξυνε-
> δεῖσθε. (*Tim.* 41 A, B.)

The bodies of the θεοὶ θεῶν are δεθέντα and therefore,
regarded merely as bodies, cannot be altogether ἄλυτα:
but the souls which inform them are of such a high
order that body and soul can never be parted by any
physical changes that may take place. The cohesion
of the elementary triangles into which their bodies may
theoretically be resolved is firmer than that of the triangles composing ordinary bodies, of which it is said:—

> τὰ γὰρ τρίγωνα εὐθὺς κατ᾽ ἀρχὰς ἑκάστου δύναμιν
> ἔχοντα ξυνίσταται μέχρι τινὸς χρόνου δυνατὰ ἐξαρκεῖν,
> οὗ βίου οὐκ ἄν ποτέ τις εἰς τὸ πέραν ἔτι βιῴη.
>
> > (*Tim.* 89 C.)

There is no μέχρι τινὸς χρόνου to be taken into account
in the bodily existence of the θεοὶ θεῶν: consequently
their souls will never be called upon to fly to another

habitation. Thus the θεοὶ θεῶν are exempt from death and metempsychosis; their bodies change indeed, but the change is gradual and not violent.

We may now return to the course of Plato's allegorical narrative. Having created the θεοὶ θεῶν the δημιουργός bethinks him of the creation of the θνητὰ γένη, mortality being the necessary counterpart of immortality. He cannot create them, however, in the same way as he created the θεοὶ θεῶν: if he were to do so, they would be even as gods, immortal. For everything that the δημιουργός himself creates, that is to say everything which in the form in which it exists is only one degree removed from the ultimate unity of νοῦς itself, is as such indestructible. Now in Plato's view there must be mortal creatures in the world in order that a real meaning may be given to immortality: in this way the universe is made as complete as it can possibly be. Since, then, mortal things have to be created somehow, and since for the reason given above the δημιουργός cannot directly create them himself, he delegates this part of the work to the θεοὶ θεῶν, the gods whom he has himself created:—

ἵνα οὖν θνητά τε ᾖ τό τε πᾶν τόδε ὄντως ἅπαν ᾖ, τρέπεσθε κατὰ φύσιν ὑμεῖς ἐπὶ τὴν τῶν ζῴων δημιουργίαν, μιμούμενοι τὴν ἐμὴν δύναμιν περὶ τὴν ὑμετέραν γένεσιν.

(*Tim.* 41 C.)

Thus the creation of the θνητὰ γένη by the θεοὶ θεῶν is an *imitation* of their own creation by the δημιουργός. In each case the act of creation consists in joining together soul and body. But it must be borne in mind that the work of the θεοὶ θεῶν is nothing more than an imitation of the work of the δημιουργός: it is not

precisely the same in kind: else nothing would be gained
by the delegation of this particular work to them. The
results of their workmanship have not the same permanence that they themselves have ; for anything which
they originate is no longer one but two degrees removed
from νοῦς. Thus the θεοὶ θεῶν, who in the mode of
their actual existence are products of the direct thinking
of absolute Mind, have the power up to a certain point,
though they are finite beings, of thinking for themselves
in a manner which may be considered an imitation of
the thinking which gives them their own existence.
But they cannot provide their own material to work
on as the δημιουργός has provided his ; consequently
the δημιουργός prepares a second blending of soul not
so pure as that of which the souls of the stars are
composed, but such as may appropriately be yoked
with mortal bodies. These souls are δεύτερα καὶ τρίτα :
that is to say, they are of varying degrees of purity
corresponding to the various kinds of animal and vegetable bodies to which they are to be joined. I do not
think anything is to be gained by pressing the phrase
δεύτερα καὶ τρίτα very closely : these inferior souls are
really all of one class, though according to the particular
form of life they may at any given time be leading,
they may be more or less pure.

The incarnation of these souls, then, as each embodiment is not intended to be permanent, is delegated by
the creator to the gods whom he has already created.
Accordingly he leaves in their hands these inferior souls
which are to undergo incarnation in mortal bodies. He
gives one soul to each of the gods :—

ξυστήσας δὲ τὸ πᾶν διεῖλε ψυχὰς ἰσαρίθμους τοῖς
ἄστροις, ἔνειμέ θ᾽ ἑκάστην πρὸς ἕκαστον. (*Tim.* 41 D.)

The ἄστρα mentioned here are of course the fixed stars,
which are the visible representations of the θεοὶ θεῶν.
The expression διεῖλε ψυχὰς ἰσαρίθμους τοῖς ἄστροις
appears simple enough; but Mr Archer-Hind seems to
be somewhat perturbed by it, and in a note on the
passage makes the following comment:—"What the
δημιουργός did, I conceive to be this.   Having completed the admixture of soul he divided the whole into
portions, assigning one portion to each star.   These
portions, be it understood, are not particular souls nor
aggregates of particular souls; they are divisions of
the whole quantity of soul, which is not as yet differentiated into particular souls."   For my own part I
am quite at a loss to understand the purpose of this
refinement; in fact it seems to me to introduce unnecessary confusion into the interpretation of the passage.   Plato's language certainly seems to imply that
the ψυχαί here mentioned are differentiated individual
souls.   If he does not mean this, why does he not say
distinctly that they are not individual souls but have
yet to be further differentiated?   Moreover it looks as
if Mr Archer-Hind supposes the differentiation of soul
to be something which is done in time, though he does
not explain how this can be so, and it does not seem
to me to be metaphysically possible.   Nor can I see
what after all is gained by supposing these two stages
in the process of differentiation; for the final differentiation into individual souls must in any case be
accomplished by the δημιουργός himself, this function
not being among the attributes of the θεοὶ θεῶν.   This
is admitted by Mr Archer-Hind himself, who in the
course of the same note goes on to say that "it would
seem that the differentiation of the souls into individual
beings was done by the δημιουργός himself, before they

were handed over to the created gods. In fact this is
metaphysically necessary." How this is to be reconciled
with the earlier part of the note I do not know. That
the δημιουργός does the final differentiating into individual souls can hardly be doubted ; such is the natural
inference from the language used a little later on : —

ἔσπειρε τοὺς μὲν εἰς γῆν, τοὺς δ' εἰς σελήνην, τοὺς δ'
εἰς τἆλλα ὅσα ὄργανα χρόνου· τὸ δὲ μετὰ τὸν σπόρον
τοῖς νέοις παρέδωκε θεοῖς σώματα πλάττειν θνητά.

(*Tim.* 42 D.)

The creative function of the stars is performed in space
and time ; they cannot, therefore, actually create souls,
nor can they cause a quantity of soul to be differentiated
into individual souls. Their powers of thought are indeed of a much higher order than ours, but not to so
great an extent as this would imply. They are Mind
externalised and therefore finite ; and it is impossible
for finite beings, however highly organised they may
be, to think in the same way as the infinite Mind of
which they are parts. The continuous thinking of νοῦς
causes pluralisation : the thinking of the θεοὶ θεῶν cannot
of itself cause pluralisation, but finds its function in
influencing in a certain way and to a certain extent the
course of pluralised existence. This being so, it may
perhaps be said that it is misleading to use the word
think to describe the operation of the stars on the
inferior γένη : does it not rather consist in an act of
will ? There is some truth in this : but I think nevertheless that it is best to keep the word even as applied
to the function of the θεοὶ θεῶν, because it serves to
keep before us the fact that everything is to be traced
back ultimately to the thinking of νοῦς. The *thought*

of the various forms of animal and vegetable life is
transmitted by νοῦς to the θεοὶ θεῶν, who actually think
the combination of the particular ψυχαί with bodies.

Thus it is clear from the mythical account that the
function of the θεοὶ θεῶν, though in a sense similar, is
yet different in kind from that of the δημιουργός: what
they have to do is to fit with mortal bodies the souls
which he entrusts to their care. They do not provide
the souls for themselves; nor can they by any creative
power of their own furnish the material out of which
the bodies for these souls are to be constructed. This
is clear from the account given of the mode of their
operation:—

νοήσαντες οἱ παῖδες τὴν τοῦ πατρὸς διάταξιν ἐπεί-
θοντο αὐτῇ, καὶ λαβόντες ἀθάνατον ἀρχὴν θνητοῦ ζῴου,
μιμούμενοι τὸν σφέτερον δημιουργόν, πυρὸς καὶ γῆς
ὕδατός τε καὶ ἀέρος ἀπὸ τοῦ κόσμου δανειζόμενοι μόρια,
ὡς ἀποδοθησόμενα πάλιν, εἰς ταὐτὸν τὰ λαμβανόμενα
συνεκόλλων, οὐ τοῖς ἀλύτοις οἷς αὐτοὶ ξυνείχοντο δεσμοῖς,
ἀλλὰ διὰ σμικρότητα ἀοράτοις πυκνοῖς γόμφοις ξυντή-
κοντες, ἐν ἐξ ἁπάντων ἀπεργαζόμενοι σῶμα ἕκαστον, τὰς
τῆς ἀθανάτου ψυχῆς περιόδους ἐνέδουν εἰς ἐπίρρυτον
σῶμα καὶ ἀπόρρυτον. (*Tim.* 42 E, 43 A.)

In this passage the words ἀπὸ τοῦ κόσμου δανειζόμενοι
μόρια are especially significant. The θεοὶ θεῶν can only
borrow the material which they are about to use: they
cannot create any for themselves. All the matter in
the universe, not only that of which their own bodies
are composed, has been already created by the δημιουργός. The δημιουργός, then, is directly responsible
for matter as well as for spirit. Accordingly we find
subsequently, when the mythical form of narrative is

dropped, that there are ideas corresponding to the four so-called elements, the fire, earth, water, and air of the present passage. It is convenient to call them ideas, because they represent permanent modes of the thought of absolute νοῦς: but we need not therefore suppose that they are on the same level with the ideas of animal and vegetable *life*. They are more like what we should call natural laws, in accordance with which the higher ideas manifest themselves in actual existence; nevertheless they spring directly from absolute Mind. For us matter is objective; consequently Plato endeavours to explain matter in terms not of finite Mind but of infinite Mind, which thinks space and things occupying it. The θεοὶ θεῶν, then, borrow their material from the σῶμα τοῦ κόσμου, which as such is the work solely of the δημιουργός. But though they cannot *create* matter, they can in a sense *differentiate* it; that is to say, they can assign a certain portion of matter for a certain time to a particular individual soul; and herein is demonstrated the fact that their power of thought (or, if we like to call it so, of will) is on a higher plane than our own or that of any other finite being. Thus the δημιουργός is directly responsible for the material as well as for the spiritual aspect of all things, but there is this difference: whereas he is responsible for the individual souls of the θνητὰ γένη, he is not responsible for their individual bodies. Mortal bodies, in so far as they may be regarded merely as matter, may be traced directly to the working of absolute Mind: but regarded as organic bodies, each guided by a particular soul, they can be referred only indirectly to this supreme cause: they are due to the direct agency of the subordinate minds of the stars. Thus matter as a whole, like everything else which is directly created by the δημιουργός, is indestructible; but the combination of material elements which forms the body of a particular living creature upon earth, inasmuch as it is the work not of the δημιουργός but of the θεοὶ θεῶν, is not indestructible: in time it must inevitably suffer dissolution, and, as far as that particular living creature is concerned, the result is death. Similarly, the δημιουργός is directly responsible for the souls of the θνητὰ γένη only in so far as they are souls; in so far as they are souls in conjunction with particular bodies the θεοὶ θεῶν are immediately responsible for them: that is to say, the δημιουργός creates not ἔμψυχα but ψυχαί. We must remember, however, that to him must be ascribed the creation not only of *soul*, but of the whole number of differentiated individual *souls*.

The conclusion to which I am coming must now for some time have been obvious. Whatever God himself creates we know to be indestructible. We know also that he is himself the creator of the individual soul. From these premisses can we possibly arrive at any other conclusion except that the individual soul as such is indestructible? And for the individual soul indestructibility can mean nothing less than personal immortality. Thus Plato's belief in the personal immortality of the soul is assuredly a natural inference from his own cosmology as set forth in the *Timaeus*, the Dialogue which embodies his most profound metaphysical thought. The statement which he puts into the mouth of the δημιουργός speaks plainly enough— δι᾽ ἐμοῦ ταῦτα γενόμενα καὶ βίου μετασχόντα θεοῖς ἰσάζοιτ᾽ ἄν. The matter of which our bodies are composed is, in so far as it is matter, indestructible; our souls likewise are severally indestructible: hence if he had himself joined body and soul together, there would have been nothing to distinguish us, the animals so constructed, from the gods. Therefore he does not so join them but leaves that task to the gods, who are not all-powerful. The result is that man and the other animals are subject to death; but even death cannot destroy the individuality of the souls which are the work of a creator who *is* all-powerful—whose will is stronger than those physical laws which only express a part of the truth: for he and Nature are one and the same.

It would seem, then, that Plato is at some pains to find a place for immortality in his cosmology. We have now to consider how this theory works in with the rest of his metaphysical system. In the first place we have to notice that no such theory as that of personal immortality is in any way essential to the working of that system so far as its cardinal principles are concerned. Soul, the universal principle of life, must of course be indestructible, and a continually existing world of pluralised existence is a necessary counterpart to the spaceless and timeless unity of Mind; but from the ontological point of view personal immortality is quite a side-issue. It is necessary on Platonic principles that absolute Mind should exist in the form of a plurality of individual souls; but there is no metaphysical reason why the whole quantity of soul should always be distributed into the same personalities or even into the same number of individual souls. In fact the doctrine of personal immortality, connected as it is with the allied doctrine of metempsychosis, raises certain questions, when we come to apply it to the general metaphysical

scheme of the *Timaeus*, to which Plato does not seem
to have given any explicit answer, and which it is not
very easy to answer for him.   Yet after all we have
but slight ground for complaint if on some points we
are left rather in the dark.   It is only to be expected
that the details of a philosophical system at once so
original and so elaborate should when pressed become
involved in a certain amount of obscurity.   And it
should be noted that Plato does not claim that his metaphysical scheme, as actually unfolded in the *Timaeus*,
is anything more than an εἰκὼς λόγος : it would be out
of place, therefore, to enforce a rigorous interpretation
of its minor details.   For much of the obscurity that
arises the allegorical form of the *Timaeus* is no doubt
responsible.   We have already had occasion to notice
the confusion which the doctrine of metempsychosis
has introduced into the interpretation of the allegorical
narrative, where under the image of a process in time
and space there is described at the same moment both
a logical succession, which is spaceless and timeless,
and a process which does actually go on in time and
space.

It is this doctrine of metempsychosis which causes
most of our difficulties in explaining the position
occupied by the theory of personal immortality in the
Timaeus.   Yet I think there can scarcely be any doubt
that Plato does literally maintain this doctrine.   We
cannot everywhere explain his allusions to it as metaphor or allegory; for it should be noted that we hear
of the transmigration of souls not only in the metaphysical part of the *Timaeus* but in the physical part
as well, and we meet with it again in the *Laws*.   But
it must be admitted that Plato has not explained as

clearly as we could wish how his theory of metempsychosis fits into his metaphysical system as a whole.
How does it harmonize with the Theory of Ideas, which
has now been developed into a theory of natural kinds?
So long as souls migrate only within each several species,
all goes well; but what happens when a human soul,
for instance, at its next incarnation enters into some
other animal form? It would seem that such a soul
must in such circumstances cease to represent one idea
and begin to represent another. Plato has provided
for the mutual interchange of the elements of fire, air,
and water; but he has given us no explicit answer to
this metaphysical question which arises out of the
doctrine of metempsychosis. It may be said no doubt
that the εἰσιόντα καὶ ἐξιόντα representing each idea
must meet with appropriate material conditions before
they can become immanent in εἰκόνες of the particular
idea which they represent. But these εἰσιόντα καὶ
ἐξιόντα are of course quite distinct from particular
souls. Both may be said to inform the body, but in
a different sense: the soul causes the body to be alive,
while the εἰσιὸν καὶ ἐξιόν causes it to represent a particular idea. The εἰσιόντα καὶ ἐξιόντα cannot be the
same as souls; they have no personality and are purely
transitory reflexions of ideas.

Thus it can hardly be denied that the inner working
of metempsychosis from the metaphysical point of view
is wrapped in a certain amount of obscurity. It is to
be observed also that this question, which the doctrine
of metempsychosis brings into special prominence, is
in reality only part of a larger question. What is the
precise relation between souls and ideas? In view of
the scantiness of any information bearing upon this

point it is impossible to say with any approach to certainty what Plato's answer to this question would have been. As Bonitz says of Aristotle, "*difficile est ea interpretari quae philosophus ipse non satis distincte et perspicue explicuerit.*" If one may hazard a suggestion in a matter which must always, I fear, remain doubtful, I should say that Plato's theory was something to this effect. The ideas are thoughts of God: that is to say, they are *permanent modes of the operation* of supreme νοῦς. Individual souls are the creatures of God : that is to say, they are *permanent determinations* of supreme νοῦς. Νοῦς necessarily exists throughout time in the form of particular souls, which also exist as such throughout time. But νοῦς also conceives itself as existing, let us say, in the form of man, in the form of pig, and in the form of each of the four so-called elements. Now here we have the ideas, the thoughts of God, one for each natural kind. From these we must carefully distinguish the particular souls or aggregates of particular souls which at a given time represent the idea of man, the idea of pig, and so on. Νοῦς thinks man-life and pig-life, but it does not determine itself directly into man-souls and pig-souls, but simply into souls, which as far as their essential nature is concerned may equally well be man-souls or pig-souls. Whether at a given time they are the one or the other depends upon their own previous conduct, which the stars take into account in bringing about their next incarnation. Thus the actual representation of the ideas at a given time is the work of the stars, and in directing that work the subordinate ideas of the four elements come into play. Νοῦς ordains that there shall be certain kinds of matter in the universe, by the combination of which suitable

bodies may be composed for the purpose of bringing
into actual existence the various kinds of life; but the
actual bringing of it into existence is left to the dis-
cretion of the stars, who by allotting to a particular soul
a particular kind of body cause that soul temporarily to
represent a certain idea.   In point of dignity the ideas
are arranged according to a graduated scale; and if in a
particular existence a man-soul does not rise to the proper
dignity of man-life, in its next existence through the
operation of the stars it may become a pig-soul with the
necessary accompaniment of a pig-body.   Conversely, if
a pig-soul proves itself too good for the representation of
pig-life—the idea of pig—in a pig-body, its tutelary star
may provide it in its next incarnation with a man-body
so that it may have its chance of successfully representing
the idea of man.   I do not think we are transgressing
the bounds of probability in supposing Plato's theory
to mean something of this kind.   But the fact remains
that he has not chosen to explain fully the metaphysical
working of details of this sort.   Perhaps he considered
that such matters were not suited to dogmatic treatment
and were better left to the individual imagination;
and no one would be disposed to quarrel with such a
conclusion.   For our purposes it is sufficient to know
that there were certain things which he felt to be true
of the soul, but which he could not altogether account
for by means of strict metaphysical theory.   In these
circumstances he contented himself with assuming them
to be true and with telling us in an allegorical fashion
how they came about.

Foremost amongst these truths are the doctrines of
immortality and metempsychosis.   In reading the account of the creation of the soul in the *Timaeus* we

can hardly help feeling that the strange thing which
Plato considers it his duty to account for somehow is
not *immortality* but *death*. The belief in immortality
comes naturally to him and scarcely seems to call for
justification; but death is a phenomenon which is hard
to understand and seems to call for some sort of explanation. Consequently he is at some pains to show
that mortality is in some way necessary as a counterpart to immortality; and he explains the functions of
the stars in such a way as to make it clear that
death is simply a necessary incident in the process of
metempsychosis. As I have said, I do not think it can
reasonably be doubted that Plato had a profound belief
in the transmigration of souls. We are continually
coming across allusions to this doctrine throughout his
works from the *Phaedrus* and the *Meno* to the *Timaeus*
and the *Laws*. In the earlier Dialogues it is closely
connected with the theory of ἀνάμνησις: and in a sense
this is also true of the *Timaeus*, where we are told that
the laws of nature are declared to souls before incarnation. Plato does not any longer believe, as he once
did, that our souls have at some period in the past had
direct knowledge of the reality of things as they are in
themselves: but the doctrine of metempsychosis still
enables him to maintain a sort of theory of 'innate
ideas.' He can still say, as he has said in the *Phaedo*,
ἦσαν αἱ ψυχαὶ καὶ πρότερον (though not now χωρὶς
σωμάτων) καὶ φρόνησιν εἶχον. Each soul, as it is de-
scended from νοῦς has φρόνησις, but the degree to
which its φρόνησις is operative depends upon the idea
which it is at any particular time representing and
upon the closeness of its approximation to the perfect
embodiment of that idea. It is in details of this sort

that the difference between the earlier and the later
Platonism is chiefly apparent; for in his general attitude
towards the question of the immortality of the soul the
Plato of the *Timaeus* is in much the same position as
the Plato of the *Phaedo*. The most important difference
between the earlier and the later forms of the doctrine
of immortality is that upon which I have already insisted. In the *Timaeus* Plato no longer looks forward
to the possibility of an actual immaterial existence for
individual souls. His belief in personal immortality is
now in fact co-extensive with his belief in metempsychosis. With this important exception his position in
regard to the general question involved remains the
same throughout. The essential indestructibility of 'all
soul', the universal principle of life, is a necessary corollary of his metaphysical system in both its earlier and
its later stages. The immortality of the individual soul
is never actually proved in the *Phaedo*; but it is obviously believed, and the belief is to a certain extent
justified in so far as the reasons which may be advanced
against such a belief are shown to be ill-founded. In
the *Timaeus* the question is approached in a somewhat
different manner; Plato makes no attempt to *prove* that
souls are individually immortal. The doctrine of individual immortality is in no way essential to the truth
of the general system of metaphysics which is evolved
in the *Timaeus*: in fact it obscures to some extent the
working out of the system. But here no less than in
the *Phaedo* individual immortality is to Plato an article
of belief. He does not, however, any longer seek to
indicate his belief by attempting to prove what no-one
can ever hope to prove: he does so in a way peculiarly
his own. In an allegorical account of the generation

and history of the soul he describes the origin of individual souls in such a manner as to emphasize and after a fashion to account for the fact that they are immortal. In its dogmatic aspect Plato's position is substantially that of Lord Beaconsfield's Signor Paraclete, with whom he says in effect:—" I know that I have a soul, and I believe that it is immortal."

CHAPTER XI.

THE DEGENERATION OF SOULS.

THERE remains one special feature of Plato's theory of immortality about which it will be well to say a few words. We have seen that according to the Platonic cosmology souls are subject to a process of degeneration. Why this should be so, why it is necessary that souls should degenerate at all, is a question which must occur to everyone. It is one of those questions, however, to which Plato has given us no explicit answer, and one which it is perhaps impossible for us adequately to answer for him. Indeed it is probable that he did not himself see his way to a solution which would be completely satisfactory. In the *Phaedrus* we are told that souls degenerate συντυχίᾳ τινί. This is of course no answer at all; and in the *Timaeus* we naturally look at any rate for some indication of a more satisfactory explanation. Nor are we altogether disappointed, though the explanation is still little more than metaphorical. Corresponding to the συντυχία of the *Phaedrus* we have in the *Timaeus* the provision of the δημιουργός that the γένεσις πρώτη of all souls shall be in human form, ἵνα

μή τις ἐλαττοῖτο ὑπ' αὐτοῦ: that is to say, the principle
of metempsychosis secures that, if there must be other
creatures in the world besides men, at any rate they
all have an equal chance. This, however, does little
more than present the problem in a new light: it
vindicates nature from the charge of unfairness to individuals, but it does not explain why it is necessary
that there should be some forms of life less perfect
than others.

We have to remember also that in the *Timaeus*
there are two forms of degeneration to be distinguished.
First there is what may be called the *logical* degeneration, which does not affect the individual but is merely
a way of representing the logical evolution of all things
through successive stages from the primal unity, this
evolution being described allegorically as though it
were a process taking place in space and time. And
secondly, there is the *actual* degeneration, which is or
may be an incident in the life of the individual and
really does occur in space and time through the process
of metempsychosis. It is to be observed further that
this process of individual degeneration is counteracted
by a similar process in the opposite direction. The
consideration of this question leads naturally to the
consideration of the larger question concerning the
place of evil in Plato's philosophy; and on this point
he has unfortunately left us somewhat in the dark. It
would be beyond the scope of this essay to endeavour
to deal exhaustively with this problem; but in view of
its connexion with our present subject it will be best
perhaps not to leave it altogether unnoticed.

Plato tells us in a manner *how* it is that evil arises.
What we know as evil is a necessary consequence of

the evolution of pluralised existence from the absolute
unity of Mind. The principle of evil, if such it may be
called, he discovers in a force which he terms ἀνάγκη.
The significance of this doctrine of ἀνάγκη has been
admirably explained in a paper by D. D. Heath entitled 'Some further observations on Ancient Theories
of Causation' (*Journal of Philology*, vol. VIII). He
shows conclusively that Plato's ἀνάγκη, like Aristotle's
τύχη and ταὐτόματον, is no 'irregular agency' such as
Grote and Mill supposed it to be, but simply the necessary operation of natural laws: in Heath's words it is
"the sum of the laws of interaction primarily imposed
on the materials with which the Demiurge is to work
out his 'constructive' or 'artistic' purpose: laws which
he cannot alter, but must bend and guide skilfully to
work his Will as far as possible." Thus we see that
ἀνάγκη, though in a sense it is the evil principle inasmuch as evil necessarily arises from it, is not of its own
nature evil. On the contrary it is good, as we should
see if we could view it apart from its undesigned con-
sequences which often are or seem to be evil; it is good
in so far as it represents the perfect working out of
divinely or naturally constituted laws. Νοῦς and ἀνάγκη,
then, are not two distinct forces or principles existing
in nature and acting continually in opposition to each
other like the φιλότης and νεῖκος of Empedocles. Ἀνάγκη
is really nothing more than the 'friction' which necessarily accompanies the working of νοῦς in the world of
phenomena. Unity must exist in the form of multiplicity, and in the spatial and temporal existence of
multiplicity evil is somehow necessarily involved. From
the mythical point of view the creator is on Plato's
assumption absolutely good: evil arises indirectly, there

being no such direct evil agency as the ordinary Greek was wont to discover in the φθόνος of his gods. As Browning expresses it in *La Saisiaz*:—

> "There is no such grudge in God as scared the ancient Greek, no fresh
> Substitute of trap for dragnet, once a breakage in the mesh."

But a creator, however good he may be, must create; and the process of creation necessarily brings evil in its train, though the evil is not, as such, intentional.

This is *how* evil arises. But the further question *why* it is necessary that creation or evolution should take place in such a manner that it inevitably produces evil still remains unanswered. We cannot hope to find a complete solution to this problem in the Platonic or perhaps in any other system of philosophy. We might as well expect Plato to tell us why νοῦς exists. In every system of philosophy there must come a stage after which metaphysical analysis can go no farther. But so far as Plato's conception of the nature and *raison d'être* of evil is concerned the difficulty may perhaps be moved back a step: we may be able to discover a partial though not a complete answer to the question why evil is a necessity in the nature of things.

We have seen that on Platonic principles, if there is to be a pluralised κόσμος, there must be evil in it. Why, then, must there be a κόσμος of this sort? Let us go back to the beginning of the mythical account of the creation. The purpose of the creation is explained by Timaeus as follows:—

λέγωμεν δὴ δι' ἥντινα αἰτίαν γένεσιν καὶ τὸ πᾶν τόδε
ὁ ξυνιστὰς ξυνέστησεν. ἀγαθὸς ἦν, ἀγαθῷ δὲ οὐδεὶς περὶ

οὐδενὸς οὐδέποτε ἐγγίγνεται φθόνος. τούτου δ' ἐκτὸς ὢν
πάντα ὅ τι μάλιστα γενέσθαι ἐβουλήθη παραπλήσια
ἑαυτῷ. (*Tim.* 29 D, E.)

The last words here quoted are translated by Mr Archer-
Hind "he desired that all things should be as like unto
himself as possible": but it should be noticed that the
word which Plato uses is not εἶναι but γενέσθαι. I think
there is some significance in this. The creator was
good, and so he wished to establish a *process* of things
which should be like himself, that is to say good. In
other words, the δημιουργός desired to realise his own
goodness. Now goodness in order to be realised in this
world must be seen in actual working. Thus a process is
necessary, and further it must be a process towards good.
The αὐτὸ ἀγαθόν is simply another aspect of νοῦς, both
aspects being united in the conception of the δημιουργός: he is not only the moving cause but also the
final cause of the κόσμος, which is created by him in
order that it may progress towards him. He symbolizes
real existence, and to Plato real existence necessarily
implies goodness. Thus we see that in order to the
realisation of good the logical existence of evil becomes
necessary; for as the general process of things has to
be towards good, some things must at any rate be less
good than others, and the process must be conceived as
proceeding from evil in the direction of good. But for
this logical existence of evil good could have no meaning. The actual process from evil to good involves the
logical process from good to evil; otherwise the actual
process in the direction of good could not take place,
for all would be good already, though it could not be
known to be so. Yet evil as such can have no real

existence; pure evil would be simply the negation of good, and just as good can be an attribute of things only in so far as they truly exist, evil can similarly be an attribute of things only in so far as they fall short of true existence :—

"The evil is null, is nought, is silence implying sound."

The same point of view is represented in a more popular form in the *Theaetetus* :—

ἀλλ᾽ οὔτ᾽ ἀπολέσθαι τὰ κακὰ δυνατόν, ὦ Θεόδωρε· ὑπεναντίον γάρ τι τῷ ἀγαθῷ ἀεὶ εἶναι ἀνάγκη· οὔτ᾽ ἐν θεοῖς αὐτὰ ἱδρύσθαι· τὴν δὲ θνητὴν φύσιν καὶ τόνδε τὸν τόπον περιπολεῖ ἐξ ἀνάγκης. (*Theaet.* 176 A.)

The use of the expression ἐξ ἀνάγκης here is noteworthy, foreshadowing as it does the more technical use of the word ἀνάγκη in the *Timaeus*. In this world we cannot help seeing that some things are at least less good than others; and any notion we may form of absolute good —not merely more good as opposed to less good— implies a corresponding notion of absolute evil. Absolute good, however, is really the whole, whereas absolute evil is really nothing.

From another point of view it may perhaps be said that the necessary existence of evil in the world is in a sense due to ourselves and our necessarily incomplete knowledge of the course of nature. The more we understand the whole nature of things, the less evil we shall see in the world; and if we could put ourselves in the position of the δημιουργός, we should see that there is really no evil in the world at all. Everything in so far as it exists at all must be good; more than this, everything is in its way perfect, though its way is

not always our way: and consequently its perfection,
so to speak, is apparent only to God: it cannot be
apprehended by finite minds. It may be true that from
our standpoint the descent of a stone upon our heads
is not perfect; but in the eye of God it is perfect in
the sense that it necessarily represents the result of
the perfect working of the law of gravitation and is so
far good: we, however, do not estimate it in regard to
what it is in itself but only in the light of our personal
relations with it, and these certainly do not seem good
to us. Just as ἀνάγκη, so far from being an 'irregular
agency,' is really a mode of the operation of νοῦς itself,
it may be said that in a sense there is a sort of ἀνάγκη
which directs νοῦς: that is to say, good must manifest
itself in a form which to finite minds often seems evil,
the evil arising from the mutual relations or interactions
of things which, if they could stand alone, would be
perfectly good. Thus what seems to us to be evil must
in a sense be good; but we cannot appreciate the fact
because our minds are finite, and therefore to us evil
is a reality. Only the absolute Mind itself can see and
appreciate the essential goodness of everything. We
can never hope to attain to this ideal point of view,
but we can nevertheless make some approach towards
it. Our business is to make the best possible use of
our intelligence in order to look at everything in its
bearing on the whole. This doctrine is strongly insisted upon from the educational standpoint in the
Laws:—

πείθωμεν τὸν νεανίαν τοῖς λόγοις, ὡς τῷ τοῦ παντὸς
ἐπιμελουμένῳ πρὸς τὴν σωτηρίαν καὶ ἀρετὴν τοῦ ὅλου
πάντ᾽ ἐστὶ συντεταγμένα, ὧν καὶ τὸ μέρος εἰς δύναμιν
ἕκαστον τὸ προσῆκον πάσχει καὶ ποιεῖ. τούτοις δ᾽ εἰσὶν

ἄρχοντες προστεταγμένοι ἑκάστοις ἐπὶ τὸ σμικρότατον
ἀεὶ πάθης καὶ πράξεως, εἰς μερισμὸν τὸν ἔσχατον τέλος
ἀπειργασμένοι· ὧν ἓν καὶ τὸ σόν, ὦ σχέτλιε, μόριον εἰς
τὸ πᾶν ξυντείνει βλέπον ἀεί, καίπερ πάνσμικρον ὄν. κ.τ.λ.

(*Laws* 903 B, C.)

What we have to realise as far as we can is that the
universe itself is a perfect ζῷον, of which we are, so to
speak, members.

Creation, then, though we have to regard it as a
process which inevitably carries evil with it, is the
means taken by the creator in order to the realisation
of his own goodness. In other words, absolute Mind
—the νοῦς βασιλεύς which is the same thing as ὄν and
ἀγαθόν—being of its own nature essentially good, is in
a manner proved to be so in the general progress of
pluralised existence, in which evil is found necessarily
to attach to the separate existence of the individual
units that together make up the actually existing universe. In proportion as these units are able to realise
their natural affinity with νοῦς, they are better and
have a greater share in true existence. The essential
goodness of everything may best be realised by attempting to take as comprehensive a view as possible of each
part of the κόσμος in its bearing on the whole. Every
form of existence from the highest to the lowest is to
be traced back ultimately to the absolute idea, the αὐτὸ
ἀγαθόν. Thus the whole sum of existence is arranged
on a logically descending scale, and the αὐτὸ ἀγαθόν,
symbolically represented by the δημιουργός, is the type
of all goodness and the source of all existence. This
it could not be unless, to use Plato's terms, ταὐτόν
existed also in the form of θάτερον, and unless θάτερον
contained within it the principle of ταὐτόν so that it

might be brought into actual existence. That is to
say, in the phenomenal world what we look upon as
evil is necessary in order to make possible a continued
approximation to the type.

This rough sketch of what I take to be the nature
and origin of evil in Plato's cosmology is perhaps sufficient for our present purpose, which is to explain the
rationale of what I have called the *logical* degeneration
of souls. Plato starts from the observed fact that some
forms of existence are of a higher order than others;
and he explains this fact on the hypothesis that all
these different forms of life of varying degrees of excellence are, as it were, links in a chain, which is logically
regarded as extending downwards from complete existence to complete non-existence, from absolute good to
absolute evil. As he states it himself in metaphorical
language, the creator πάντα ὅ τι μάλιστα γενέσθαι ἐβουλήθη παραπλήσια ἑαυτῷ. What Plato wishes to establish
is the reality of a general progress of things in the
direction of good; and this necessitates the establishment logically of evil as the starting-point of this
progress. Absolute evil, therefore, which can only be
an attribute of complete non-existence, must be conceived logically as a counterfoil to absolute good, the
special attribute of transcendental existence. Neither
absolute evil nor absolute good, however, actually exists
as such : what does actually exist is a world of pluralised
Being having for its ultimate object the realisation of
its fundamental unity and goodness. Nothing which
actually exists is completely good or completely evil;
but everything is to be regarded as more or less good
according as it realises more or less clearly the true
nature of existence.

Once the necessity for the existence or apparent existence of evil in the world has been recognised, the *actual* degeneration of particular souls in time, though at first sight seeming to contradict the notion of a general progress of things towards good, does not really present so great a difficulty as the problem of the actual origin and nature of evil itself. It is one of the chief features of Plato's theory of metempsychosis that souls migrate not only within each separate species but from a higher species to a lower and *vice versa*. This doctrine has an obvious ethical application, as we shall see in the next chapter. Metaphysically it seems to be important in so far as it provides for the carrying out of the principle of οὐδεὶς ἐλαττοῦται already noticed. Plato finds it necessary to maintain it in view of the present actual condition of the world, in which there undoubtedly are some souls whose mode of life is inferior to that of others; and he feels that these souls must have their chance of climbing the ladder of existence. But there does not seem to be any equally valid reason why there should always be a downward migration as well as an upward. At present there are both processes going on, but in the future things may be different. At any stage in the downward course of a soul a lost step may be regained. We are not told of any fixed laws which determine when and where each soul is to halt and proceed in the other direction; all we know is that it depends upon the merit of the life lived by the soul during any particular incarnation. There will always be the possibility of descent as well as the possibility of ascent; but there is no reason why all souls should not finally ascend to the πρώτη καὶ ἀρίστη ἕξις. And in this connexion it is worth noticing that in the *Timaeus*,

while there is no mention of any final state of degradation such as we find in earlier Dialogues, Plato does
seem to hold out the hope of our attaining to a state
of existence higher than any with which we are at
present familiar :—

    καὶ ὁ μὲν εὖ τὸν προσήκοντα χρόνον βιοὺς πάλιν εἰς
τὴν τοῦ ξυννόμου πορευθεὶς οἴκησιν ἄστρου βίον εὐδαίμονα
καὶ συνήθη ἔξοι. (*Tim.* 42 B.)

What exactly is meant by this βίος εὐδαίμων καὶ συνήθης
it is perhaps impossible to determine ; but it does not
seem unreasonable to suppose that Plato did actually
contemplate the possibility of a higher life in which
figuratively or literally the souls of men may hold
communion with the stars.   There is nothing in his
metaphysical or ethical philosophy, so far as we can
see, that tells definitely against such a notion; in fact
his theory of general mental and moral progress seems
distinctly in favour of it.   But we must carefully distinguish this notion of a higher life from that which
he entertained at an earlier period.   There is no
question of an immaterial existence in which the soul
can know the ideas; that would imply that a finite
existence could be perfect, and we know that perfection can belong to the infinite alone.   All finite
forms of life, even the life of the stars themselves, must
necessarily be imperfect; but a continued approach
towards perfection is always possible.

    By his theory of metempsychosis, then, Plato secures
that in spite of the present condition of the world οὐδεὶς
ἐλαττοῦται.   An individual soul must remain imperfect,
simply because it *is* an individual soul ; but all individual souls may in time be moving upwards.   He

could not suppose that the universe was constructed on
such a principle that there must always be some souls
which are necessarily degenerating simply in order to
counterbalance the upward march of others more fortunate than themselves. There must always be evil in
the world, it is true; but this would be giving evil
a firmer footing than Plato was disposed to allow it.
The power of evil is not so great that it cannot be
continually lessened; in fact the possibility of lessening
it is the very corner-stone of his theory of progress.

We have seen that Plato assumes from the outset
that the source of all things is good; and he supplements this assumption by equating the αὐτὸ ἀγαθόν with
Mind, the only thing which in the truest sense exists.
It is true that pure undifferentiated Mind (the ταὐτόν
aspect of things) which would be absolutely good, like
pure uninformed matter (the θάτερον aspect), which
would be absolutely evil, can exist as such only in a
logical sense: what actually exists and always must
exist is ταὐτόν qualified by θάτερον, for the one aspect
can only exist in combination with the other. Yet good
and evil have not the same degree of dignity: good
is always superior in that it is the special attribute of
the fountain-head of existence, whereas evil as such is
a mere negation. However potent the reality or apparent reality of evil in the universe may be, it can
never be real in the same sense in which good is real.
In this respect Plato is a thoroughgoing optimist. Any
theory that placed evil on an equality with good would
be intolerable to him; to do so would be the same
thing as to place matter on an equality with mind, and
against this he protests with all the fervour of a convinced idealist. Still less will he listen to the assertions

of the materialists, who say that all that exists is
matter. Mind is the ultimate source of all things, and
as such it must be good. Ἀγαθὸς ἦν, he says of the
δημιουργός: and the same thing is repeated in various
ways and in various places. The following passage is
especially noteworthy:—

τὸν μὲν οὖν ποιητὴν καὶ πατέρα τοῦδε τοῦ παντὸς
εὑρεῖν τε ἔργον καὶ εὑρόντα εἰς πάντας ἀδύνατον λέγειν.
τόδε δ᾽ οὖν πάλιν ἐπισκεπτέον περὶ αὐτοῦ, πρὸς πότερον
τῶν παραδειγμάτων ὁ τεκταινόμενος αὐτὸν ἀπειργάζετο,
πότερον πρὸς τὸ κατὰ ταὐτὰ καὶ ὡσαύτως ἔχον ἢ πρὸς τὸ
γεγονός. εἰ μὲν δὴ καλός ἐστιν ὅδε ὁ κόσμος ὅ τε
δημιουργὸς ἀγαθός, δῆλον ὡς πρὸς τὸ ἀΐδιον ἔβλεπεν·
εἰ δὲ ὃ μηδ᾽ εἰπεῖν τινὶ θέμις, πρὸς τὸ γεγονός. παντὶ δὴ
σαφὲς ὅτι πρὸς τὸ ἀΐδιον· ὁ μὲν γὰρ κάλλιστος τῶν
γεγονότων, ὁ δ᾽ ἄριστος τῶν αἰτίων. (*Tim.* 28 C, 29 A.)

Commenting here on the phrase πρὸς τὸ γεγονός Mr
Archer-Hind remarks:—"It may reasonably be asked,
how could the creator look πρὸς τὸ γεγονός, since at that
stage there was no γεγονὸς to look to? Plato's meaning,
I take it, is this: the γεγονὸς at which the Artificer
would look can of course only be the γεγονὸς that he
was about to produce. Now if he looked at this, instead
of fixing his eyes upon any eternal type, that would
mean that he created arbitrarily and at random a universe that simply fulfilled his fancy at the moment and
did not express any underlying thought: the universe
would in fact be a collection of incoherent phenomena, a mere plaything of the creator. But, says
Plato, this is not so: material nature is but the visible
counterpart of a spiritual reality; all things have their
meaning. Creation is no merely arbitrary exercise of

will on the part of the creator; it is the working out of an inevitable law." This note, so far as I understand it, gives a fair account of Plato's general position ; but I think that the true significance of the expression πρὸς τὸ γεγονός has been missed. Is Mr Archer-Hind right in saying that "at that stage there was no γεγονὸς to look to"? It seems to me that according to the *mythical* account there was. There was no *cosmos*, it is true, but there was a *chaos*:—

οὕτω δὴ πᾶν ὅσον ἦν ὁρατὸν παραλαβὼν οὐχ ἡσυχίαν ἄγον ἀλλὰ κινούμενον πλημμελῶς καὶ ἀτάκτως, εἰς τάξιν αὐτὸ ἤγαγεν ἐκ τῆς ἀταξίας, ἡγούμενος ἐκεῖνο τούτου πάντως ἄμεινον. (*Tim.* 30 A.)

Thus the function of the δημιουργός is conceived to be the bringing of order out of disorder: he *found* (παραλαβών) his material ready to his hand like any other artificer. Now the chaos upon which he worked might, in so far as it was ὁρατόν, be spoken of as γεγονός, as we see from another passage:—

γέγονεν· ὁρατὸς γὰρ ἁπτός τέ ἐστι καὶ σῶμα ἔχων, πάντα δὲ τὰ τοιαῦτα αἰσθητά, τὰ δ' αἰσθητά, δόξῃ περιληπτὰ μετ' αἰσθήσεως, γιγνόμενα καὶ γεννητὰ ἐφάνη.
(*Tim.* 28 B, C.)

What Plato means here is that γίγνεται and not ἔστιν is to be predicated of the visible world, which belongs to the sphere of γιγνόμενον, not to that of ὄν. So when Plato says that in creating the world the creator looked not πρὸς τὸ γεγονός but πρὸς τὸ αΐδιον, he surely means simply that the highest place in the universe is to be assigned to mind and not to matter : for good resides in the νοητόν rather than in the αἰσθητόν. To give the highest place to matter would be to Plato a profanity:

it would be the same thing as calling the creator evil—ὃ μηδ' εἰπεῖν τινὶ θέμις.

We see, then, that the essential supremacy of mind over matter according to Plato implies the essential goodness of the universe. If mind were derived from matter, there would be no true unification, no permanent source of good. But there *is* a permanent source of good : conversely, therefore, the essential goodness of the universe implies the essential supremacy of mind over matter. Thus all things must be conceived as in some way representing the αὐτὸ ἀγαθόν or universal Mind, a law of whose being it is that it should evolve itself in such a way as to form a world of pluralised existence : and since it is essentially good, the universal Mind evolves itself in such a way as to cause the world to be as like as possible to itself. In order that this may be so, the image as opposed to the type must take the form of a process in space and time, which are the necessary conditions and limitations of its existence. Since, then, there must be a process of some sort, it would be inconsistent with Plato's philosophical principles for him to hold that this process can be anything but a general progress towards good, though such a progress must logically presuppose evil as a starting-point. Thus the logical evolution of souls from the highest to the lowest is counteracted by their actual evolution from the lowest to the highest.

16

CHAPTER XII.

THE PLACE OF IMMORTALITY IN PLATO'S PHILOSOPHY.

NOW that we have determined in what sense Plato believed the soul to be immortal and have discussed certain special features of his theory of immortality, it remains to discover, if possible, what bearing this theory has upon his philosophy as a whole and upon what convictions he was led to maintain it to the end. The particular motive which caused him to affirm the doctrine of immortality with such earnestness in the *Phaedo* cannot have influenced him at a later time when his metaphysical researches had convinced him that the hope of a future immaterial existence in which we may know the ideas could in the nature of things never be realised. When we come to the *Timaeus*, we cannot help seeing that the doctrine of personal immortality does not belong to the essence of the metaphysics of that Dialogue; the system would work quite well without it. In fact, introduced as it is under the form of metempsychosis in the middle of the allegorical exposition of that system, it renders the interpretation to a certain extent difficult and confused. Yet it is evident that Plato set some store by his doctrine; else why should he introduce it in such a context and in so prominent a manner? It can hardly be doubted that it embodies his personal conviction; for Plato does not give utterance to opinions at random. But it is not so easy to say upon what this personal conviction is based. So far as his metaphysical opinions are concerned, such necessity as there may have been for maintaining the doctrine of personal immortality seems to have decreased rather than increased ; nor can the doctrine be regarded as fairly deducible from any ethical necessity. Plato's ethics, like his metaphysics, would remain substantially unaltered whether he considered the soul to be immortal or not. It is noticeable that in none of the later Dialogues does he attempt to prove the immortality of the soul. Still despite changes of doctrine consequent upon the attainment of clearer metaphysical insight he remains to the end faithful to his conviction that, whether the fact can be proved or not, the soul *is* immortal. This being so he works the doctrine of personal immortality into his system, so far as that can be done, with consummate skill. He introduces it into that part of his metaphysical allegory with which it has naturally the greatest affinity, namely the part where an account is given of the genesis and nature of all soul; and then he proceeds by means of the supplementary doctrine of metempsychosis to connect it with his system of ethics.

If, then, the doctrine is essential neither to his metaphysics nor to his ethics, why does Plato continue to maintain it? I have said that in his philosophy there is no ethical *necessity* for the doctrine. But to say this is not to say what Mr Archer-Hind says in the Introduction to his edition of the *Phaedo* (p. xiv):—"In the

16—2

true Platonic system of ethics immortality plays no
part. Plato's morality is founded in the very depths
of his ontology; for the principle of good and the
principle of being are one and the same. It matters
nothing whether we live or die: that alone is good which
is like the idea of good." Now in so far as Plato's system
of ethics is founded upon his metaphysics this is no
doubt a fair statement of his position. But, as we have
seen, Plato was forced to abandon his belief that it was
possible for the philosopher eventually to discover the
αὐτὸ ἀγαθόν: and that being the case a complete system
of ethical science cannot be deduced from metaphysics.
Hence although it is doubtless true that the essence of
Plato's ethical teaching would remain the same whether
he accepted the doctrine of the soul's immortality or
not, I cannot help feeling that Mr Archer-Hind's statement that "in the true Platonic system of ethics immortality plays no part" is somewhat too sweeping. It
seems to me that immortality does play a part, if a
subordinate one, in Plato's ethics. If the question is
of no real importance in his eyes, why does he insist
upon the doctrine of immortality so strongly as he does
in the *Phaedo*, and why does he introduce the subject
afresh in a metaphysical Dialogue like the *Timaeus*,
where it could safely have been omitted without leaving
any gap in the metaphysical system which he is there
primarily concerned to establish? The truth is that
according to Plato a belief in the immortality of the
soul possesses a real importance, not only for the
common man, but also for the philosopher himself,
whose life thus becomes, as Aristotle would say, ἱκανῶς
κεχορηγημένος. This is made clear in the *Phaedo*, as we
may see from the following passage :—

XII.] IN PLATO'S PHILOSOPHY 245

ἔστι δὲ δὴ τὸ κεφάλαιον ὧν ζητεῖς· ἀξιοῖς ἐπι-
δειχθῆναι ἡμῶν τὴν ψυχὴν ἀνώλεθρόν τε καὶ ἀθάνατον
οὖσαν, εἰ φιλόσοφος ἀνὴρ μέλλων ἀποθανεῖσθαι, θαρρῶν
τε καὶ ἡγούμενος ἀποθανὼν ἐκεῖ εὖ πράξειν διαφερόντως
ἢ εἰ ἐν ἄλλῳ βίῳ βιοὺς ἐτελεύτα, μὴ ἀνόητόν τε καὶ
ἠλίθιον θάρσος θαρρήσει. (*Phaedo* 95 B, C.)

And many other passages might be quoted which show
the same point of view. In fact in the *Phaedo* the
necessity of proving the immortality of the soul arises
for this very reason, that it is a belief in immortality
which more than anything else enables the philosopher
to view with cheerfulness the approach of death and is
an incentive to him and anyone else who will listen to
him to lead a truly philosophic life; for after death the
worth of it will be made manifest. There is also another
striking passage in the *Phaedo* which seems to argue for
the doctrine a more direct application :—

ἀλλὰ τόδε γ', ἔφη, ὦ ἄνδρες, δίκαιον διανοηθῆναι, ὅτι,
εἴπερ ἡ ψυχὴ ἀθάνατος, ἐπιμελείας δὴ δεῖται οὐχ ὑπὲρ
τοῦ χρόνου τούτου μόνον, ἐν ᾧ καλοῦμεν τὸ ζῆν, ἀλλ' ὑπὲρ
τοῦ παντός, καὶ ὁ κίνδυνος νῦν δὴ καὶ δόξειεν ἂν δεινὸς
εἶναι, εἴ τις αὐτῆς ἀμελήσει. κ.τ.λ. (*Phaedo* 107 B, C.)

Here is an incentive to morality which is derived directly
from the doctrine of immortality. We have to regard
the health of the soul not merely in respect of this
particular phase of existence which we call life, but with
reference to the whole life of the soul, which never
ceases. Were it otherwise, as Socrates goes on to say,
the sinner's best course might be to commit suicide; as
it is, however, the best course for everyone is to do his
utmost to improve himself both mentally and morally.

It would appear, then, that regarded from an ethical standpoint the doctrine of immortality is not without its importance in Plato's philosophy. But we must be careful to guard against misapprehension in discriminating the use which he makes of it. For the philosopher at least, the immortality of the soul brings a great and serious responsibility; and the greater our progress in philosophy and the consequent understanding of the real meaning of immortality, the greater will our sense of responsibility become. Some men, it may be, have no wish for immortality; the notion may even be repugnant to them : but whether we wish it or not, our souls *are* immortal; we cannot alter the fact, and therefore we must live in the full knowledge that life does not end with death. When the soul leaves the body, it carries nothing away with it except the effects of such mental and moral training and education as it may have received upon earth; and the character of this training is what determines the nature of its next life. It is this more than anything else that gives life its meaning. The wicked and idle may escape in this life, but we may be sure that they will receive their due measure of punishment hereafter in that they will be forced to enter upon some inferior course of existence as members of a lower species. It is important to notice, if we are to understand Plato's ethics aright, that this is really the kind of punishment that is inflicted, not the terrible retribution of which we read in the myths of the *Gorgias*, the *Republic*, and the *Phaedo* : such terrors are described in myths only and cannot be intended to be taken literally. There is no hell with which we can frighten the immoral man into morality; morality, if it is to be worthy of the name, must come

from a higher source than that, for δίκαια πράττειν is
not the same thing as δίκαιον εἶναι. Virtue, if it is not
exactly the same as knowledge, at any rate implies in the
virtuous man a certain knowledge of what virtue means.
And if there is no hell to frighten us into virtue, neither
is there any heaven in the commonly accepted sense
of the word to lure us into it. It is true that in the
Phaedo the hope is held out that the soul of the true
philosopher will pass to an immaterial region and there
contemplate the αὐτὸ καλόν, αὐτὸ δίκαιον, and the rest
of the ideas; and in the *Timaeus* we are told that the
soul which lives a good life has the prospect of finally
returning εἰς τὴν τοῦ ξυννόμου οἴκησιν ἄστρου, where it
will enjoy a βίος εὐδαίμων καὶ συνήθης, that is to say
a life of contemplation. But it may well be doubted
whether the vicious man would look upon the prospect
of an existence of this sort as more attractive than that
of becoming a pig or some other animal, which would
be the worst that could happen to him. Thus Plato
cannot fairly be charged with founding his morality
upon a system of future rewards and punishments as
generally understood. Before the bad man can be
brought to regard the one as a reward and the other
as a punishment, he must become in Plato's sense a
good man; for then and then only is he capable of
estimating the comparative worth of the lower and the
higher life. The αὐτὸ καλόν and the αὐτὸ δίκαιον will
possess no attraction for a man so long as his life is
neither καλός nor δίκαιος. It is only the good man who
appreciates these qualities and desires to realise them
more fully; and it is in virtue of his goodness that a
fuller realisation of them is made possible for him.
A complete realisation of them is of course impossible;

for according to Plato's later theory, as there are no self-existent ideas of καλόν, δίκαιον, and the like, so there is no final state of bliss for the soul untrammelled by the fetters of the body, in which such ideas, if they existed, could be apprehended. Ψυχή in so far as it is distributed into individual ψυχαί must always contain within it an ἐπιθυμητικόν and a θυμοειδές as well as a λογιστικόν: and the two former, however much they may be kept in subjection by the latter, necessitate the existence of soul in conjunction with body of some sort. But, as I have before suggested, it is quite conceivable that Plato in his dislike of technical terminology may have continued to speak of εἴδη of καλόν and δίκαιον without meaning that there are any self-existent ideas or καθ᾽ αὑτὰ γένη, to use Aristotle's accurate phrase, of these qualities. We know that in the *Sophist* he speaks of ταὐτόν, θάτερον, στάσις, κίνησις, and οὐσία as εἴδη without implying that they are ideas in the special sense. Such ideas as καλόν and δίκαιον are in Plato's later theory merged in the ideas of the natural kinds, which necessarily imply these ideal qualities; for existence and goodness have now come to be recognised as two aspects of the same thing. Καλόν and δίκαιον are not self-existent types; but they are still in a sense ideas obtained by abstraction, which we may, if we please, set before us as ideals to be striven after, though they can never be entirely realised. We must remember, however, that the idea to which we are really endeavouring to approximate is the idea of man. The fuller realisation of the idea of man necessarily carries with it the fuller realisation of such ideas or ideals as καλόν and δίκαιον. The idea of man, regarded from this ethical point of view as the ideal to which the life of man should be made as far as possible to conform, seems to be sometimes, as it were, personified in the term θεός. This connotation of the word seems to be implied in one of the earlier and again in one of the later Dialogues, though there is, I think, a significant change of expression in the one as compared with the other. In the *Phaedrus* we read :—

ἰχνεύοντες δὲ παρ' ἑαυτῶν ἀνευρίσκειν τὴν τοῦ σφετέρου θεοῦ φύσιν, εὐποροῦσι διὰ τὸ συντόνως ἠναγκάσθαι πρὸς τὸν θεὸν βλέπειν, καὶ ἐφαπτόμενοι αὐτοῦ τῇ μνήμῃ, ἐνθουσιῶντες, ἐξ ἐκείνου λαμβάνουσι τὰ ἔθη καὶ τὰ ἐπιτηδεύματα, καθ' ὅσον δυνατὸν θεοῦ ἀνθρώπῳ μετασχεῖν.

(*Phaedr.* 252 E, 253 A.)

In the *Theaetetus* the same doctrine is expressed in a slightly altered form :—

διὸ καὶ πειρᾶσθαι χρὴ ἐνθένδε ἐκεῖσε [*sc.* 'from earth to heaven'] φεύγειν ὅ τι τάχιστα. φυγὴ δὲ ὁμοίωσις θεῷ κατὰ τὸ δυνατόν· ὁμοίωσις δὲ δίκαιον καὶ ὅσιον μετὰ φρονήσεως γενέσθαι. (*Theaet.* 176, A, B.)

Of course I do not mean to assert that the ideas are directly referred to in either of the above passages ; but it is noteworthy nevertheless that the form in which the ethical doctrine is stated in each case reflects the phraseology of the Theory of Ideas. In the *Phaedrus* the earlier form, in the *Theaetetus* the later form of the theory is suggested : the μέθεξις θεοῦ of the one becomes the ὁμοίωσις θεῷ of the other ; but the ethical doctrine which underlies both notions is essentially the same.

Ὁμοίωσις θεῷ—this is the mainspring of Plato's ethics: a continual upward progress is what he contemplates as the good for man. Through countless incarnations in all the various forms of life the soul must travel in a ceaseless effort to attain to the unattainable ideal, θεός. In a very real sense Plato utters the exhortation to

> "Arise and fly
> The reeling Faun, the sensual feast;
> Move upward, working out the beast,
> And let the ape and tiger die."

The objection is sometimes made to the Platonic as compared with the Aristotelian ethics that, whereas Aristotle aims at a complete reconciliation between the desires and the will, Plato never achieves this reconciliation: that is to say, Plato's good man possesses only what Aristotle calls ἐγκράτεια, the complete control of the desires by the will, and never arrives at true σωφρο-σύνη, the complete harmony of the two. The distinction may perhaps be admitted: but at the same time it may reasonably be questioned whether Plato's system is on this account fairly open to disparagement. Aristotle's psychology undoubtedly strikes deeper and reaches farther than Plato's; yet it may be doubted whether, as the result of his more scientific method and greater experience of human nature, he has any better ethical ideal to set before us. Aristotle's view of ethics is as a whole intensely practical, and the chief part of the interest and value of his treatise to us is derived from the fact that it is so practical and so nearly related to actual life; but this ideal σωφροσύνη is surely something more than human. Plato is by nature more of a metaphysician than Aristotle, and consequently his ethical system is more subordinate to metaphysics than Aristotle's. With his views concerning the necessity of evil in the constitution of things as a counterpart to

good, he could hardly have recognised as actually
possible such a perfection of human nature as Aristotle
seems to contemplate. In the sphere of ethics no less
than in that of metaphysics good would be meaningless
if there were no evil to make it capable of realisation.
Absolute mental and moral perfection would in Plato's
eyes necessarily imply absolute independence of the conditions of space and time, and this for the individual
he recognises as metaphysically impossible. Universal
soul, which we may think of in the abstract as existing
logically out of time and space, might be conceived as
being completely σώφρων: but particular souls, which
must actually exist in and throughout these conditions,
can never be so. There will never be an end of time
and space ; hence there can never be any state of existence for the individual soul which is not temporal and
spatial. All that the individual soul can do is by means
of dialectical studies to increase its knowledge of the
true nature of time and space and all that they imply,
so that it may become ever more and more free, though
never entirely free, from the influence of their limitations.
Similarly on the part of the moral nature what Plato
calls ὁμοίωσις θεῷ may be continually developed : that
is to say, ψυχή in the sphere of morals as well as in that
of knowledge can obtain ever more and more control
over σῶμα and its attendant evils; for Plato draws no
hard and fast line between mental and moral excellence.
But for every individual soul a condition of absolute
purity must always remain an unattainable ideal. The
process of ὁμοίωσις θεῷ may go on for ever, but man
will never become θεός. Thus, according to Plato, the
business of philosophy, in so far as it deals with human
conduct, is

"To sway
The heart of man: and teach him to attain
By shadowing forth the Unattainable;
And step by step to scale that mighty stair
Whose landing-place is wrapt about with clouds
Of glory of heaven."

This is not Aristotle's view. His moral standard does not profess to be *ideal* but *real* in the sense in which he understands reality: that is to say it has nothing transcendental about it; it is something which can be actually realised here and now, something κτητὸν ἀνθρώπῳ. Accordingly he gives us a number of practical rules by which our conduct should be ordered. To him moral virtue consists in a variety of μέσα which are to be attained by avoiding this and that extreme of vice; to Plato it is rather a μέτριον, a fixed but transcendental standard which we can never actually reach, though we may make continual progress towards it. This is only one instance of the fundamental difference between the two philosophers, a difference which is more marked perhaps in metaphysics, but which appears unmistakably also in their ethical views. Aristotle regards the individual man mainly as a *citizen*: the state must educate the individual in order that the individual may afterwards be useful in maintaining the state; the πόλις is πρῶτον φύσει: hence φύσει πολιτικὸν ζῷον ἄνθρωπος. Plato regards the state mainly as a collection of *individual men*: the individual must support the state because the state secures the proper education of the individual, who may thus attain to the philosophic life. Aristotle, therefore, does not concern himself with the question of immortality: it matters nothing to the state whether the individual members composing it possess immortal souls or not. But Plato is, if we may say so without

causing misapprehension, more *spiritual* than Aristotle;
he thinks of man as an individual *soul* whose every concern is of importance, and whose immortality is a matter
that calls for serious consideration. To Plato a man
who is not an active member of a πόλις is not necessarily in Aristotle's sense ἢ θεὸς ἢ θηρίον; he is something between the two, and has in him some of the
elements of each; but his duty is to try to make
himself as unlike θηρίον and as like θεός as possible.
His true πόλις is no earthly commonwealth, but a
heavenly city which it should be his endeavour to represent as far as may be in his own person. This point of
view is admirably expressed in the remarkably fine
ending of the ninth book of the *Republic*, of which the
concluding words are specially suggestive in their
magnificence:—

οὐκ ἄρα, ἔφη, τά γε πολιτικὰ ἐθελήσει πράττειν,
ἐάνπερ τούτου κήδηται. Νὴ τὸν κύνα, ἦν δ᾽ ἐγώ, ἔν γε
τῇ ἑαυτοῦ πόλει καὶ μάλα, οὐ μέντοι ἴσως ἔν γε τῇ
πατρίδι, ἐὰν μὴ θεία τις ξυμβῇ τύχη. Μανθάνω, ἔφη.
ἐν ᾗ νῦν διήλθομεν οἰκίζοντες πόλει λέγεις, τῇ ἐν λόγοις
κειμένῃ. ἐπεὶ γῆς γε οὐδαμοῦ οἶμαι αὐτὴν εἶναι. Ἀλλ᾽,
ἦν δ᾽ ἐγώ, ἐν οὐρανῷ ἴσως παράδειγμα ἀνάκειται τῷ
βουλομένῳ ὁρᾶν καὶ ὁρῶντι ἑαυτὸν κατοικίζειν. διαφέρει
δὲ οὐδέν, εἴτε που ἔστιν εἴτε ἔσται. τὰ γὰρ ταύτης μόνης
ἂν πράξειεν, ἄλλης δὲ οὐδεμιᾶς. Εἰκός γ᾽, ἔφη.

(*Rep.* 592 A, B.)

To sum up. The basis of Plato's ethics is ὁμοίωσις
θεῷ, a continual striving after unattainable perfection;
the same notion in short which underlies his metaphysical teaching. Aristotle considers that man's moral
nature may be completely developed; but as an indis-

pensable condition of its complete development he demands a βίος τέλειος, a life of sufficient length to make
such complete development possible. We can never
indeed be sure that a βίος τέλειος will be accorded to us;
but if it is, our moral nature may under favourable
conditions—if we are, that is, τοῖς ἐκτὸς ἀγαθοῖς ἱκανῶς
κεχορηγημένοι—be completely developed, and then we
shall be completely happy. Thus, though Aristotle sets
before us a standard of attainable moral perfection, this
part of his ethical doctrine can scarcely be of anything
like universal application. A man may fail of a βίος
τέλειος; he may not meet with sufficiently favourable
external circumstances—and for him life has lost the
chief part of its power and meaning and purpose. Plato,
aiming in a sense not so high and in a sense higher,
gives us a doctrine that must appeal to all from the
highest to the lowest. In his ethical system the notion
of moral development is a still more important feature
than in Aristotle's: so important, so essential, does he
regard it that it can never come to an end, never be
complete. In his view it is the very eternity of development that itself gives meaning to life; for the practical
good of life consists in no final and attainable ideal:
it lies precisely in progress itself. Where there is no
progress there is no real good, no real existence, that we
can recognise: there is either retrogression or at best
stagnation. And this continual progress, which itself
constitutes the ἀνθρώπινον ἀγαθόν, demands something
more than Aristotle's βίος τέλειος: the life must be
co-extensive with the progress and so must never end.

CONCLUSION.

PERHAPS I have now said enough to show what I consider to have been the cause of Plato's bestowal of so much thought on the great problem of the immortality of the soul, and what place I imagine his own doctrine of immortality to hold in his philosophy. From a vague belief it is developed till it becomes a philosophical theory analogous to the Theory of Ideas; and it ends by obtaining an abiding place in his ethics. Not that he in any way bases his ethical system upon it: it would indeed be nearer the truth to say that he bases it upon his ethical system. Having first established his system of morality on a basis as lofty and as little egoistic as is humanly possible, he considers himself fairly entitled to take into account τὰ μέγιστα ἐπίχειρα ἀρετῆς: and the character of these ἐπίχειρα turns out to be such that the doctrine of immortality upon which the hope of them is founded, so far from invalidating his defence of morality upon its own merits, is seen to be the natural outcome of his ethical theory.

If it be allowable to compare the teaching of a poetical philosopher with that of a philosophical poet, one would be strongly tempted to compare Plato with Browning; and I do not think the analogy would be by any means fanciful. Browning's philosophy has been truly said to be based upon two fundamental doctrines, from which an optimistic theory of the universe and man's position in it may be derived. It has been pointed out that much of his poetry is characterized by the hope which lies in a consciousness, first, of 'the imperfection of God', and secondly, of 'the imperfection of man'. Both these doctrines may be said to be contained at least implicitly in the philosophy of Plato. The first, the doctrine of *Saul*, fairly expresses the doctrine that forms the basis of all Plato's metaphysics: the very perfection of the αὐτὸ ἀγαθόν is in a sense imperfection, as we may judge from the fact that it must evolve itself into a world that is not wholly good in order that its own goodness may be realised. The second embodies an ethical theory which is almost exactly that which I have attributed to Plato; and with it the doctrine of immortality is closely connected. For Browning, as for Plato, the very fact of mortality seems to imply the truth of immortality. It is a paradoxical doctrine perhaps; but it is nevertheless

"A paradox
Which comforts while it mocks."

Plato's theory of evil again is very like Browning's, and so is his notion of the good of unrealised aspiration. We need not look further than *Abt Vogler* and *Rabbi Ben Ezra* to discover the similarity. And 'the hope that lies in the imperfection of man' leads as naturally to a belief in immortality as Plato's ὁμοίωσις θεῷ. There are many passages in *La Saisiaz* which inevitably suggest Plato. We may note especially the following :—

"This life has its hopes for this life, hopes that promise joy: life done—
Out of all the hopes, how many had complete fulfilment? none.
'But the soul is not the body': and the breath is not the flute;
Both together make the music: either marred and all is mute."

And again:—

> "In this first
> Life I see the good of evil, why our world began at worst:
> Since time means amelioration, tardily enough displayed,
> Yet a mainly onward moving, never wholly retrograde.
> We know more though we know little, we grow stronger though
> still weak,
> Partly see though all too purblind, stammer though we cannot speak."

In Plato, then, as in Browning, it is a belief in the immortality of the soul which gives the final touch to his ethical teaching. It is closely linked with his conception of progress as the good for man. It is

> "The glory of going on and still to be"

that makes his ethical philosophy at once so universal and so stimulating: universal, because no soul can have fallen so low in misery or degradation as to be incapable by its own efforts of bettering its estate, if not now, at least hereafter ; and stimulating, because nothing in this world can be so good but our minds can conceive and our efforts can command something still better.

Καὶ πῶς, εἰ μὴ Φοῖβος ἀν' Ἑλλάδα φῦσε Πλάτωνα,
ψυχὰς ἀνθρώπων γράμμασιν ἠκέσατ' ἄν;
καὶ γὰρ ὁ τοῦδε γεγὼς Ἀσκληπιός ἐστιν ἰητὴρ
σώματος, ὡς ψυχῆς ἀθανάτοιο Πλάτων.

DIOGENES LAERTIUS.

For EU product safety concerns, contact us at Calle de José Abascal, 56–1°, 28003 Madrid, Spain or eugpsr@cambridge.org.

www.ingramcontent.com/pod-product-compliance
Ingram Content Group UK Ltd.
Pitfield, Milton Keynes, MK11 3LW, UK
UKHW020320140625
459647UK00018B/1940